D1531452

CIVIL WAR

A NOVEL OF THE MARVEL UNIVERSE

ADAPTED FROM THE GRAPHIC NOVEL
BY MARK MILLAR AND STEVE McNIVEN

MARVEL

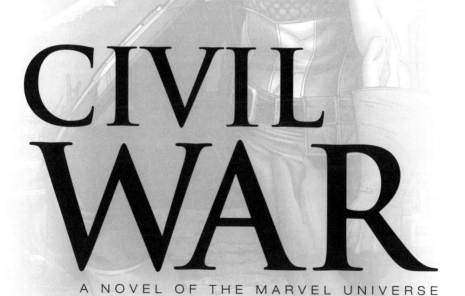

CIVIL
WAR

A NOVEL OF THE MARVEL UNIVERSE

STUART MOORE

CIVIL WAR PROSE NOVEL. First printing 2012. Published by MARVEL WORLDWIDE, INC., a subsidiary of MARVEL ENTERTAINMENT, LLC. OFFICE OF PUBLICATION: 135 West 50th Street, New York, NY, 10020. Copyright © 2012 Marvel Characters, Inc. All rights reserved.

ISBN# 978-0-7851-6035-9.

$24.99 per copy in the U.S. and
$27.99 in Canada (GST #R127032852); Canadian Agreement #40668537.

Printed in the U.S.A.

ALAN FINE, EVP - Office of the President, Marvel Worldwide, Inc. and EVP & CMO Marvel Characters B.V.; DAN BUCKLEY, Publisher & President - Print, Animation & Digital Divisions; JOE QUESADA, Chief Creative Officer; TOM BREVOORT, SVP of Publishing; DAVID BOGART, SVP of Operations & Procurement, Publishing; RUWAN JAYATILLEKE, SVP & Associate Publisher, Publishing; C.B. CEBULSKI, SVP of Creator & Content Development; DAVID GABRIEL, SVP of Publishing Sales & Circulation; MICHAEL PASCIULLO, SVP of Brand Planning & Communications; JIM O'KEEFE, VP of Operations & Logistics; DAN CARR, Executive Director of Publishing Technology; SUSAN CRESPI, Editorial Operations Manager; ALEX MORALES, Publishing Operations Manager; STAN LEE, Chairman Emeritus. For information regarding advertising in Marvel Comics or on Marvel. com, please contact John Dokes, SVP Integrated Sales and Marketing, at jdokes@marvel.com. For Marvel subscription inquiries, please call 800-217-9158. Manufactured between 4/2/2012 and 4/30/2012 by SHERIDAN BOOKS, INC., CHELSEA, MI, USA.

First printing 2012
10 9 8 7 6 5 4 3 2 1

COVER ART BY MICHAEL TURNER AND PETER STEIGERWALD

Marie Javins, Editor
Design by Spring Hoteling

Senior Editor, Special Projects: Jeff Youngquist
Senior Vice President of Sales: David Gabriel
SVP of Brand Planning & Communications: Michael Pasciullo
SVP & Associate Publisher, Publishing: Ruwan Jayatilleke
Editor In Chief: Axel Alonso
Chief Creative Officer: Joe Quesada
Publisher: Dan Buckley
Executive Producer: Alan Fine

For Mark Millar, who turned the blank page into gold; Steve McNiven, who brought it to life; and Liz, who sat through all my jabber about Captain America and Iron Man.

WARRIORS

SPEEDBALL could barely stand still. That wasn't unusual. Ever since the accident in the lab, his body had become a barely controlled generator of highly volatile kinetic-force bubbles. His teammates in the New Warriors were accustomed to his constant bouncing around, his inability to stay focused on anything for more than ninety seconds at a time. They barely even bothered to roll their eyes anymore.

No, Speedball acting antsy wasn't new. But the reason for it was.

"Earth to Speedball." The producer's voice was tinny in his ear. "You gonna answer my question, kid?"

Speedball smiled. "Call me Robbie, Mister Ashley."

"You know the rules. When you're miked and in the field, it's code names only. *Speedball.*"

"Yes sir." He couldn't resist tweaking Ashley. The man was such a suit.

"So," Ashley said.

"So?"

"The villains. *How many?*"

Speedball brushed crabgrass away from his leg. He leapt up into the air past Namorita, who stood leaning against a tree, bored. He bounced off Microbe's massive frame—the big guy sat sprawled in the grass, snoring—and came in for a featherlight landing right behind Night Thrasher, their black-cowled leader.

Thrash was all business, his hidden eyes peering through a pair of high-tech binoculars. Speedball looked past him at the house, old and wood-framed, concealed from its neighbors by a high fence. The Warriors—and their camera crew—stood about fifty feet away, hidden behind a pair of big oak trees.

A trio of muscular men appeared in the doorway of the house, all dressed in casual clothes: jeans, work shirts. Speedball touched a button on his earpiece. "Three villains."

"Four," Thrasher said.

Speedball squinted, managed to make out a muscular woman with dark hair. "Oh yeah. I see Coldheart in the back, emptying the trash." Speedball giggled. "Emptying the trash. Man, these guys are hardcore."

"Actually, they're all on the FBI's most wanted list." Ashley sounded almost worried now. "Cobalt Man, Speedfreek, Nitro...they all broke out of Rykers Island three months back. And they all got records as long as your arm."

Microbe had shambled up behind them—all 350 pounds of him—dressed in green and white with a thick belt full of compartments. "What's up?"

Thrasher motioned him to silence.

"Coldheart fought Spider-Man a couple of times," Ashley continued. "And get this. Speedfreek almost took down the Hulk."

Thrasher lowered the binoculars. "He what now?"

Microbe scratched his head. "These guys sound out of our league."

"Out of your league maybe, lardo."

"Shut up, 'Ball."

"I told you not to call me that."

"'Ball," Microbe repeated, a lazy smile on his face.

"Enough." Namorita turned her head, barely interested. "What's the plan?"

Speedball smirked. "Plan is you spend five more minutes in makeup, Nita. You think people wanna see that big ugly zit on your chin?"

She shot him the finger and turned away. Pierre rushed up to her, foundation brush in his hand.

Namorita was a blue-skinned beauty, an offshoot of the royal family of Atlantis. Cousin or niece or something to Prince Namor, ruler of the undersea city. One time, Speedball had tried to get into her pants; she'd held his head underwater for five minutes.

"I don't know," Thrasher said. He cast a worried glance back toward the house. "I'm not sure we should do this."

"What?" Speedball almost jumped up into the air, then realized just in time he'd be blowing their cover. "Think of the ratings, Thrash. We're dyin' here. Six months we been driving around the country looking for goofballs to fight, and the best we've managed was a bum with a spray can and a wooden leg. This could be the episode that really puts the New Warriors on the map. We beat these clowns and everyone'll stop bitching about Nova leaving the show to go back into space."

Fernandez, the cameraman, cleared his throat. "I just wanna remind everybody that the crew's on shift for another twenty minutes. After that, we go to time and a half."

Everyone turned to Night Thrasher.

"Okay, listen up everyone." Thrasher held out a tablet computer, displaying profiles of the four villains. "Nitro and Cobalt Man are the real threats here. Coldheart's a hand-to-hand expert; we should take her out from a distance if possible. I don't know the current state of Cobalt's armor, but..."

"'Ball," Microbe said again, leaning over to whisper in Speedball's ear. "'Ball 'ball 'ball 'ball 'ballllll."

Speedball pulled out his iPhone, thumbed on some Honey Claws. Electronic riffs and a pumping bass line. Mercifully, it drowned out both Microbe's taunts and Thrasher's boring tactical briefing.

Speedball was tired and cranky. They all were, he realized. It had been Thrasher's idea to turn the New Warriors into a reality show, and at the beginning it seemed exciting. Times were tough for teenage heroes, and this was a chance to transform their frankly third-rate team into pop stars. The show enjoyed a brief spurt of attention, and Speedball became addicted to the public acclaim, the guest appearances on The Colbert Report and Charlie Rose.

But then Nova had quit, and the less said about his replacement— "Debrii"—the better. She'd washed out after two episodes. As the season wore on, the strain of travel and constant reshoots had worn on all of their nerves. And the ratings took a sharp dive, straight into the toilet. A second season looked really, really unlikely.

It's too bad, he thought. *When this started, we were all friends.*

Nita elbowed him roughly in the ribs, and he yanked off the earbuds. "What?"

"We've been marked."

Speedball looked over at the house, just as Coldheart turned to stare right at them. Then she ran inside, yelling, "Everybody in costume. *It's a raid!*"

The Warriors were on their feet. Fernandez hefted his camera, preparing to follow them.

"Standard attack pattern," Thrasher called out. "Form on me—"

Speedball just grinned and leapt, kinetic-energy bubbles blasting out from him in all directions. "GO!" he yelled.

He could almost feel Thrasher's exhausted sigh.

As Speedball arced in for a landing, halfway across the lawn, he thumbed his iPhone to another track. The show wasn't broadcast live, but somehow, the stentorian theme music in his ears always got him pumped. And Speedball lived to get pumped.

"SPEEDBALL!" the announcer's voice called in his ear. "NIGHT THRASHER! MICROBE! THE SULTRY NAMORITA! AND...THE MAN CALLED *NOVA*!"

He hated that part.

"IN A WORLD OF GRAYS...THERE IS STILL GOOD AND EVIL! THERE ARE STILL..."

"...*THE NEW WARRIORS!*" Speedball shouted the words along with the announcer—just as he crashed into the front door, splintering it to toothpicks.

The other Warriors ran up behind him, surveying the scene. The living room was stripped bare, like a crack den. A long-haired man whirled to greet them, half clad in a metal exoskeleton.

"Speedfreek," Thrasher said.

"Holy crap." Speedfreek reached for a silvery, red-visored helmet.

Grinning again, Speedball body slammed him, sending the helmet flying. They crashed together through the far wall, into the backyard. 'Freek stumbled back over an old stump, surrounded by overgrown grass and weeds.

"I'd heard that clothes make the man, Speedfreek." Speedball punched him hard, a solid left cross. "And in your case, it's *totally true!*"

"Ungh!" Speedfreek flew back, fell to the lawn.

Fernandez, the cameraman, tapped on Speedball's shoulder. "Sound cut out for a minute there, bud. Any chance of that last part again?"

Speedball grimaced, motioned to Namorita. She rolled her eyes and stalked over to the dazed Speedfreek. She lifted him easily up into the air, tossed his limp form toward the cameraman.

Speedball crouched down and leapt up high, swooping back down with a flying kick. As his foot made contact with Speedfreek's jaw, he called out clearly: "In your case, Chuckles, it's *totally true!*"

Fernandez lowered the camera, gave a bored thumbs-up.

Speedball looked around. Night Thrasher and Microbe had Coldheart and Cobalt Man cornered against the far fence. Cobalt was struggling to fasten his high-tech suit over his big frame, while Coldheart slashed her energy swords through the air, keeping the Warriors at bay.

Microbe turned lazily to glance at Speedball. *Probably hoping I get my head kicked in,* Speedball thought.

"Wait a minute." Coldheart paused, holding up her energy swords in a defensive posture. "I know you guys. You're those idiots from that reality show."

"That's right," Thrash replied. "And *this* is reality."

Speedball shook his head. *Lame catchphrase, boss.*

"No," Coldheart continued. "No way. I'm not gettin' taken down by Goldfish Girl and the Bondage Queen." She sliced a crackling sword-arc through the air.

But Namorita was already inside Coldheart's defenses. Nita slammed a blue fist, hardened to withstand the ocean's depths, straight across the villainess' jaw. "Beg to differ, sweetheart."

Night Thrasher followed up with an acrobatic kick to Coldheart's stomach. "Can we edit out the part where she called me the Bondage Queen?"

"Yeah." Nita smirked. "Because Night Thrasher sounds *so* much straighter."

Coldheart was down—but where had Cobalt Man gone? And what the hell was Microbe doing, just standing there in the corner of the lawn, his back to them?

Speedball leapt over to Microbe. Surprisingly, the manchild stood over a writhing, subdued villain in an overcoat. Beneath the coat, an armored exoskeleton seemed to be dissolving away before their eyes.

"I got Cobalt Man!" Microbe said. "My bacterial powers are rusting his suit away. Guess I'm not such a loser after all, huh?"

"Learn to count, loser." Speedball looked around. "Where's the fourth bad guy?"

Nita leapt high up, the small wings on her feet fluttering madly. She stopped, hovering in midair, and pointed out over the house toward the road beyond. "I'm on it." She turned to soar up and over the roof.

Thrasher and Microbe whirled back toward the house. They marched through the hole in the wall, heading after Namorita.

Speedball started to follow, then turned back at a sound. On the ground, Speedfreek grunted, trying to rise. Speedball kicked him hard, then turned toward the house. Fernandez followed, shouldering his camera.

Halfway through the living room, Speedball stopped in his tracks. Fernandez shot him a look, and Speedball motioned him ahead. The cameraman trotted on toward the front door.

Speedball took a long, careful look around the room. Beer cans were everywhere. On a folding table, pizza dripped and rotted, the one remaining slice soaking through a greasy box. A meth pipe still glowed, discarded on a pile of Xbox disks. Ancient paint cracked and peeled from the walls; stuffing leaked from the old sofa.

This house, he realized. *It's where you end up. When it all goes wrong, when things don't turn out the way you expect. When you make all the wrong decisions, and end up running for your life.*

Speedball had peaked early during the fight; now his adrenaline levels were crashing. He felt suddenly tired, useless, futile. He was glad the others weren't around—he'd expended a lot of energy, no pun intended, keeping his bipolar condition a secret from them. He felt very unreal, as though he were watching his own actions from a distance. Like some bored, faceless audience member, just getting ready to click away to another channel.

"Speedball!" Ashley's voice lanced into his ear. "Kid, where are you? You want to miss the climax?"

No, he realized. *No, I don't want to miss it.*

Speedball bounded out through the shattered front door in a burst of kinetic energy. He pivoted on the front step, posing briefly in case one of the cameras was recording him, then bounced out into the street.

Across the road, a crowd of elementary school kids had gathered at the edge of a playground. Some of them held books, computers; one kid carried a baseball bat. Night Thrasher and Microbe held them back, motioning firmly, while Namorita swooped down through the air toward a parked school bus.

A small figure dashed across the street, toward the school bus: purple-and-blue costume, long silver hair. Cruel eyes that looked like they'd seen—and done—terrible things.

Nita crashed down onto him from above, slamming him into the bus, caving in its side. Shattered window glass hailed down, covering both figures.

The man made no sound.

"On your feet, Nitro." Namorita stood in full battle stance, arms upraised, legs planted firmly for the camera. "And don't try any of your stupid explosions, because that's only going to make me hit you harder."

Speedball moved in to back her up.

Nitro knelt crouched on the pavement, leaning up against the dented bus. When he looked up, his eyes blazed with hate...and deadly fire.

"Namorita, right?"

Fernandez moved in, swinging the camera back and forth from Nitro to Nita.

Nitro smiled, and his eyes glowed brighter. "I'm afraid I'm not one of those bargain-basement losers you're used to, baby."

Nitro's whole body was glowing now. Nita took a step back. Night Thrasher watched, tense and unsure. Microbe just stared, his mouth slack, eyes wide.

The kids had moved out into the street, also staring. One of them dribbled a basketball absently, nervously.

Thrasher strode forward, sudden alarm in his eyes. "Speedball... Robbie. Help me get these kids out of here!"

Ashley was chattering too, in his ear.

Speedball didn't move, didn't even nod. Once again, he felt like he was watching events, images, moving in a prerecorded pattern on some high-def screen. *Does any of this matter?* he wondered. *If it all goes wrong, if it doesn't follow the right script, can we just do another take?*

Or is this the last, the only take?

Nitro was a ball of fire now. Only his glaring eyes were visible, searing into Namorita's.

"You're playing with the big boys now," Nitro said.

The energy flared out from him, consuming Namorita first. She arched in pain, let out a silent scream, then dissolved into skeletal ash. The shockwave continued to spread outward, engulfing camera, cameraman, school bus. Night Thrasher, then Microbe. The house, and the three villains sprawled in its backyard.

The children.

Eight hundred fifty-nine residents of Stamford, Connecticut died that day. But Robbie Baldwin, the young hero called Speedball, never knew that. As Robbie's body boiled into vapor, as the kinetic energy inside him burst forth for the last time into the void, his final thought was:

At least I won't have to get old.

PART ONE
LAST GLEAMING

ONE

ENERGY tingled across his skin, dancing along the millimeter-thick sheath covering his body. Wireless sensors reached out, touched matching circuits on boots, chestplate, leggings. Microprocessors winked to life, each one faster than the last. Armor plates snapped open, seeking out his body, locking into place, completing each circuit in turn. Gloves clicked onto fingers, one two three four-five-ten.

The helmet came last, wafting easily into his hands. He lifted it onto his head and snapped the faceplate down.

With the first light of dawn, Tony Stark rose up into the Manhattan sky.

Avengers Tower dropped away below. Tony looked down, executed a vertical half-turn. The Manhattan skyline spiraled into view, majestic and sprawling. To the north, Central Park lay like a green blanket on a bed of gray. Southward, the tall, tapering maze of Wall Street narrowed to a sharp point in the water.

New York was home, and Tony loved it. But today he was restless.

A dozen indicator lights clamored for Tony's attention, but he ignored them. *Where,* he wondered, *should I go for breakfast this morning? The Cloisters? Quick jaunt to the Vineyard? Or maybe a longer hop, down to*

Boca? Serena would just be setting up for the day at the Delray Hyatt—she'd be stunned to see him again.

No, he realized. Today he was restless. Today would be different.

With a quick mental command, he dialed Pepper Potts. The call went straight to voice mail.

"Cancel my morning," he said. "Thanks, doll."

Pepper was never off duty. The voice mail meant she was deliberately ignoring him. No matter; she'd be acting on his instructions within minutes.

Tony banked sideways, cast a quick glance down at Central Park. Then he fired up his boot-jets—and the invincible Iron Man shot out across the city, over the East River.

The phone-messages light was winking, but Tony couldn't deal with that yet. He clicked the autopilot on, making sure the special FAA notification beacon was activated. He soared over LaGuardia Airport, banked left, and blinked twice at the RSS feed. Before his eyes, a menu of headlines appeared.

More economic trouble in the European Union; he'd have to double-check his holdings later. Another Mideast war looked ready to break out, maybe as soon as today. Pepper had flagged a magazine feature on the Mexican subsidiary of Stark Enterprises too. Tony would have to make sure Nuñez, that division's COO, remembered the company's strict no-munitions policy.

And the Senate Metahumans Investigations Committee was in the news again. That reminded Tony of another duty, so he clicked over to email. Scanned a couple hundred messages: charities, contracts, old friends, old supposed friends who wanted money, invitations, Avengers business, financial statements...

...there it was. Confirmation of his own testimony before the Meta-humans Committee, next week. That was an important one—there'd be no long-distance flight to blow off steam that day.

The Committee had been formed to investigate abuses of superhuman power, and to recommend standards and regulations to govern the actions of metahumans. Like many Congressional committees, it served largely to score political points for its members. But Tony had to admit that, as the world had grown more dangerous, super-powered beings had become less and less popular among civilians. As the highest profile Avenger with a publicly known identity, Tony felt a special obligation to make sure both sides of the issue were heard.

Below, a passenger ship was just pulling into Pelham Bay. Tony waved down at them, and a few tourists waved back. Then he soared up and out, over the wide expanse of the Atlantic Ocean.

Scattered ships below, at first. Then just waves: massive, rolling, a pure, endless display of natural power. The sight calmed Tony, focused him. Slowly, the real source of his anxiety rose to the surface of his mind.

Thor.

The messenger from Asgard, home of the Norse gods, had appeared suddenly. Twelve feet tall, massive and stern, hovering in a mist of smoky fog above Avengers Tower. Tony had greeted the messenger on the roof, with Carol Danvers—the Avenger called Ms. Marvel—hovering just above. She floated tall and graceful, her body lithe and strong in flowing blue and red. Captain America stood with them, in full uniform, alongside Tigra, the orange-furred cat-woman.

For a moment, the messenger said nothing. Then he unfurled a parchment scroll, yellowed with age, and began to read.

"RAGNAROK HAS COME," he said. "I AM SENT TO NOTIFY YOU OF THE THUNDER GOD'S FATE. YOU WILL SEE HIM NO MORE."

Tigra's eyes went wide with alarm. Captain America, teeth gritted, stepped forward. "We're ready. Tell us where to go."

"NO. IT IS DONE. RAGNAROK HAS COME AND PASSED, LAYING WASTE TO ALL ASGARD."

Tony flew up into the air, confronting the messenger directly. "Look," he began.

"THOR HAS FALLEN IN BATTLE. HE IS NO MORE."

At those words, a terrible, sunken feeling had taken hold of Tony. He felt dizzy, almost tumbled out of the sky.

"I AM HERE OUT OF RESPECT FOR WHAT HE MEANT TO YOU. BUT HEAR ME: THIS IS FATHER ODIN'S FINAL MESSAGE. FROM THIS DAY, THERE WILL BE NO FURTHER CONTACT BETWEEN MIDGARD AND ASGARD, BETWEEN YOUR REALM AND OURS.

"THOR IS DEAD. THE AGE OF GODS IS DONE."

And with a peal of dull, echoing thunder, the messenger was gone.

That was four weeks ago. Now, soaring out over the ocean, Tony heard the words again in his head: THE AGE OF GODS IS DONE.

Well, he thought. *Maybe. Maybe not.*

Tony had grieved for Thor, this past month. The Avengers had discussed their sorrow and also their frustration: After dozens, hundreds of battles together, their friend and comrade had apparently died alone, in a war fought far away, on some other plane of existence entirely. Not only had the Avengers been powerless to help their friend, but they probably couldn't even have *perceived* the battle that took his life.

Now, though, Tony began to realize that something else was nagging at him. Thor hadn't just been his friend; the thunder god had been the linchpin, the very center of the Avengers. Tony and Cap were both strong-willed men, each with his own strengths and flaws: Cap was ruled by heart and instinct, Tony by a faith in the power of industry and technology. Several times since the founding of the team, they'd almost come to blows over some matter of strategy or sacrifice. And each time, Thor had spoken up with that booming voice that left no room for argument. He'd remind them of their duties or laugh at their folly, and his gigantic mirth always brought them together. Or else he would just walk up behind and clap both men both on the back, so hard it nearly fused Tony's armor to his skin.

Tony had tried to reach out to Cap, but the super-soldier had been very quiet these past weeks. Tony had a terrible feeling that Thor's death had driven some permanent wedge through the heart of the Avengers.

Otherwise, things were going well. Stark Enterprises was flush with Homeland Security contracts, and if there was no one special woman in Tony's life right now, there were four or five incredibly hot ones. Overall, the last few years had been a very good time to be Tony Stark.

And yet, he couldn't shake this dread. The feeling, deep in his metal-sheathed heart, that something profoundly horrible was about to happen.

Another light winked on. Happy Hogan, Tony's chauffeur.

"Morning, Hap."

"Mister Stark. You need me to pick you up?"

Something loomed up ahead, bobbing on the choppy water, barely visible through the cloud layer. Tony peered at it, briefly distracted.

"Mister Stark?"

"Uh, not this morning, Happy. I don't think you could bring the car around where I am."

"Another hotel room? Who is she this time?"

Tony dipped below the clouds, banked around in an arc—and spotted a small, 24-foot fishing vessel. Probably Portuguese, but a *long* way out from home port. It was listing, taking in water over the choppy sea. Crewmen struggled on deck, trying to bail out water with buckets, but they were losing ground.

"Ring you later, Hap."

Tony swooped in toward the ship. A massive wave swelled beneath it, tipping it up on its side. The crewmen grabbed frantically for masts, supports. But the wave pushed relentlessly. The ship was about to capsize.

As Tony dove, he called up a web listing for 24-foot ships. Weight would be somewhere between 3400 and 4200 pounds, not counting crewmen or cargo. A strain, but with the new microcontrollers on his shoulder-muscle augmenters, it should be doable. The ship's stern rose up before him, pointing almost straight up into the air now. He grabbed hold of the stern, kicked in the microcontrollers with a mental command, and pushed.

To his shock, the boat continued to press against him, forcing him downward toward the sea. His armor, he realized, had stalled; the controllers had failed to engage. Four thousand pounds of fishing boat pushed down now against Tony's normal, human muscles.

Just then a call rang through—an Avengers Tower priority number. Tony swore; he couldn't take it now. With half a thought, he activated the auto-text reply: *Will call back.*

Below him, fishermen hung from the masts, crying out in panic. They'd be underwater in seconds.

Tony couldn't fire repulsor rays; at this range, they'd shatter the boat to splinters. He forced himself to breathe and executed a force-reboot of the microcontrollers. Lights danced before his eyes...and then, this time, the controllers engaged. Energy flowed into his metallic exoskeleton. Tony pushed, too hard at first, and grabbed at the boat to correct its course. Then he eased it back down, settling it gently into the water.

The sea had calmed, temporarily. Tony called up an internal translation memo, chose PORTUGUESE.

"You'd better head back to port," he said. The armor translated his words seamlessly, amplifying them to the fishermen below.

A relieved, soaked captain smiled sheepishly back up at him. His mouth formed words in Portuguese, and Tony heard the armor's metallic voice: "Thank you, Mister Anthony Stark."

Huh, Tony thought. *They even know me in Portugal.*

He swooped upward, high enough to make out the coastlines of Portugal and Spain. The water seemed calm enough for safe passage, so he waved farewell to the ship and shot off toward the shore.

Those microcontrollers were trouble. Tony had always had trouble with microcircuitry; the smaller his work got, the more likely it was to misfire. He should consult someone about it...maybe Bill Foster? Before he'd become the hero called Goliath, Foster had specialized in miniaturization.

"Memo," Tony said aloud. "Call Bill Foster tomorrow."

Spain's beach-dotted coastline loomed, tempting him. Did he dare stop for tapas? No. Not today. He pulled up the phone menu and selected CALL BACK LAST NUMBER. An option popped up: VIDEO? He selected YES.

A nightmare apparition appeared before Tony, filling his field of vision. A glistening, insect-like creature, gleaming metallic gold and red, slim arms and legs crackling with electric power. Elongated gold lenses hid its eyes, lending it an air of inhuman malice. Its shape was vaguely human—except for the four additional, metallic tentacles sprouting from its back, flicking back and forth in random, jerky motions.

Tony tumbled in midair, quickly righted himself. He'd passed clear over Spain now, heading over the Tyrrhenian Sea toward Italy.

"Tony? You there?"

The voice was friendly, medium-pitched and familiar. Tony laughed.

"Peter Parker," he said.

"Gave you a heart attack, huh? Sorry, not funny."

"That's okay, Peter." Tony shifted south, away from Bosnia, to swing around the tip of Greece. "I should recognize that suit...I built it, after all. Just never seen anyone actually wearing it before."

On Tony's video feed, Peter Parker—the amazing Spider-Man—leapt up onto a table, all grace and speed. "Well." He vamped, adopting a comical "Vogue" pose, metallic tentacles framing his face. "What do you think?"

"It's you, baby."

Tony double-checked the call-origination info; it was Avengers Tower, all right. That explained the video capability. It also gave him a good sense of why Peter had called.

"Seriously, Tony...and you know me, I don't say 'seriously' very often. This costume is Da. Bomb."

"If I were you, I wouldn't say that very often either."

Spider-Man tapped at the gold lenses. "What's in these things, anyway?"

"Infrared and ultraviolet filters. The earpiece has built-in fire, police, and emergency scanners." Tony smiled; he loved explaining his own work. "The mouth covering has carbon filters to keep out toxins, and there's a full GPS system built into the chestplate."

"Whew! I'll never get lost in the West Village again. What's with those diagonal cross streets, anyway?"

"Well, you...hang on a minute, Peter..."

Jordan loomed up ahead, with Saudi Arabia just beyond. Tony kicked in his armor's stealth field, felt the familiar tingling throughout his entire frame. Now he was invisible to radar, satellites, and the naked eye at any range past forty feet.

"...you never know where you'll find yourself." He called up a detailed dossier on Peter, scanned it quickly. "How's your aunt?"

"Better, thanks. That heart attack turned out to be minor."

"Glad to hear it."

"Tony, I'm grateful as hell to you. You know I am. That old cloth suit I sewed when I was fifteen…it was looking pretty ragged."

"I've also incorporated mesh webbing that should let you glide for short distances," Tony said.

"Tony…"

"The whole thing is made of heat-resistant Kevlar microfiber. Anything less than a medium-caliber shell won't even penetrate it."

"Tony, I'm not sure if I can accept."

Tony frowned, kicked in his afterburners. The desert sped by, a blur of brown hills under the unforgiving sun.

"The suit is a gift, Peter."

"I know. I mean the other thing."

Peter's back tentacles twitched. *He hasn't gotten used to the mental controls yet,* Tony realized.

"I need you, Peter."

"I'm flattered. Believe me, I haven't heard that from too many *chicas* lately."

"I might be able to help with that, too."

"Tony, I just don't think I can replace a god."

So that's it.

Tony paused, gathered his thoughts. These next few moments, he realized, were critical. They could set the course for the rest of his life, and of Peter's too.

Peter added: "I've never been much of a joiner, either. I'm just a friendly neighborhood Spider-Man. You guys operate on a whole other level."

Tony notched up the sensitivity level on his microphone. When he spoke again, his voice had a subtly greater resonance to it.

"Peter," he began, "there's a lot going on right now. Have you heard of the Senate Metahumans Investigations Committee?"

"No, but I already want to party with them."

"They're mulling over a number of measures that will have profound effects on the way you and I live our lives. The age of the lone wolf is ending, Peter. The whole *world* is your neighborhood now.

"If you plan to continue—if you want to carry on saving lives, helping people, using your gifts for the betterment of mankind—you're going to need a support structure."

Spider-Man said nothing. His expression was unreadable, behind the metal-mesh façade.

"I have a strong team in the Avengers," Tony continued. "Cap, Tigra, Ms. Marvel, Hawkeye, the Falcon, Goliath. Even Luke Cage is starting to fit in. But there's no one else who *thinks* the way I do—who understands science and technology, and who always has one eye on the future."

"Ha! All I do these days is worry about the future."

"Peter, I'm not asking you to *replace* Thor. No one could do that. But I need your raw strength, and I need your sharp mind. You're a crucial part of Project Avenger now."

Spider-Man leapt up, scuttled nervously across the ceiling of the Tower conference room. His tentacles flashed and whipped around. He looked more like a spider than ever before.

India whizzed by below, then Thailand. Indonesia.

"Full medical?" Spidey asked.

"Better than that Obamacare you're on now."

"Then I'm in."

"Excellent." The gray bulk of Australia loomed ahead. "I'll be home in three hours. Celebratory drink at the Tower, say two PM?"

"Club soda, of course."

"You know me well." Tony paused. "Peter, I'm having a little satellite trouble. See you this afternoon."

"Satellite trouble? Where are you, anyway?"

"You wouldn't believe me."

"Everything okay?"

"Little trouble with the new microcontrollers in my armor...never mind. I'm fine."

"Good. Well, uh, thanks. Again."

"We're going to do great things, Peter. Thank *you*."

Tony severed the connection.

He glanced down just as New Zealand slid by. He kicked left, banked north, and slammed on the afterburners full blast. The first sonic boom barely penetrated his armor; the second one rattled his ears slightly.

Tony had grown bored with the flight. He was eager to get home, to return to work. To set the next phase of his life into motion.

Enlisting Peter into the Avengers had been a top priority. Tony genuinely liked the young man, and he hadn't been lying when he'd flattered Peter's scientific ability and quick mind. He found himself looking forward to mentoring Peter.

But there was another factor he hadn't brought up. Tony wasn't just interested in Peter Parker, science prodigy. As Spider-Man, Peter was one of the most powerful metahumans currently roaming the planet. That made him a resource to be tapped...and a potential danger to be watched, too.

Better to keep him close.

Tony glanced down at the Pacific Ocean, watching as the tiny islands of Hawaii appeared. He slowed briefly, picturing himself on a hotel deck with a Virgin Colada in hand. Beautiful women glistening as they splashed and strode from the water.

No. Not today.

By the time Tony reached California, he had eight voice mails from Pepper. Appointments, calls, contracts. With each successive message, her voice grew just a tiny notch angrier.

Well, Tony thought. *She's waited this long...*

The salt flats of Utah rushed by, then the beautiful snowcapped Colorado mountains. The bare plains of Kansas, the lush forests of Missouri.

So beautiful. All of it.

When the Appalachian Mountains rose into view, he dialed Happy.

"Gonna need a pickup, Hap."

"You still in the hotel room, boss?" Happy chuckled. "Whatever's in your veins, they oughta bottle it an' sell it like Via*grrrrrrrr*"

A rush of lights and alarms assaulted him, blocking out Happy's voice. Tony blinked, wobbled over Pittsburgh, and cleared all notifications with a mental command.

"Still there, Happy?"

"Yeah, boss."

"Stand by."

Tony called up the RSS feed; it loaded slowly. He flipped through the cable news channels. The incoming reports all seemed very confused, even panicked. Something about hundreds dead...a huge crater, right in the middle of...

He could make out Avengers Tower now, jutting up above the Manhattan skyline ahead. "Meet me at the Tower, Happy," he said. "Fast as you..."

Then his optical sensors picked up a column of smoke rising up into the air, over to the left. Couple miles north. No...farther away than that, past the city limits. Forty miles, at least.

A *big* column of smoke.

Something horrible had happened.

"Change of plans, Hap—stand by for instructions. I'm changing course now, to..."

He paused, locked GPS on to that thick, rising plume of black smoke.

"...Stamford, Connecticut."

TWO

THE first thing Spider-Man thought as he entered Stamford was: *This is a hell of a first mission as an Avenger.*

On the outskirts of the city, ambulances squealed. People stood outside their homes, chattering fearfully. A few businessmen stabbed at phones, frustrated; cell service was overloaded. Everyone kept glancing north, toward the thick black cloud at the center of the explosion.

Spider-Man stopped at an intersection, glanced up. The smoke had thinned out now, but a dull artificial haze blanketed the whole city. The lenses in his new costume could probably analyze that fog's composition, but somehow he didn't really want to know.

Spidey knew he needed to be here. But Tony wasn't answering his calls, and as embarrassing as it sounded, he didn't know how to reach anyone else in the Avengers. So he'd hopped a ride on a northbound truck and, when traffic slowed to a stop, he'd hoofed it the last three miles.

An Avengers quinjet whizzed by overhead, heading toward Ground Zero. Spider-Man raised his arm, shot a strand of webbing up to wrap around a lamppost, and set off after his new teammates.

Half a mile out, a line of police barricades blocked the main road.

Beyond, Spidey could see devastation: collapsed buildings, flashing emergency vehicles, shards of cloth wafting down rubble-strewn streets. Frantic civilians argued with cops, threatening and cajoling, desperate for news of their loved ones.

Just outside the barricade, a small crowd had gathered, pointing upward. An old four-story library building, topped with an ornate cupola, creaked and tottered. Spider-Man focused his lenses and spotted the cause: a shard of concrete projecting from one wall, apparently flung there from all the way inside the disaster zone. An old woman and a man on crutches straggled out of the library's front door, urged on by local police.

But that wasn't what the crowd was staring at. Along the side of the cupola, near the top of the building, crept the deep red form of Daredevil, the Man Without Fear.

Spider-Man tensed and leapt. He almost overshot—the muscle-augmenters in the new suit had kicked in automatically. But he pivoted in midair and, in less than a second, touched softly down on the outer wall. His fingers clung easily, spider-style, to the brick facade.

If Daredevil was startled, he didn't show it. His radar sense had probably warned him. "Peter," he said. "Is that you?"

"In the flesh, Matt." Spider-Man paused, tapped a finger against his metallic eye-lens. "And steel, I guess."

Beneath them, the building creaked and lurched.

"There's a kid trapped inside," Daredevil said. "Back me up?"

"Always."

Daredevil grabbed at a window latch, tried to pull it open. Locked. Spider-Man tapped him on the shoulder, then—concentrating—reached out with one of the tentacles protruding from his costume's back. The tentacle quavered before the window, then *rapped* it hard, just once. The glass shattered.

Daredevil turned to him. "Where'd you get the suit?"

"Fellow named Anthony Stark built it for me. Perhaps you've heard of him?"

Daredevil frowned, his mouth grim beneath his red cowl. Then he turned and dove into the building.

Spider-Man shrugged and followed, using his tentacles to sweep away the glass remaining in the frame.

The office was bare, quiet. No power; computers sat dark on a pair of paper-strewn desks. "You know where this kid is?" Spider-Man asked.

But Daredevil was concentrating, sending his radar sense fanning out through the floor. He pointed toward the door, and again Spidey followed.

"Matt. How you doing, anyway? I know that whole identity thing's been a strain for you."

Daredevil didn't answer right away. Six months ago, a tabloid paper with organized crime connections had outed his secret identity, revealing him publicly as Matt Murdock, crusading attorney. This had led to a flood of civil suits and public harassment. Matt had made the risky decision to deny everything, to publicly swear he was *not* Daredevil—which, of course, was a lie. Spider-Man wasn't sure he agreed with his friend's decision; the morality seemed pretty murky. But Matt had made a persuasive case that it was his only workable option.

"I'm all right," Daredevil said. He didn't sound convincing. "Hey. Hey there!"

In a room full of cubicles, a seven-year-old girl sat cowering on the floor against a barrier. The building lurched, and she whimpered.

Then she saw Spider-Man, and screamed.

Guess not everyone's used to the new look, he thought.

"Let me get this one," Daredevil said.

Five minutes later, they were back down on the ground. Daredevil handed the girl over to her mother, while a brace of cops watched carefully. The woman cast suspicious eyes across Daredevil, then Spider-Man. Then she took off at a run.

"Gratitude," Spidey said.

Daredevil turned back to him. "Do you blame her, after what happened today?"

"I don't *know* what happened today."

"It's bad, Peter. For all of us."

Spider-Man frowned. "Can I get a tiny little clue here?"

"I'm talking about the Superhuman Registration Act."

Spidey shrugged helplessly. With both arms and four tentacles.

Daredevil shot a look upward, and Spider-Man followed his gaze. The red-and-gold figure of Iron Man streaked by, headed for Ground Zero.

"Ask your new BFF," Daredevil continued.

When Spidey looked down, Matt was gone.

SWINGING over the barricade proved no problem. A cop yelled up at Spider-Man once, halfheartedly, then returned to his duties. The Stamford police had more than enough to deal with today.

Inside the barricade, the streets turned quickly to chaos. Some houses had collapsed inward; others lay fallen under piles of rubble. Emergency crews bustled all around, transferring the dead and injured to ambulances or, where the roads were too rough, to hastily outfitted Jeeps.

And the sky...the sky was filled with ash, with a gray haze. The sun shone through weakly, casting no shadows, a dull red orb barely visible through the cloud of dust.

A flutter of wings caught Spider-Man's attention. The Falcon, a muscular black man costumed in red and white, fluttered downward a block away. Spidey followed his descent and spotted Captain America, in full costume, speaking with a couple of medics.

Cap and the Falcon had been partners, off and on, for years. They exchanged a few terse words—Spidey was too far away to hear—and then set off at a run toward a still-smoking house.

"Cap," Spidey called.

Captain America turned, squinted at Spider-Man, and flashed him a quick frown. Then he turned and resumed course for the burning building.

Spidey shook his head. *What was that about?* He raised his hand to fire off a webline, planning to follow Cap and the Falcon—

"Hey. You an Avenger?"

A rescue worker had lowered his breathing mask. He looked exhausted, impatient.

"Yeah," Spider-Man said. "I guess I am."

"We could use some help." He pointed to a collapsed pile of stone, the remains of an old city administrative building. "Motion detectors are picking up something, twenty feet down. But we don't got our diggers here yet."

"I got it." Spidey leapt through the air. "Clear a little space, guys?"

Time to give this new suit a workout.

And then he was digging, using his tentacles to clear away stone and mortar, the splintered remains of desks, walls, collapsed ceilings. He reached ground level and kept burrowing, down into the building's basement, then its sub-basement. Climbing down carefully, steadying himself with web-braces, sweeping the tentacles around to clear debris and punch through layers of flooring. In the old days, he would have had to do this the hard way, lifting ceilings with his webbing and forcing his way through blocked passageways using muscle power alone.

This seemed easier. More natural, even.

Almost before Spider-Man knew it, the rescue workers had followed

him down on grappling ropes. They fanned out around the sub-basement, while Spidey reinforced the creaky ceiling with layer after layer of
webbing. When they'd located all five survivors, they rigged up rescue
pulleys and began lifting the injured out. The civilians had inhaled a lot
of dust; one had a broken leg. But they would all survive.

Peter crawled back up to ground level, to scattered applause from the
rescue workers. And two other figures, too: Tigra, the catlike were-
woman, and Luke Cage, Power Man.

Tigra reached out her arms and half-hugged, half-hoisted Spider-
Man up out of the building. Her furry body was warm and muscular; her
bikini costume barely covered her at all. She held Spidey close, just a little
too long.

"Welcome to the Avengers." Tigra smiled, ran flirty eyes down Spider-
Man's thin frame. "'Bout time we got some hot guys in this group."

"Thanks. Wish it was under less..." He gestured around. "Well, less
horrifically apocalyptic circumstances."

"The Avengers saved my life." Tigra seemed serious now. "After my
transformation. Cap and Iron Man...if I hadn't had this team for support,
I don't know what would have happened to me."

Cage, a working-class hero from Harlem, wore dirty jeans, a black
muscle shirt, and shades that hid his eyes. His dark face was covered with
dirt and soot. He clapped Spider-Man on the back.

"How 'bout you?" Spider-Man asked. "Being an Avenger, has it been
good for you?"

"Only been a couple months. This was prison, I wouldn't even be
eligible for parole yet." Cage lowered his shades, peered closer at Spidey.
"Interesting threads."

"It's a Tony Stark designer original. They'll be selling it at Target next
year."

"Come on," Tigra said. "Let's see if we can help Cap out."

She set off on all fours, picking her way over downed stoplights, across fallen telephone poles. Cage gave Spidey a quick nod, and together they followed.

Straight ahead, a single, freestanding brick building still raged with fire. Goliath, the latest in a long line of size-changing heroes, stood twenty feet high, picking debris off the roof. He reached down, recoiled from a blast of flame, and grabbed a loose chunk of tar. He threw it high into the air, and Ms. Marvel swooped down under it. She fired off a blast of radiant energy, incinerating the roof chunk instantly.

Spider-Man frowned. "Is that a firehouse? On *fire*?"

"Former firehouse." Falcon swooped in for a landing in front of them. "Now it's condos. Well, *now* it's a disaster area."

Cage stepped forward, gave Falcon a half-hug. The two had grown up in the same neighborhood. "Cap's inside?"

"Straight up. Said to hang tight out here."

"Where are the firemen?" Spidey asked.

Falcon gestured around, at the chaos and flashing lights. "On their way."

A middle-aged man stumbled out of the building, coughed, and dropped to his knees. Falcon rose up into the air and whistled; a pair of medics came running.

Hawkeye the marksman followed the man out of the building, balancing two small children on his wiry arms. His purple costume was singed and torn; one of his quiver's straps had been burned clear away. He deposited the kids in the medics' hands and staggered, dizzy.

Above, Goliath picked another piece off the roof. "Gas fire," he called down. "It's still burning."

Falcon landed next to Hawkeye, led him over to Spidey and the others. "Good work, Hawk. Where's Cap?"

Hawkeye coughed, grimaced. "Still inside. I thought we got everybody, but he said…he insisted—" He burst out hacking again, doubled over.

"You oughta see the medics, too."

But Hawkeye slowly straightened, a playful look creeping into his eye. He grabbed an arrow from his quiver, reached out and poked Spider-Man in the chest with it.

"And miss this mook's hazing?" He smiled. "Welcome to the Avengers, Webs."

For once, Spider-Man found himself lost for words. He stood for a long moment…

…and then an explosion burst forth from the firehouse. Flames flared out the door. Goliath took a giant stride back, almost fell. Ms. Marvel swooped backward in midair, watching with the others in horror.

"Cap," Falcon said.

Then a figure appeared in the doorway, silhouetted against the raging fire. A tall, muscular man in a tattered red-white-and-blue uniform. Captain America, the living legend of World War II, took one careful step after another out of the inferno, carrying an unconscious woman in his strong arms.

Medics swarmed around him, took his burden from him. "Third degree burns," one said. "But she's still alive."

"Get her into the Jeep."

"Cap!" Tigra cried.

Cage, Falcon, and Hawkeye followed her toward the building. Cap coughed once, waved them off. He smiled at Falcon, clapped Hawkeye on the back, and rested a steadying arm on Tigra's slim frame.

Then he turned toward Spider-Man, and his face turned dark.

"Spider-Man's just arrived," Tigra said. "It's his first mission as an Avenger."

Still glaring, Cap held out his hand. Spidey took it, unsure, and felt Cap's strong grip as they shook.

"Not the look I was expecting," Cap said.

Behind them, a fire engine finally squealed up. Firemen unrolled hoses, began aiming them at the burning building.

Cap held Spider-Man's hand for a long moment. Cage and Falcon exchanged a look. Hawkeye rubbed his neck, uncomfortable.

Beneath his mask, Spider-Man frowned. He felt like he was back in high school, fidgeting under thick glasses while some popular kid stared him down.

"I, uh, I should check in with Tony," he said at length. "Anybody know where he is?"

WHEN Spider-Man reached the crater, he realized the true extent of the devastation. An area covering one-and-a-half city blocks had been totally flattened, reduced to ash and hard-packed dirt. Half a school building stood at the edge of the blast zone. Its other half had been incinerated, fallen off into the dead hard ground of the crater itself.

The Avengers' quinjet sat parked in the bowl-like depression, alongside the Fantastic Four's custom-built plane. The haze was thicker here, seeming to shroud the crater in an eerie midday twilight.

Spidey leapt over the quinjet. "Boss," he said.

Iron Man held up a hand to Spider-Man: Wait a minute. Tony stood talking to Reed Richards, Mister Fantastic of the FF. Reed had assembled a makeshift network of laptops, Wi-Fi nodes, and sensory detectors, right in the dead center of the crater. Ben Grimm, the Thing, strained his orange-rock biceps to lift a massive computer system out of the plane.

The other members of the FF stood watching them: Sue Richards, Reed's wife, known as the Invisible Woman, and her brother Johnny

Storm, the Human Torch. Johnny's eyes were wide; he almost seemed in shock. Little fires flared on and off, involuntarily, across his arms and shoulders.

A sudden motion caught Spider-Man's eye. He turned to see Wolverine, crouched down over by the crater's far lip. Sniffing the air.

"...think that's all the survivors," Reed said, peering into a screen. "There weren't too many, this close to the blast."

"What..." Johnny stopped, caught himself. "What caused this?"

"The New Warriors," Tony replied. "I just watched the footage...it was broadcast remotely to their studio. In the name of *ratings*, they tried to take down a gang of villains way above their power level."

"Well, they paid for it." Reed was grim. "I read no survivors in the blast zone."

"I confirm that," Wolverine called. "No livin' scents."

"Not even Nitro?" Tony asked. "He set off the explosion."

Spidey frowned. "What kind of crook blows himself up, knowing he'll die along with his victims? Do we have *suicide bomber* super villains now?"

Tony turned glowing eye-slits toward Spider-Man for the first time. "If I could ask him, I would. But that doesn't seem to be an option."

"Kids," Johnny said. He held up a shred of blue-and-gold cloth, a tiny piece of Speedball's costume. "They were just kids."

Spider-Man crossed to Johnny, lay a hand on his old friend's shoulder. "Matchstick. You okay?"

But Johnny shrugged him off, grimaced, and burst into flames. He took off, wordless, into the gray-fogged sky.

Sue grimaced, turned toward the FF's plane. "I'll follow him, make sure he's okay. You can catch a ride home?"

"Sure," Reed replied. Their eyes met for a moment in profound, silent understanding.

Spider-Man found himself wondering: *Could I ever be that close to a woman?*

"Reed," Tony said. "I'm gonna need all the data you can assemble. The Senate hearing is next week...this is the worst possible time for a disaster like this."

"Tony," Spider-Man called. But Iron Man was already in flight, arcing up and out of the crater.

Spider-Man followed, unsure what to do next, at a slight distance. Behind him, Reed Richards turned to the Thing, began setting up some new piece of machinery.

Captain America stood just outside the crater, watching the last of the casualties being loaded into an ambulance. Tony touched down next to him. "Cap."

Captain America turned slowly toward him.

"All these children, Tony." Cap's voice was hoarse, even deeper than usual. "The FEMA chief said there could be as many as nine hundred casualties. All for a TV show."

"They should have called us," Tony replied. "The New Warriors, I mean. Night Thrasher knew they were out of their league."

Cap stared at him for a moment, then turned away. He strode quickly over to an ambulance, began speaking with the driver.

Spider-Man stepped forward. "Tony," he repeated. "I'm at your service. Tell me what to do."

"There's nothing *to* do, Peter—I mean, Spider-Man. Get your tux out of the closet and prepare to be respectful. We've got funerals to attend."

"But—"

"This isn't a crime to be solved, or an adventure, or a villain to be fought. It's just a tragedy."

"Or an opportunity. Right, bub?"

Wolverine had crept up behind them, silent. His face was hostile, but not with animal savagery. This was something deeper, more personal.

"You're headin' for Washington soon, right? To talk to Congress about the state of superhumans in this country."

"That's right, Logan."

"Well, I don't give a rat's whisker what you do with these clowns." He gestured up at Falcon and Ms. Marvel, hovering just above. "But I got a message from the X-Men: We're neutral. The mutant community's stayin' out of this scrap."

"You're also an Avenger, Logan." Tony stepped toward Wolverine, repulsors glowing.

Immediately, the mutant fell backward into a defensive crouch. Unbreakable claws burst forth from his hands, stopping half an inch from Iron Man's chestplate.

Behind Tony, the other Avengers had gathered: Goliath, Cage, Hawkeye. Tigra crouched low, growling softly.

Captain America stood off in the distance, over by the ambulance. He looked down at a stretcher, shook his head at the body.

Tony rose up a few inches off the ground, right at the lip of the crater, and stared down at Wolverine like a god. When he spoke again, his voice was a metallic hiss. "Maybe you should take a leave from the Avengers."

Wolverine turned and strode away. "Way ahead of you. *Boss.*"

"Watch your step, Logan."

The mutant turned, snarled. "You think about comin' after me, Tone, you better watch *more* than your step."

Then he took off like a wild animal, loping away at incredible speed.

The Avengers seemed to all exhale at once. They looked around awkwardly, watching as the last of the rescue vehicles rumbled away.

"Tony," Spider-Man said. "What *are* you gonna say to the committee?"

Tony Stark made no reply. He just stood, staring out over the crater, as the black-gray mist slowly faded to reveal a low, setting sun.

Spider-Man stood with him, with his new teammates. He was an Avenger now; this was supposed to be his new beginning. But for nine hundred residents of Stamford, Connecticut...

"...it's the end," he whispered.

Tony turned sharply toward him. For a moment, Spider-Man had the crazy idea that Tony was about to snap at him. But the armored Avenger just looked upward, activated his boot jets, and flashed silently up into the blood-red sky.

THREE

FROM outside, the Blazer Club didn't look like much. Just a greasy glass double-door, its small velvet rope projecting out onto the sidewalk. Old-style movie marquee with plastic letters spelling out TONIGHT: ACTS OF VENGE NCE.

The bouncer looked Sue Richards up and down, from her flat shoes to her old jeans to her bob haircut. His eyes were hidden behind thick shades, but his mouth betrayed a slight smirk. He didn't even bother to shake his head.

Sue grimaced and stepped back into the crowd. It was an unusually showy group for New York. A clutch of Wall Street execs, laughing loud and showing off big rings. Two tourist girls, impossibly skinny and bejeweled, trying hard to look cool. Smallish, muscular black man with a girl on each arm and a hot pizza slice hanging from his hand. A seven-foot-tall Amazon woman in revealing white dress, cleavage threatening to spill out onto the streets of Manhattan.

Inside and out, Blazer was a bit more L.A. than most New York clubs. Maybe that was why Johnny Storm, Sue's brother, liked it so much.

A muscle-shirted Latino man with a goatee shoved past Sue, towing a small Asian woman in his wake. The bouncer moved the rope aside, let them in.

Sue clenched her fists. She'd been hunting for Johnny all afternoon, and these were the only civilian clothes she'd had stored in the plane. If she didn't look fabulous enough for the Blazer Club, that was *their* problem.

She closed her eyes, concentrated, and vanished from sight.

Susan Richards, the Invisible Woman, strode back up to the doorway and stepped easily around the rope. As she passed the bouncer, she willed her force field to expand slightly, shoving him up against a suburban-trash nerd who was trying to talk his way in. The bouncer turned, puzzled, but saw nothing.

That was petty, Sue thought. But she smiled.

Blazer's main hall was enormous, at least half the size of a football field. Low lighting, forty-foot walls rising up to a vaulted ceiling. Colorfully garbed people danced casually or stood in clumps, yelling to be heard over the pounding techno hip-hop. Men in suits, rich kids, lingerie and fetish models casting painted eyes around for the right agent, the right photographer.

Sue pushed her way through the throng of humanity, keeping herself invisible for now. Up on the stage, a dominatrix dressed like the Black Widow raised a stiletto heel onto "Daredevil's" back, whipping him lightly as he crouched on all fours. The costumes, Sue noticed, were really sharp: every zipper, choker, and billy club in place. But none of the patrons seemed to care.

Sue stopped to watch, more thoughtful than aroused. *I've missed a lot these past few years. While I was raising Franklin and little Valeria.*

She realized she couldn't even identify the song playing.

Johnny had taken the Stamford disaster harder than anyone else.

He'd always been an emotional kid, and the death toll had shaken all of them. But Sue realized something else: Johnny was closer in age to the New Warriors than anyone else on the scene today.

And Johnny had made plenty of mistakes in his own life.

I could have been an Olympic swimmer, Sue thought suddenly. *When I was fifteen. I used to practice every day; I even passed the prelims. I was on my way.*

But I gave it up when Dad...stopped trying. Gave it up to take care of my little brother.

Years later, she was still taking care of him.

Johnny wasn't the sort to mope around when he felt bad. He went looking for trouble. Which meant—

A young man in a skinny tie bumped into Sue, nearly spilling one of his four drinks. He looked around, puzzled. Sheepishly, she faded back into view, mumbling an apology that vanished into the roar of music. The young man blinked twice, frowned momentarily, then shrugged and held out a brown cocktail.

Sue started to shake her head, then smiled and took the drink.

Just then the music blipped off. Some sort of technical glitch. Sue turned at the sound of raised voices.

Across the room, a freestanding metal staircase led up to a platform and a door set halfway up the wall. A mixed group of clubgoers stood gathered around, ogling someone or something at the top of the stairs. A bright orange flame flared up from the platform, and the crowd shrank back, oohing.

Johnny.

Sue pushed her way through the crowd, leaving Skinny Tie behind. She tried to call out to her brother, but the room was too noisy. When she reached the base of the staircase, she could see Johnny standing before the door, waving a flaming hand down at the crowd. Some of them seemed impressed; others were...well, it was hard to tell. A trashy blonde hung on Johnny's arm, gesturing drunkenly.

At the top of the staircase, a bouncer swung open the door. "VIP Room, Mister Storm. Paris and Lindsay are waiting."

"Thanks, Chico." Johnny pulled out a fiver, then accidentally set it aflame. "Ha, sorry! Wait, here you go."

Sue grimaced, then moved toward the staircase. But a big woman in a tight backless dress clanked a boot up onto the steps, blocking her way. "How come that loser gets into the VIP Room?" the woman asked.

Johnny paused at the door, turned slowly around.

No, Sue thought. *Don't do it, kid.*

"Tell you what, Gorgeous." Johnny's eyes flashed. "Next time *you* save the world from Galactus, you can borrow my *pass.* '?"

"How 'bout the next time you blow up a school?"

The woman's companion, a trim man in an all-black shirt, laid a hand around her shoulders. "Yeah, jackass. How 'bout the next time you kill some *innocent kids?*"

Johnny tottered drunkenly, took a step toward the edge of the staircase. "Hell are you talking about, hipster?"

The bouncer watched, eyes narrowing. Johnny's date disengaged from his arm, casting a quick worried look his way.

Sue tensed, prepared to will herself invisible again...but stopped as a look of shame crossed Johnny's face. "Look," he began. "I mean..."

"Man," said a heavy man, "you got some nerve swaggering around town after that. I was you, I'd be ashamed to go outside."

Johnny lurched forward, suddenly angry, and almost fell down the staircase. "Shut your cakehole, Tubby. I got nothing to do with Speedball or the New Warriors. Those guys were strictly C-List."

"Baby killer!"

The crowd charged up the stairs.

Everything happened very fast, then. Sue reached out with her force field, clearing a path up the metal staircase. People stumbled up against the railings, a few of them toppling the few feet down to the floor. Sue leapt up the steps, three at a time. Heard a sickening *crack*, and a cry of pain.

The music faded back up, harder and louder than ever.

When Sue reached the top, Johnny was lying on the platform floor, his hands wrapped around his bloody head. The Tight Dress woman stood over him, face twisted with hate, a broken bottle clutched in her fist. The bouncer stood at the edge of the platform, warning people away.

Johnny's date let out a little shriek and disappeared into the VIP Room, slamming the door behind her.

Sue charged Tight Dress, projecting invisible force from her hands. The woman got in one more good kick at Johnny's head before Sue rammed into her. Sue lifted up with her force field, pushed the woman over the rail, and watched as she fell into the crowd of humanity below.

Johnny was rolling around, writhing, blood dripping through the metal mesh of the platform, like red rain falling onto the patrons below. His arms flashed briefly aflame, then his legs. He clutched his skull, let out a horrible *huh huh huh* noise.

More patrons were rushing the staircase now. Furious, pent up, some of their faces spattered with Johnny's blood. *They want to kill him,* she realized. *They want to kill all of us.*

Bouncers closed in, trying to stop the human tide. But the club-goers kept advancing, like maddened nineteenth-century villagers. As they reached the top of the stairs, Sue crouched down next to her brother and reached out, surrounding them both with an impenetrable force field. The first two attackers bounced off hard, tumbling back into the wave behind them.

Johnny wasn't moving now.

"My brother," Sue called, struggling to shout over the music and screams. *"CALL MY BROTHER AN AMBULANCE!"*

FOUR

"FIRST of all, I'd like to thank you all for coming. It means a lot...to me, and most of all to your friends, neighbors, and family who lost loved ones in yesterday's *utterly avoidable* tragedy."

```
Subject: Henry Pym

Aliases: ANT-MAN, GIANT-MAN, YELLOWJACKET

Group Affiliation: Avengers (former)

Powers: assorted size-changing abilities, flight,
stinger-weapons

Power Type: artificial

Current Location: New York, NY
```

Tony Stark called up the iPhone's onscreen keyboard, jotted a note: *Retired. Harmless.*

"At times like this, it's crucial that a community come together. We cannot allow ourselves to descend into hatred and bitterness. Judgment belongs to the Lord, not to us."

```
Subject: Robert Reynolds

Aliases: SENTRY

Group Affiliation: Avengers (occasional)

Powers: extreme strength, invulnerability, and
unknown other capabilities

Power Type: inborn

Current Location: unknown
```

Tony frowned, wrote: *Potential trouble. Find and recruit.*

"That said..." The minister looked down, removed his glasses. "...in our grief, we must not forget the causes of this tragedy, nor forgive its perpetrators. Forgiveness, too, is reserved for the Lord."

```
Subject: Robert Bruce Banner

Aliases: THE HULK

Group Affiliation: none

Powers: anger-fueled strength—
no measurable limit

Power Type: inborn

Current Location: exiled to deep space
```

Tony shivered.

The church was huge, with several hundred pews; but every one of them was filled today. Old people and young, men and women, every one of them dressed in mourning black.

Tony sat five rows from the front, his mind racing. He hadn't slept last night. Since the incident he'd slipped into overdrive, the way he did when confronted by a sticky engineering problem. His subconscious whirled around and around, tackling the situation from a thousand different angles.

"...and so we ask you, Lord, for your mercy."

So many heroes. Hundreds of them, and who knew how many villains besides. Tony already kept dossiers on most of them, but now he found himself compulsively updating the entries.

There's a lot of power here, he thought. *A lot of potential Nitros.*

"Mercy. Not only for the souls of the children who perished..." The minister paused, looked out over the crowd. "...but also for the so-called *super-people* whose carelessness led us to this sad place."

A news-alert icon flashed in the corner of Tony's phone. He slipped on his earbuds, casting a brief, guilty glance around. A bald man appeared on the phone screen behind a cable-news logo, his voice tinny in Tony's ears.

"*...like Speedball, for example. Nobody likes to speak ill of the dead, but here was a boy who, by all accounts, couldn't even name the president of the United States. Shouldn't a kid like that be* tested *before he's allowed to work in our communities?*"

Tony frowned, clicked to another channel. The phone screen filled with a close-up of Johnny Storm's bloody, unconscious face as he was loaded into an ambulance. Blinding lights flashed in the Manhattan night.

"*—details in the brutal assault on Johnny Storm, the Human Torch, last evening. This, the latest in a series of attacks on New York's super-community. More on the hour, plus the growing pressure on the president as the people of Stamford ask: What are his proposals for super hero reform?*"

Click.

"*A ban on super heroes?*" She-Hulk leaned forward and removed her glasses, rattling the talk-show host. "*Well, in a world full of super villains that's obviously impossible, Piers. But training them and making them carry badges? Hell yes, I think that's a reasonable response."*

Tony felt a prickling on his neck, looked up suddenly. The two women next to him were glaring at him through their veils. He flashed them a sheepish smile.

Then he noticed the other set of eyes boring into him, from the end of the row. Captain America.

Tony yanked off the earbuds, slipped the phone into his pocket.

When the service ended, Tony beelined for the door. People were already gathering together, weeping and comforting each other. He had no desire to intrude on their grief. Several other Avengers, including Tigra and Ms. Marvel, had wanted to come, but they'd all agreed it was best to keep the superhuman contingent as small as possible. No one wanted to turn the people of Stamford's grief into a media circus.

Tony strode quickly out of the church. He didn't really feel like arguing with Cap right now, either.

Just outside the door, Tony felt a hand on his shoulder. He turned to see Peter Parker, smiling sheepishly. "Boss," Peter said.

"Peter. I thought we agreed Cap and I were going to represent the Avengers."

Peter shrugged. "Who's an Avenger? You're looking at a humble photojournalist from the Daily Bugle."

Tony smiled despite himself, eyed Peter up and down. The rented tux looked good on Peter, but those shoes were scuffed. And brown.

Baby steps, Tony thought. *This one's a project.*

"Besides," Peter continued. "I just wanted to be here."

The church's driveway was small and curved, on the edge of an open field. Cars clogged its full length, pulling up one at a time to pick up the oldest mourners. Down the line, Tony spotted Happy Hogan leaning against the limo.

"Walk with me, Peter."

Peter fell in beside Tony. They passed the minister, who stood comforting a pair of grieving widows. A very old woman was with them, weeping uncontrollably into a lace kerchief.

Captain America stood off to the side, solemnly shaking hands with a pair of firemen.

The minister raised his head, locked eyes briefly with Tony. Tony looked away.

"I feel like I should be snapping pics," Peter said.

"That part of your life is over," Tony replied. "No more scrambling for rent money."

"You mean I'm part of the one percent now?"

Tony stopped, touched the boy's shoulder. "Things are about to happen fast, Peter. I'm glad you're with me."

"Things. Like the Superhuman Registration Act."

Tony raised an eyebrow. "Not many people have heard that phrase yet."

"But it's why you're going to Washington next week, right?"

"Tonight, actually. The Committee has moved up their timetable, in light of..." He gestured around, taking in the church and the mourners. "The president has asked to meet with me this evening, and the hearings take place tomorrow."

"What would it mean? This Act?"

"All metahumans would be required to undergo registration and training in order to practice their...their gifts in public. It also gives the government extremely broad powers of enforcement. Broader, even, than anything the Senate was considering before."

"And you support it?"

"It's a tricky piece of legislation." Tony frowned. "If it's enacted into law, it would have to be administered with great wisdom. Great care."

"Tony Stark?"

Tony whirled around—just in time for a stream of spittle to strike him in the face.

"You *filthy piece of crap!*"

The woman was crying openly, tears streaming down her cheeks. Peter moved to restrain her, but Tony held out a hand.

Happy Hogan was already behind the woman. "Ma'am, I'm going to have to ask you to leave." He laid a meaty hand on her shoulder.

"Leave what? My own son's *funeral?*" She shrugged him off angrily, turned to point at Tony. "*He's* the one you should be dragging away."

Tony grimaced, wiped his face dry. "Ma'am, I appreciate that you're upset. But the New Warriors'...tragic actions...had nothing to do with me."

"Oh yeah? Who finances the Avengers? Who's been telling kids for years that they can live outside the law, as long as they're wearing *tights?*"

Peter Parker cleared his throat. "I, uh, don't think Mister Stark says that."

"Cops have to train and carry badges," the woman continued, "but that's too *boring* for Tony Stark. All you need are some powers and a badass attitude, and bang! You've got a place in Joe Billionaire's private super-gang."

Tony opened his mouth to speak, and then something happened that had only happened once before. His mind went utterly, completely blank.

She's right, he realized.

Happy reached for the woman again. She shrank away from him, doubling over with a piercing wail of sorrow. A crowd was gathering now, watching with hostile eyes.

"Jerome left me," the woman sobbed. "When they took away his pension, he just...he couldn't take the pressure. All I had left was my little Damien. And now...and now..."

"Hap," Tony said, "Let's go."

"You, Stark." The woman straightened, stabbed a finger out at Tony's retreating form. "You *fund* this sickness. With your billions. My Damien's blood is—it's on your hands. Now, now and forever."

Tony strode toward the limo, flanked by Happy and Peter. A thousand eyes followed them, glaring in judgment.

"Well, that was fun." Peter grimaced. "And only a little scary."

"They're the scared ones," Tony said. "All of them. They grew up thinking they'd have jobs, pensions, a few bucks to spend in their old age. Now they're terrified. Can you blame them?"

"Maybe you could give them 'a few bucks.'"

"Maybe I can do more than that." Happy yanked open the limo door, and Tony stepped inside. He paused for a moment, fixed his gaze on Peter's questioning eyes. "I can make them safe."

Peter nodded slowly.

He knows, Tony thought. *He understands.*

The door slammed shut, and suddenly Tony was alone. Alone in the dark quiet limo, walled off by metal and glass from the sea of grief outside. Just a billionaire and his private thoughts, dark and heavy.

Happy slid around to the front, slipped behind the wheel. "Home, boss?"

"Straight to the airport, Hap." Tony peered out the tinted window at the dark-suited mourners. "I know what I have to do."

FIVE

THE Baxter Building, home of the Fantastic Four, had seen its share of battles. The Sinister Six once tore up the square in front so badly, the FF had been without water for a week. Galactus, Devourer of Worlds, had been fought off from the roof. Doctor Doom once launched the entire building into space.

The people of midtown Manhattan, understandably, had a love-hate relationship with the FF. They loved having heroes in their midst, especially heroes as public and friendly as the Four. But the constant brawling and property damage had brought on civil suits, protests, and even the occasional death threat.

Still, Spider-Man had never seen anything like the scene outside today.

A solid wall of protesters formed a semicircle in front of the Baxter Building, blocking Broadway where it met Seventh Avenue at the north end of Times Square. They chanted angrily, waved signs reading:

FF OUT OF NYC!

(NEW) WARRIORS OF DEATH

REGISTRATION NOW

HEROES = MURDERERS

And perhaps most succinctly:

REMEMBER STAMFORD

Spider-Man swung over the crowd, as swiftly as he could manage. A few people pointed, and the chants stopped. The crowd grew silent for a moment, as though confused.

Great, he thought. *Doesn't* anybody *recognize me in the new threads?*

Then a low rumble rose up, followed by a barrage of boos and whistles. A rock flew past Spidey's head; he dodged it easily, spider-sense kicking in automatically. Then a tomato.

He let go of his webline and spread his arms wide. He felt a moment of panic; he'd only used the costume's gliding mechanism once before, and he really didn't want to plummet face-first into that angry mob. But at a certain point, he reflected, you had to trust something.

Or some*one.* Tony Stark, in this case.

Then Spider-Man was soaring, almost flying through the air. He reached out and made contact with the outer wall of the Baxter Building, then scuttled upward like his namesake, circling around the building to avoid the huge vehicle hangar doors on the top levels. Below, the crowd's booing seemed to fade like a bad dream.

At the second level from the top, he spotted a concealed doorway built right into the brick facing. He started to reach for it—

—and turned in alarm.

"Dasvidanya."

Natasha Romanov, the Russian super-spy called the Black Widow, sat casually on a ledge, gorgeous as always in tight black leather. She was eating a salad from a takeout container.

"Natasha," Spider-Man said. "What—how did you get here?"

She turned, gave him a withering look. "You have airplanes in this country?"

"What are you doing?"

"Waiting for you. Well, someone like you. Preferably taller." She stood, stretched precariously on the ledge. Spidey started to reach for her; the street was forty stories below. Natasha didn't seem concerned.

"I just flew in from the Mother Country," she continued. "Tony was kind enough to tell me about the gathering, but apparently Reed Richards didn't get the message. I was not on the approved list at the door." She gestured down at the crowd, now distant dots of color. "And security is a bit tight today."

"So you just..."

"There was bound to be an airborne visitor sooner or later."

Spidey paused, digested this for a moment. Then he shrugged and turned back to the hidden doorway.

"Johnny Storm gave me access to this," he said. "Man, I hope he's okay."

"Yes, yes." He heard her yawn.

At Spider-Man's touch, the doorway glowed. The word AUTHENTICATING appeared, holographically superimposed over the bricks; then AUTHORIZED. The hatch swung inward.

A quick crawl through an air duct, and they dropped down into a corridor near the FF's main operational center.

"So are you here as an Avenger?" Spider-Man asked. "Or representing S.H.I.E.L.D.?"

The Widow shrugged, as if the question had no meaning.

A flurry of laughter, and a tiny girl stumbled into sight, tripping over her own feet. A slightly older boy with a thick mop of blond hair came chasing after her. They both stopped simultaneously, eyeing the Widow. She glared back down at them.

Then the boy turned to Spider-Man and grinned. "Hey, Uncle Spidey. Cool costume!"

"*Thank* you, Franklin," Spider-Man said. "You're the first person I've met today with any taste."

The girl—Valeria—had recovered, and looked at them with witchy, glowing eyes. "Everybody's in Daddy's lab," she said.

"Cool." Spidey reached down and ruffled her hair. Valeria stood stock still, watching him, as though they were conducting an experiment together.

Then Franklin slapped her arm and ran. She whirled, laughing, and took off after him.

Spider-Man watched them go. Franklin and Valeria were great kids, and he knew how much they meant to Reed and Sue. He felt a twinge of regret, of envy. If only things had worked out differently with...

"While we're young?" the Widow said.

Spidey grimaced, and followed the Widow down the hall.

He always felt like a twelve-year-old around her.

REED Richards's laboratory was huge, windowless, high-ceilinged, and utterly packed with scientific equipment. Particle beam microscopes, giant lasers, alien spaceships laid out like frogs ready to be dissected. Supercomputers, ranging from the latest SUN systems to antique Cray assemblages, all custom-networked together in a tangled system that only Reed's incredible brain could understand. Johnny Storm had once observed to Spidey that, if anything ever happened to Reed, nobody would even be able to toast a slice of bread in this lab, ever again.

It seemed an odd place for the biggest gathering of super heroes ever assembled. But Spider-Man quickly realized: It was the only room in the Baxter Building large enough.

Hawkeye, Goliath, the Falcon, Tigra, and Ms. Marvel stood together, talking intensely. These, Peter realized, were the core Avengers, the nexus of Tony's premier super hero team. Hawkeye gestured wildly, nearly banging into one of Reed's big electronic devices. A time machine, maybe.

Luke Cage stood apart, in street clothes and dark shades, speaking in low tones with Cloak, a young African-American hero in a swirling blue costume. Nighthawk and Valkyrie, representatives of the off-and-on team the Defenders, milled about uncomfortably, drinks in their hands. Spider-Woman, the red-and-yellow-clad masked Avenger, stood alone in the group, tapping at her phone. The Young Avengers—Hulkling, Patriot, Wiccan, Stature, and Speed—seemed to huddle together, eyeing the older heroes suspiciously.

Dagger, a willowy young girl with light powers, danced around the room, flitting excitedly from one of Reed's machines to the next. Reed stood in the back, near the Negative Zone portal, his neck stretched out like a ten-foot snake. His head bobbed back and forth, following Dagger's path. Every time she touched something, he winced.

Spider-Man felt a stab of claustrophobia. Here, among all his fellow heroes, he felt somehow, paradoxically, exposed. Vulnerable.

You're not wanted by the law anymore, he reminded himself. *You're an Avenger now.*

He spotted Daredevil over in a corner, talking in soft low tones with the green-skinned She-Hulk. *Get two lawyers together,* he thought...they were probably deep into the legal implications of the Superhuman Registration Act by now.

Spider-Man started over toward Daredevil, but Natasha elbowed past him. She slinked up to Daredevil, laid a hand on his chest. She-Hulk rolled her eyes and turned away.

Ben Grimm, the Thing, clapped a hand on Spider-Man's back—not too hard; Ben had learned not to cripple ordinary people with friendly gestures. "Hey, Spidey. Glad ya came."

"Ben."

Spidey leaned against an intricate machine, a latticework of glass and metal. Ben frowned. "Y'better not touch that."

"Oh, sorry. Reed'll get mad?"

"Worse. He'll spend twenny minutes tellin' you what it does."

Spidey followed Ben's gaze. Across the room, Reed was gesturing expansively with elongated arms, explaining something to a clearly confused Dagger. Cloak, her partner, had joined her. He seemed equally befuddled.

"Hey," Spider-Man said, "how's Johnny doing?"

"Better...he's stable, mostly conscious. Suzy's with him now." Ben slammed a rocky fist into his palm. "I shouldn't think about it too much. Makes me wanna clobber somebody."

"Yeah. Any news about the Registration Act yet?

"Not yet." Ben gestured up at a huge wallscreen tuned to CNN. The sound was muted, but a graphic read: BREAKING NEWS - SENATE IN CLOSED SESSION ON SRA. "Should be any minute."

Ms. Marvel glided over to join them, tall and statuesque in blue and red. The other Avengers followed in her wake. "Tony's been incommunicado all day," she said to Spider-Man. "We were just wondering if you've heard from him."

Tigra, smiled, baring pointed teeth. "Spider-Man is Tony's new *favorrrrrrite.*"

"Not me," Spidey said. "Haven't heard a word." He felt uncomfortable again, like an invader in a private club.

"Tone only texts me about babes. An' I ain't got a single pic from him today." Hawkeye, the archer, looked up from his phone. "That *really* worries me."

"Hey." Spider-Man looked around. "Where's Captain America?"

"Called away. Top secret." Falcon shrugged. "'Sall he'd say."

"Gotta be S.H.I.E.L.D.," Hawkeye said. "It's always S.H.I.E.L.D."

Nighthawk was staring at the TV screen. "Pension plans and annual vacation time? Are they trying to turn us into civil servants?"

Luke Cage frowned. "I think they're trying to close us down."

"Or make us more legitimate," Ms. Marvel replied. "Why shouldn't we be better trained and publicly accountable?"

Patriot, leader of the Young Avengers, spoke up tentatively. "Somebody said we should go on strike if they mess with us. Does anybody think that's a good idea?"

Reed Richards stepped forward, frowning. "I don't think anyone here would seriously advocate a super hero strike, son."

"Becoming public employees makes perfect sense," Ms. Marvel continued, "if it helps people sleep easier."

"I can't believe I'm hearing this." Goliath grew slightly, rising to eight feet in height, and all eyes turned to him. "The masks are a tradition. They're part of who we are. We can't just let the government turn us into super-cops."

"Actually," Spider-Woman said, "we're lucky people have put up with this for so long. Why *should* we be allowed to hide behind these things?"

Hawkeye bristled. "Because the world ain't so nice outside your ivory tower, babe."

"I've never really understood the secret identity fetish," Reed said. "The Fantastic Four have been public since the very beginning, and it's always worked for us."

"For you, maybe." Spider-Man felt the claustrophobia, the panic, rising inside him again. "But what about the day I come home and find the woman who raised me impaled on an octopus arm?"

Awkward silence.

Parker, Spidey thought, *you sure know how to bring down a room.*

As the conversation slowly resumed, he slinked into a corner. Behind a refrigerator-sized electron microscope, Daredevil and the Black Widow stood very close together, their lips almost touching. At first Spidey couldn't tell if they were arguing or making out.

"...being paranoid," the Widow said. "It's all just speculation at the moment."

"No," Daredevil replied. "This has been building for a long time. Stamford was just the final straw."

"You Americans." She nuzzled his chest, a hard look on her lovely face. "So *spoiled* with freedom. The slightest hint of a threat, and you throw a tantrum."

Daredevil flicked blind eyes toward Spider-Man.

"If that Act passes," DD said, "It's the end of the way we do business. The end of everything. You can smell it in the air."

"Spoiled," the Widow repeated. Whispered it softly, into his chest.

"Quiet, everyone!"

Spidey turned to see Reed Richards raising a remote control toward the screen. Below a stern-looking female reporter, a headline crawl read: BREAKING NEWS.

"They're about to announce the results of the vote."

The chatter of TV noise rose in the room, drowning out the speculation of two dozen costumed heroes. Wings rustled; drinks were placed down. Masks, eyes, and lenses all turned to stare up at the screen.

The blank visage of Iron Man stared down at them, accompanied by the legend: AFTER THE REPORT: EXCLUSIVE INTERVIEW WITH ANTHONY STARK, THE INVINCIBLE IRON MAN.

Peter Parker, the amazing Spider-Man, felt yet another panic-twinge in his gut. *Oh, Tony,* he thought. *Man, I hope you know what you're doing.*

SIX

ONCE, the world had been simple. Countries fought wars over lines on a map, occupying conquered territories with tanks, armies, fleets. Men battled on land, at sea, or in fighter planes. They fought, they fell, and they died.

Except for Captain America. In 1945, near the end of the Second World War, he fell in battle...but he didn't die. Through a fluke of nature, he was preserved in a state of suspension, fated to awaken decades later in a very different world. A world of global communications, satellite tracking, of cameras and computers smaller than a speck of dust. A world where wars were fought very differently, for different causes, with startling new technologies.

Technologies such as the S.H.I.E.L.D. Helicarrier.

Built during the Cold War, the Helicarrier served as command post and staging point for all major operations of the Strategic Hazard Intervention Espionage Logistics Directorate. Half a mile wide, the size and bulk of a small city, it soared above the Earth, powered by several breakthrough technologies developed by Stark Enterprises. Current location: six miles over New York City.

On the carrier's flight deck, Captain America watched an F-22 Raptor glide in for a landing. The sleek stealth plane dropped wheels at the last minute, skidding just slightly as it touched down. It taxied to the end of the long deck, past a virtual museum of military aircraft past and present, and decelerated to a full, graceful stop.

They just stopped making the F-22, Cap thought. He hoped the new models would perform as well. You never knew.

He turned to peer down over the edge of the deck's metal balcony, wind whipping at his face. Somewhere down below, Earth's super heroes were gathering. But he couldn't see the city. Too much cloud cover.

"Cap? The director'll see you now."

Armored S.H.I.E.L.D. agents led him inside, through high, gray-metal corridors dotted with window portals. Captain America's duties had brought him to the Helicarrier many times before. But this time, something was different.

It feels cold. Alien, almost.

The corridor opened up into a wide, low-ceilinged room crisscrossed with walkways. No more windows. A proud woman stood facing him in full S.H.I.E.L.D. braid, with short-cropped hair and striking features. Two male agents flanked her, their hands held loose near high-tech side-arms. One had cruel eyes and broken-looking features; the other wore shades and sported a mustache.

"Captain," the woman said.

"Commander Hill."

She smiled, a cold reptile smile. "It's Director now. Well, Acting Director."

Cap frowned. "Where's Fury?"

"You've been out of the loop, haven't you?" She stepped closer to him. "I'm sorry to report that Nicholas Fury was lost at sea, four months ago.

You've heard of the Poseidon Protocol?"

"Only the name."

"And that's all you're ever going to hear. Suffice it to say, Nick Fury gave his life for his country."

Cap felt a sick feeling in his stomach. He'd lost comrades before, but this was a shock—especially so soon after Thor's death. Like Cap, Fury was just a man, but an extraordinary one. He'd been around at least as long as Cap, fought in even more wars, and had beaten the odds time and again.

Gave his life for his country.

"I'm told that twenty-three of your friends are meeting in the Baxter Building right now to discuss the super-community's reaction to the Superhuman Registration Act. What do *you* think they should do?"

"I..." Cap paused, startled by the abruptness of Hill's question. "I don't think that's for me to say."

"Cut the crap, Captain. I know you were tight with Fury, but I'm acting head of S.H.I.E.L.D. now. If nothing else, I expect you to respect the badge."

Captain America frowned, took in a long breath. Turned away briefly to gather his thoughts.

"I think this plan will split us down the middle. I think you're going to have us at war with one another."

"What's the matter with these guys?" The cruel-looking agent gestured at Cap. "How can anyone argue against super heroes being properly trained and *paid* for a living?"

Cap turned sharply to Hill: *Get your man in line?* But she just looked to the other agent, the one with the mustache.

"How many rebels do you estimate here, Captain?" Mustache asked.

"If Registration becomes law? A lot."

"Any majors?" asked Hill.

He frowned again. "Mostly the heroes who work close to the streets. Daredevil, maybe Iron Fist. I can't be sure."

"So nobody you can't handle."

"What?"

"You heard me."

Involuntarily, Cap's hand clenched into a fist. He slipped it behind his back.

"The proposal has just passed the Senate," Hill continued. "It's *done*, Captain. The law will take effect in two weeks—which means we're already behind schedule." She gestured around at the Helicarrier, its cold gray walls. "We're developing an anti-superhuman response unit here. But we need to make sure the Avengers are on board, and that *you're* out there leading the Avengers."

"You're asking me to arrest people who risk their lives for this country, every day of the week."

"No, Captain. I'm asking you to obey the will of the American people."

More S.H.I.E.L.D. agents had filed in, he realized. Heavily armored men and women, in padded riot gear with thick visors. They gathered around Hill, and behind Cap as well. Surrounding him.

"Don't play politics, Hill. Super heroes need to stay above that stuff. We can't have Washington telling us who the super villains are."

"I thought super villains were *guys in masks who refused to obey the law.*"

Her finger barely twitched, but Cap caught the motion. Instantly, a dozen S.H.I.E.L.D. agents raised their weapons into position, rifles and lasers and tranq guns. One by one, they cocked their guns: *Chik-Chak. Chik-Chak. Chik-Chak.*

All pointed at one man. A man with a flag on his chest.

Cap didn't flinch, didn't move a muscle. "Is this the hit squad you've been training to take down heroes?"

"Nobody wants a war, Captain." Hill gestured, tried to smile now. "The people are just sick and tired of living in the Wild West."

"Masked heroes are a part of this country's history."

"So's smallpox," said Cruel Features. "Grow up, huh?"

"Nobody's saying you can't do your job," Hill said. "We're just expanding its parameters, that's all."

"It's time you went legit like the rest of us." Mustache Agent held his rifle outstretched, its red laser dot dancing across the star on Cap's chest. "*Soldier.*"

Captain America took a single step toward Hill. A dozen agents stepped forward in response.

"I knew your grandfather, Hill. Did you know that?"

She said nothing.

"His unit suffered eighty percent losses in the Bulge. They retreated along the English Channel, cut off, no supplies. The weather was brutal: huge storms, blinding snowfalls, sub-zero temperatures. One man bled out; another died stopping a Panzer division from crossing the river.

"Corporal Francis Hill kept his last buddy alive. When we found them, they were half-starved and suffering from severe exposure. But he'd held his bridge against the Germans, and saved at least one man's life."

Hill just stared at him.

"Did he ever tell you that story, Director Hill?"

"A dozen times."

"He was one of many true heroes I met in that war." Slowly, Cap turned and addressed the circle of S.H.I.E.L.D. agents. "Put your weapons down, boys."

"Captain America," Hill said slowly, "is not in command here."

She stepped forward, her teeth gritted in rage.

"*Their* war," she hissed. "Not mine."

"Weapons. Down," Cap repeated. "Or I will not be responsible for what comes next."

"Tranquilizers on. Get ready."

"This is insane, Hill."

"There's an easy solution."

"Damn you for this."

"Damn you for *making* me do thi—"

Cap jerked his arm up and out, ramming his shield into the agent's rifle just as the man pulled the trigger. Cap leapt upward, pivoted in mid-air, and grabbed the second man's neck, twisting just hard enough to knock him off his feet. The man let out a strangled cry.

"Tranquilizers!" Hill yelled. "NOW!"

Cap grabbed the third agent by his riot gear, held him up in the air. The barrage of tranq capsules struck the agent full-on, shielding Cap for a crucial second. Then he flung the agent into his attackers and took off at a run.

"Take him! Take him *down*!"

He plowed through the line of agents, punching and battering, slapping their guns away and knocking the men off balance. Armor had its drawbacks; Cap was lighter, swifter than his enemies. He flung his impenetrable shield at a pair of attackers, slicing the tips off their guns. When it boomeranged back, he snatched it out of the air without looking.

The S.H.I.E.L.D. agent with cruel features stood before the corridor leading outside, blocking Cap's way. Four more men backed him up, all armed with heavy-gauge rifles. These weren't tranq guns. Not anymore.

Cap raised his shield, and his mouth curled into a battle-grimace. "Don't even think it, little man."

Then he *charged*, head down, his shield held straight out like a battering ram. He plowed into the agent, smashing the man's jaw. He swung the shield to one side, then the other, toppling S.H.I.E.L.D. agents like tenpins.

"DIRECTOR HILL TO ALL UNITS." The loudspeakers blared now, almost deafeningly. "STOP CAPTAIN AMERICA. I REPEAT: *STOP CAPTAIN AMERICA!*"

Cap dashed out into the hallway, bullets whistling all around him. Shells, pulse beams, tranq capsules. He paused before a small window, holding his shield up behind him to block the fire.

He waited, braced against the window, for a break in the fire. Inevitably, it came.

Muscles honed in World War II coiled tight, and Captain America swiveled around and *punched out the window* with his shield. Then he leapt, out the window and into open air. A fresh barrage of bullets followed him; he twisted and dropped, surrendering his actions to pure survival instinct.

The flight deck lay below, but that was no good; he'd be a sitting duck. He bounced off a gunmount and flipped himself upward, heading toward the upper levels of the Helicarrier. Grabbed for purchase on the outer wall, grasped a disused propeller, and swung himself up again.

Below, a phalanx of S.H.I.E.L.D. agents appeared in the shattered window. They looked around, sighted him, and fired upward.

This is bad, he thought. *Six miles up and nowhere to run.*

Then he saw it: an old P-40 Warhawk, just arcing down toward the flight deck. A relic, just like him, miraculously still in service. It bore the cruel jaw and painted eye of the Flying Tigers, meticulously repainted over the years.

The P-40 must have been closing in for a landing when the shooting broke out. Eighty, ninety feet above, and dropping. Seventy. Sixty-five.

Cap leapt.

He crashed down on top of the cockpit, shield first, shattering the glass. Pain shot up through his legs. The pilot flinched away, shook his head against the sudden wind. "JEEZUS!"

Cap clamped a hand onto the man's throat.

"Keep flying, son. And watch that potty mouth."

The pilot nodded frantically, pulled up on the stick. The flight deck grew closer, faster and faster, then seemed to flatten out as the plane leveled off, less than twenty feet above the deck. The pilot kicked in the afterburners, and the plane began to rise.

Cap staggered, almost toppled off. He held on, gritting his teeth.

S.H.I.E.L.D. agents ran out onto the flight deck: two dozen, maybe three. They pointed upward, started squeezing off shots.

But Cap's plane was moving too fast. The pilot nosed it up farther, pulling up and away from the carrier. The flight deck slid past in a blur, and then they were out over open air.

Cap glanced backward. The Helicarrier was shrinking into the distance, its jagged bulk limned against the clouds. No doubt Hill was already scrambling pursuit planes, but he knew they'd be too late.

Cap steadied himself atop the cracked cockpit, riding the plane like a surfer. He looked down just as the clouds parted…revealing the spires of Manhattan, the ocean and rivers surrounding it. The sea to the east, the mountains and farms and towns to the west.

"Whe-whe-*where are we going?*" the pilot yelled.

Cap leaned forward, into the wind.

"America," he said.

PART TWO
STARTING TO BELIEVE

SEVEN

THE place: corner of 12th Street and Fifth Avenue, Manhattan. The time: 8:24 AM—morning rush hour. The robot: twelve feet tall, shaking the ground with every step, its face a gigantic, twisted mirror-image of the villain called Doctor Doom.

Tony Stark braked to a stop in midair, half a block away from the robot. He looked down, saw that the police had cleared the block. People stood behind barricades, watching, recording the scene with their phones and digital cameras.

"This is our chance," Tony said.

Ms. Marvel glided up next to Tony, waiting for instructions. Below, Luke Cage and the Black Widow sprinted down the middle of the cleared street. Spider-Man followed close behind them, webbing his way from traffic light to streetlamp.

Tony opened a radio link. "Reed, are you online?"

The robot stamped down hard, cracking open the pavement. People gasped and shrank farther back behind the barricades, pressing up against storefronts and deli windows.

"I AM DOOM!" the robot said.

Reed Richards's voice crackled in Tony's ear. "In the absence of conclusive evidence," he said, "I would assume that's the Doombot."

Tony frowned. Joking, or just stating the obvious? With Reed, it was hard to tell.

"We're ready, Tone." Spider-Man came through crisp and clear on the Stark frequency. "Friendly neighborhood rookie Avenger, reporting for duty."

Tony scanned his troops. Tigra nodded fiercely up at him; Cage looked grim, unsure. Spider-Man clung to a factory building wall, ready for action. Ms. Marvel hovered, poised and statuesque as always.

With a thought, Tony turned his armor's amplifiers up to full gain. "ATTENTION CITIZENS," he said. "I AM IRON MAN, A REGISTERED SUPERHUMAN; REAL NAME, ANTHONY STARK. THIS IS AN INITIATIVE-APPROVED SUPERHUMAN PROCEDURE, OPERATING WITHIN SRA SAFETY PROTOCOLS. PLEASE STAND BACK AND ALLOW US TO DO OUR JOBS. THERE IS NOTHING TO FEAR."

People exchanged glances, unsure.

The robot took another slow, lumbering step down Fifth Avenue. "I AM DOOM!" Its foot raised another quake, setting off a block's worth of car alarms.

"Reed," Tony said. "Quick rundown on this thing. And I mean quick."

"It's a prototype peacekeeper, built by Doctor Doom—you know who he is?"

"Yes, Reed."

Victor Von Doom was Reed's arch-foe, a brilliant, armored scientist who ruled the country of Latveria with, quite literally, an iron fist. Doom had nurtured a grudge against Reed since their days in college together.

"Right, well. Doom claims he intended the 'bot only for domestic use, within Latveria. But it developed some sort of rudimentary artificial intelligence and fled to America."

Ms. Marvel frowned. "Doom actually *warned* you about this thing? Why?"

"Maybe he sees which way the political winds are blowing in this country. I suspect he wants to get on Tony's good side. Or perhaps he has another, deeper plan." Reed hesitated. "I don't know."

Tony realized: *Those are his least favorite three words in the English language.*

"Thanks, Reed. Stark out."

Tony double-checked; all the Avengers were on his frequency. "Everyone follow my lead," he said. "This is the beginning of a new era. It's our chance to show how things will work, from now on. To regain the people's trust."

"Me like trust," Spider-Man said. "Trust good."

"I AM DOOM!"

"Aerial assault first." Tony launched himself forward. "Carol?"

Ms. Marvel fell in behind him, her long red sash waving bright in the morning sun. Together they arrowed toward the robot's head, slicing through the air in perfect formation. It turned glowing eyes toward them, lurched to one side—

—and stumbled into a parked car, smashing the trunk flat. A woman wrenched open the driver's side door and half-stumbled, half-fell out, clutching a baby. She lurched, looking around with panicked eyes, and ran—straight into the robot's leg.

Slowly, its head swiveled to look down at her.

Tony whirled toward Ms. Marvel. Her blue-gloved arms were outstretched, beginning to glow with power. Carol's half-alien physiology allowed her to generate highly charged energy bolts; she was one of the most powerful Avengers in a combat situation.

But if she fired at the robot now...

"Carol." Tony's amplified voice was sharp, deliberately piercing. "Civilian safety first."

Ms. Marvel grimaced, nodded, and swooped downward.

The robot reached a huge arm down toward the frightened woman. She stood frozen, backed up against the car, her fingers rigid around her baby. Ms. Marvel arced down between them, reaching out. But the woman shrank even farther back.

She's as terrified of us, Tony realized, *as of the Doombot.*

"Protocols," he said.

Ms. Marvel seemed to pivot in midair on the ball of her foot, coming to a stop just above the battered car. The robot's head bobbed up and down in a confused motion, looking from her to the woman and back again.

Tony found himself staring at Ms. Marvel. *She's beautiful. Statuesque, powerful, with a dancer's grace. A model for everything we're trying to achieve.*

Ms. Marvel turned to the woman and spoke in even, rehearsed tones.

"I am Ms. Marvel," she said, "a registered superhuman. Real name, Carol Danvers. I'm here to assist you. Please stand back and allow me to—"

Tony was already in motion—but a half-second too late. The robot lifted its huge metal arm and *swatted* Ms. Marvel out of the air.

"AVENGERS ASSEMBLE!"

Tony's powerful repulsor rays blasted into the robot's head. Sparks showered into the air. He retreated back a few feet and activated a multiple camera protocol. All at once, his internal monitors showed:

- Ms. Marvel had struck a building, raining bricks down onto the sidewalk. She was clearly dazed, but her pulse-rate showed even. No serious injuries.

- The woman ran off down the street, holding her baby. Safe.
- The Doombot's brain-casing had cracked open, exposing servos and circuitry. But it was still standing. Tony felt the tingle of a radar lock, and saw an unfamiliar weapon-tube extruding from the 'bot's finger.
- Spider-Man webbed through the air toward the battle. Cage and the Black Widow ran down the street, half a step behind him.

The Doombot's weapon let out a bright arc-light flash, blinding Tony momentarily. Eye-filters dropped down automatically in less than a second. It took another three seconds for his vision to clear, and by then:

The robot was still in motion, but the Avengers were on it. Cage had climbed onto its back, pounding at it with steel-hard fists. Widow stood perched on a lamp-post, blasting its chest with her stingers. The robot lurched from side to side, almost as if it could feel the pain of their assault.

"I AM—DOOM," it crackled.

Spider-Man landed light as a feather on the street, just behind the robot. He planted his feet firmly, reached out both arms, and fired off a thick barrage of sticky webbing. It struck the robot's back—elegantly missing Cage, who climbed up toward the 'bot's head. The robot stopped short, anchored back by the pull of the webbing.

Cage spotted the robot's shattered brain casing and smiled a nasty smile. He cracked his knuckles once, then reared back and started pummeling the 'bot's circuitry.

"Cage," Tony said. "Protocols."

Cage ignored Tony. He reached inside the robot's head and began yanking out wires. Electric flashes sparked harmlessly off his tough skin.

Tony moved in, repulsors glowing. "Hold it steady, Pe—uh, Spider-Man."

"You got it, boss."

"Stop calling me that."

"Yes, boss."

The webbing formed a thick cable now, stretching from Spider-Man's wrists to the struggling Doombot. With practiced ease, Spidey twirled his hands and grabbed hold of the webbing, just as the last of it shot free of his web-shooters. Then he *pulled*.

The Doombot raised a leg, tried to move forward. Spider-Man held firm, his lean muscles straining. The Doombot stopped dead, stuck in place.

Inside his armor, Tony smiled with pride. These were the new Avengers. *His* Avengers.

"Keep it up, Peter. Nice work."

"Thanks. Hey, Tone, when this is over, I need to talk to you about a few things."

"I don't have a hole in my schedule till next spring. Let's do it now."

Still gripping the webline, Spider-Man turned gold-metallic eyes upward in surprise. "Now?"

Tony switched to a private frequency. "It's called multitasking."

"Whoa! It's like you're inside my head."

Then Ms. Marvel swooped up again, in front of the 'bot. She fired off twin energy-blasts from her hands, and the Doombot's head caved in. It let out a piercing, electronic cry.

"Tick tock, Peter."

"Right. Well, first off, I got your first stipend check. And..."

"Make sure they took out the FICA. FICA will really come back and bite you."

"Tony, it was more than I made last year."

Tony blasted the robot once, twice. It lurched; its head lolled loose now, connected to its body by a thick cable.

"You're earning it, Peter. Right now."

"Well, you know. Thanks."

Cage was pounding repeatedly on the robot's stomach now, bashing a deep dent in its metal hide. The 'bot doubled forward, falling to its knees.

Tony reached out and *swatted* the robot sideways. Switching his anchor web to one hand, Spider-Man reached out with the other and webbed up the thing's optical sensors. Its head swung wildly, side to side, on the end of that cable.

"Peter, listen." Tony gestured to Ms. Marvel, who let out another fearsome energy blast. "The Superhuman Registration Act becomes law at midnight tonight. I've personally assured the president that I will take charge of its implementation."

"You?"

"Someone has to do it. Nobody wants some faceless administration bureaucrat in the job. Better that it's someone who understands the powered community, who's registered and operating publicly himself."

"I...yeah. Yeah, that makes sense."

"I'm going to need you at my side."

"For that stipend? You got it."

"It's not a simple matter, Peter." Tony flipped channels momentarily. "Natasha, sever that thing's head, will you?"

From her perch atop a lamppost, the Black Widow smiled. Her stingers flashed out, and the Doombot's head tumbled free. But its body kept moving, lurching around randomly, dangerously close to the fenced-in spectators.

"Peter, I'll need your help in some matters of...enforcement. Details will be forthcoming."

"Okay. I guess."

"And there's something else. You know what I'm talking about."

"Tony..."

"Peter, it's the right thing to do." Tony paused, turned up his volume slightly. "And as of midnight, it's the law."

Spider-Man's expression was unreadable beneath his mask. But Tony's readouts showed elevated levels of adrenaline within him, and an accelerated pulse rate.

Cage grappled with the Doombot's leg, kneecapping it repeatedly with one powerful punch after another. "This boy takes some punishment," he said.

"It's not open for negotiation, Peter."

"I...I need you to promise me something."

"Name it."

"My aunt. Aunt May. No matter what happens, you have to keep her safe."

"Peter, I swear to you right now: If you do this, I'll personally protect that sweet old lady till one of us is dead. And I suspect she'll outlive me."

Spider-Man tensed, grunted. Then, drawing on every ounce of his spider-enhanced strength, he yanked hard on the webline. Cage leapt free, the Widow jumped down. Ms. Marvel wafted upward, all grace and power.

The Doombot crashed to the pavement in a shower of sparks. One leg joint twitched briefly, rattling against a manhole. Then it was still.

Tony looked down, surveying the scene. The Doombot lay in a sprawl of cracked tar, smack in the middle of the street. The Avengers stood in a circle around it, dusting themselves off. Natasha stretched a sore muscle.

Tony made a thumbs-up gesture to the crowd, and the police

started lowering the barricades. People crept in cautiously, toward the middle of the street. Businessmen, tourists, women with strollers. They stared at the robot, hushed, for a long moment. Not speaking, barely breathing.

Then the crowd erupted in a roar of applause.

Tony reached out and took Ms. Marvel's hand. Together, like royalty, they descended to the street.

"Hear that?" Tony said. "That's the sound of people starting to believe in heroes again."

"I ain't sure." Cage approached, rubbing his knuckles. "We still gonna *be* super heroes after this, Tony? Won't we just be S.H.I.E.L.D. agents, on the federal payroll?"

"No, Luke. We're heroes. We tackle super-crime and we save people's lives." Tony glanced at Spider-Man. "The only thing changing is that the kids, the amateurs, and the sociopaths will be weeded out."

Widow raised an eyebrow, caustic as always. "Which category does Captain America fall into, Anthony?"

Tony rose up slightly, twirled around. He raised powerful arms to the crowd, and they cheered again.

Ms. Marvel smiled. Cage grimaced, looked away. Natasha nodded.

Spider-Man's face was hidden, but Tony knew he was listening to every word.

Tony swooped low over the prone, unmoving Doombot. He reached out a metal gauntlet to a teenaged couple, who stood watching with wide eyes. The boy nodded, flashed Tony a thumbs-up sign.

"Trust me, Natasha. Cap's wrong this time."

EIGHT

SUSAN Richards was tired. Tired of hospital food, of hospital coffee. Tired of chatting with her groggy brother, trying to keep his spirits up. Tired of prying information out of the doctors about how well the operation had gone. Of trying to explain to the nurses that they needed to keep Johnny's fever down *at all times,* unless they wanted to walk in one morning and find the sheets accidentally charred to ashes.

Mostly, she was just tired.

"Franklin?" She kicked off her shoes, flipped on the living room light. "Val, honey?"

Silence.

She pulled out her phone. A light was blinking: new text message. It was from Ben Grimm.

Suzie - Franklin wanted to see the new Pixar flick, so I took the rugrats out. Figred you an Big Brain could use a little alone time.

And a second message:

```
Ok, I'M the one wanted t see the Pixar flick. Val
was pushin for a documentry but Im still bigger
n her.
```

Sue smiled. At times like this, she realized what a blessing the Fantastic Four was. They weren't just a team, like the Avengers or the Defenders. They were a mutual support group, a family. A comfort when times got rough.

She padded through the living quarters. Checked the mail, flipped on the muted TV. More footage of the Stamford explosion, rising up in a thick black cloud. Were they ever going to stop showing that?

Almost ritualistically, Sue paced through the dining room, kitchen, all three bathrooms. Franklin's little room and Val's littler one. The master bedroom was dark, empty, the bed undisturbed where the robot maid had neatened it this morning.

Quit stalling, she told herself. *You know where he is.*

Reed's lab was buzzing, both figuratively and literally. Over the past week, he'd rented a dozen extra high-powered computer systems from Columbia University, airlifting them in and networking them into his existing databases. The floor was a spaghetti-tangle of cables, server boxes, routers, and switches.

And in the center: a hexagonal table strewn with laptop computers, papers, and tablets. Reed sat at the far end, his elongated neck craned up and around, eyes flicking from a tablet computer to a sheaf of hologram-stamped papers marked CLASSIFIED.

God, Sue thought, *I love him.*

She knew how Reed got when he was deep into his research. In order to get his attention, she'd have to say at least four separate outrageous things, waiting after each one for him to grunt. Sometimes punching was required.

To her shock, he looked right up and smiled at her.

"Susan!" Reed exclaimed. "You wouldn't believe what happened this morning."

She smiled, glanced at the sprawl of wiring. "I guess it wasn't the electric bill."

"I alerted the Avengers to a Doombot, helped them stop its rampage. And—and afterward, Tony came by and we talked for a long time. He's got a lot of plans, honey. A lot of very important plans."

"Mm."

"This is the biggest thing I've ever worked on." His eyes were flashing; Sue had never seen him like this. "Tony wasn't kidding when he said he'd revolutionize every metahuman in America. I haven't been this excited since I saw my first singularity."

"I'd be excited too," she said slowly, "if Tony's genius plan didn't mean jail for half our Christmas list."

"Yes, yes, I know." He turned away, activated a large wall screen. "But it's their choice. They can always register."

"About this Registration—"

"It's a must, honey. Take a look at my projections."

Frowning, Sue crossed to the wall screen. Reed's handwriting covered it, floor to ceiling: equations, notes, circles, strikeouts.

"This is gobbledygook," she said.

"No no." He stretched up behind her, pointed to the screen. "It's the exponential curve the number of super-beings is following. We're seeing more every year: mutants, accidents, artificially powered humans like Tony. Aliens. Even time travelers. It's an enormous social danger."

"They're all people," she whispered.

"We're facing an apocalypse if the unregulated activity isn't brought under control." She felt his hand, soft, on her shoulder blade. "This isn't politics, darling. It's science. I'd reached this conclusion already; Tony's plan is just the best, quickest way to prevent disaster."

She said nothing.

"You should have seen the team in action this morning," Reed continued. "Tony showed me the video. They did their job perfectly, and they did it all within the new guidelines. This can *work*, darling. Plus it's an amazing opportunity for us." He gestured wildly now, his elongated arms clicking on touch screens all over the room. "You should hear the ideas we've been tossing around. I feel like a concept machine."

Reed's arm had snapped back; his fingers caressed the small of her back now. Slowly his hand crept downward.

Sue and Reed had always had an active sex life, even after the kids were born. More than once, she'd laughed to herself about the image their friends had of them. Everyone saw Reed as a cold, obsessive scientist, and her as a cheery mother figure. They had no idea.

But this...something was deeply, profoundly wrong. Involuntarily, she flashed on her force field. Reed snatched his fingers away as though he'd been stung.

"Sorry," they both said, almost simultaneously.

Suddenly a loud, grinding noise filled the room. Sue whirled toward the Negative Zone portal. Its lights flashed; its circular perimeter whirled to life. Within the portal, a swirling mass of stars appeared, dotted with asteroids and distant, fast-moving humanoid forms.

"It's all right," Reed said. "Just running a test."

The portal ground louder, rising in pitch. Above it, near the ceiling, a display screen lit up: PROJECT 42 GATEWAY DRILL / SUCCESSFUL.

"Project 42?" Sue shouted. "What's that?"

Reed cocked his head, peered at her with an odd expression. Hesitated.

Then a sharp metallic voice cut through the noise. "It's classified."

As Sue watched, the red-and-gold figure of Iron Man appeared within the portal. His boot-jets flared, propelling him up and outward. He hovered gracefully for a moment, then swooped out into the room.

"Hello, Susan," Tony said.

"Tony," she said, keeping her voice carefully neutral.

The portal cycled to a halt. The stars faded, and the portal irised closed.

Reed smiled at Tony, stretched his upper body around to face him. "How were conditions inside?"

"Interesting." Tony flashed a red-glowing eye at Susan, then cut off Reed with a hand gesture. "I think it'll do."

"I'll collate the data on—"

"We'll discuss it later. I have to get going." Tony looked up, as if distracted by some signal coming through his armor. "The SRA becomes law at midnight. Your paperwork's done, right?"

Reed frowned. "We're already public. Our identities are known."

"Nonetheless, there are forms. We need your power levels, known weaknesses, any prison record or incidents where a member of your team has lost control."

"Of course." Reed nodded several times, his mind racing. "I also want to talk to Doctor Pym about that Niflhel Protocol you mentioned—"

"Reed." Tony leaned in, metallic eyes flashing red. *"Not now."*

Sue's eyes narrowed. Reed had never kept secrets from her before.

"Honey." Reed craned his neck around, smiled hesitantly at Sue. "Can you take care of that paperwork Tony mentioned?"

"It's all online," Tony said.

Tony was hovering just off the ground, she noticed, giving him an air of additional height and authority. He looked like a creature from a '50s sci-fi movie, an alien overlord come to rule benevolently over Earth. The

Iron Man armor covered every inch of his body, leaving no visible trace of his humanity.

And Reed seemed totally in his thrall. Like a teenager with a boy-crush.

"Sure," Sue said. "Oh, and Reed?"

"Yes, dear?"

"Your brother-in-law's doing better. The surgeon managed to get the bone fragments off his brain; they might even release him in a day or two."

"That's—"

"Just in case you give a damn."

Then she turned and stalked away, out of the room. Feeling the cold, red-laser eyes of Iron Man on her back, with every step.

NINE

TONY Stark's limo held every type of soft drink known to man. Cola, diet cola, orange, grape; fruit punch and Gatorade, eight kinds of vitamin water. Regular and decaf, plus dangerously overcaffeinated tipples from South America. Sculpted glass bottles adorned with Japanese characters, each sealed with a single marble. Vintage brands like Jolt, Patio, and New Coke, scavenged from warehouses all over the world.

The drinks sat above a trough of crushed ice, staring out at Tony like a row of glass and metal eyes. And not one of them was what he wanted.

Distract yourself, he thought. He clicked on the TV, and a coiffed blonde appeared above a cable news logo.

"...just got word about a press conference that Tony Stark has called for tomorrow," she said. "This, of course, to follow the enactment of the Superhuman Registration Act into law, just minutes from now. How does that strike you?"

The screen shifted to a fierce masculine face. Bushy brows, graying temples, a too-short mustache adorning his lip. White shirt, rolled-up sleeves. Nostrils flaring with excitement.

Below his face, the words appeared:

J. JONAH JAMESON
PUBLISHER, DAILY BUGLE

"How does it *strike* me?" Jameson repeated. "It's *great*, Megan. I mean, it's only a first step toward controlling our massive superhuman problem. But at midnight tonight, everything my newspaper has *ever campaigned for* officially becomes *law*."

Wow, Tony thought. *He's even scarier when he smiles.*

"Do you think—"

"No more *masks*," Jameson continued, cutting off the reporter. "No more hiding, and no more *creepy excuses* about *secret identities*. These clowns will *work for S.H.I.E.L.D.* or their colorful butts will wind up in *jail*. Period."

"Mister Jameson. Do you think, do you really think all the super heroes are going to just sign up?"

"No." Jameson leaned forward into the camera, and a hungry look appeared in his eyes. "Only the *smart ones*."

Tony smiled. *Sorry, old man. Peter's not your whipping boy anymore.*

Still, it was good to have a major newspaper on the side of Registration. Even one run by a borderline psychopath.

The reporter asked another question. Jameson ignored it entirely, launching instead into a long recitation of the great struggles for justice conducted over the years by the heroic Daily Bugle. Tony rolled his eyes, clicked to another channel.

The thick smoke cloud again, rising up over the ruined Stamford school. *As if I don't see that in my dreams every night.* He muted the TV.

The corner of the screen read: 11:53 PM.

"Pull over, Happy," Tony said. "Time to drink a toast."

Happy's voice came over the speaker. "You got a beer for me back there, Mister Stark?"

"You're driving, Hap." Tony glanced briefly back up at the devastation on the screen. "Let's play by the rules tonight."

"HEARD anything from Captain America, Mister Stark?"

Tony fidgeted, shifted the smartphone from hand to hand. He looked up at Happy, who sat opposite, hefting a seltzer water while leaning his bulky frame against the driver's barrier.

He looks so...at ease, Tony thought. *Will I ever feel that way again?*

"Nothing from Cap." Tony frowned. "Hawkeye's dropped out of sight too, and I can't raise Cage. I think Cap's secretly putting together his own team." He tossed the phone to Happy. "Jesus, Happy, I can't look. Tell me how many heroes have registered."

Happy peered at the screen. "Looks like...thirty-seven. Wait, make that thirty-eight. Ms. Widow's registration just came through."

"Just like Natasha to make me sweat a little." Tony took a deep breath. "Thirty-eight."

"That's about what you expected, right?"

"Pretty much. Still...Hap, are the FF's forms in?"

"Just a sec..." Happy ran a thick finger down the screen, scrolling the display. "Yep, here they are. All four of 'em."

Well. That was something, at least.

"Couple more just rolled in. Prob'ly not everyone's gonna meet the deadline head-on." Happy glanced at his watch. "Hey, it's one minute till. You want we should do a New Year's-style countdown?"

"No." Tony leaned back, closing his eyes tight. He kept them closed, squeezing till spots appeared. "I just hope we're doing the right—"

A loud sharp beeping filled the air, echoing off the limo's walls. Tony snapped his eyes open just in time to see a startled Happy toss the smartphone up into the air, like a boiling pan of oil.

Tony grabbed the phone, stabbed at a mute button. "S.H.I.E.L.D. alert," he said.

When he turned around, Happy was already holding up the Iron Man helmet.

S.H.I.E.L.D. Mobile Command Center 3A was a high-tech hovercraft designed specifically for urban operations. Tony caught up with it a few blocks north of Wall Street, among the close-packed skyscrapers of lower Manhattan. At first all he saw was a blur, like a heat wave rippling sideways in the night against the fifth-story windows. He kicked his boot-jets to full, course-correcting by trial and error. When he matched the vehicle's speed, his sensors penetrated the S.H.I.E.L.D. stealth cloak and he saw the Command Center: a low flat bus with a pointed front end, skimming its way around the tall buildings.

"IRON MAN, REAL NAME TONY STARK," he broadcast. "REQUEST APPROVAL TO COME ABOARD."

The interior was dark, cramped, and crowded with surveillance screens. A real war room. Four S.H.I.E.L.D. agents in full gear manned computer consoles.

"Unregistered minor," Maria Hill said, pointing to a flatscreen. "Tried to foil a robbery in costume. A clear violation of the Act."

Tony lifted up his helmet and peered at the screen. It showed a young masked black man, accompanied by one of Tony's own dossier entries:

Subject: Eli Bradley

Alias: PATRIOT

Group Affiliation: Young Avengers (unauthorized)

Powers: enhanced strength, agility; throwing
stars

Power Type: inborn/artificial (hybrid)

Current Location: New York, NY

Tony frowned. "Where is he now?"

Hill turned to an agent. "Russell. The new holo display online yet?"

"Yes ma'am."

"Punch it up."

She motioned Tony back. In the center of the room, a three-dimensional image flickered to life: Patriot, scared and breathing hard, lit only by sporadic streetlamps and roof lights. He ran and jumped for his life, making incredible leaps from the top of one high building to another.

"This display is state of the art," Hill said. "It uses ordinary cameras, but enhances—"

"I know." Tony waved a hand through the image; it didn't even waver. "I designed it."

"We've got him," the agent said. "NYPD surveillance cameras are locked on his heat signature. Foxtrot-Four is closing in, just a few blocks south of here."

On the image, a helicopter spotlight appeared in the air, just behind Patriot. He half-turned, a terrified look on his face. Then he sprinted away, even faster.

Hill smiled. "Run, you little freak."

Tony frowned. He'd never been sure what to make of Hill; she struck him as an extremist, the kind of soldier who always looked for the simplest, most violent solution to a problem. The loss of Nick Fury had left a vacuum at the top of S.H.I.E.L.D., a dangerous thing in an organization charged with policing the entire free world. Hill had seen her chance and grabbed for it.

And she sure seemed to be taking a lot of pleasure in this.

"The Registration Act has been law for thirty-eight minutes, Commander. Shouldn't you give this kid a little time?"

Hill raised an eyebrow at him. "First off, Stark, it's *Director* now."

"*Acting* Director, I think."

She glared at him. "Patriot and the Young Avengers—a group, I might add, that *you* allowed tacitly to be formed in the first place—have been tweeting all night against the Act." She motioned to an agent, who called up a flatscreen full of text. "Examples: 'Death before unmasking.' 'Eff S.H.I.E.L.D. forever.' 'Tony Stark: One Percenter With a Heart of Stone.'" She smiled. "Bit of poetry in that one, I thought."

"Director," the agent said, "signal from Foxtrot-Four."

On the holo, Patriot made a massive leap up and across a dark gap between buildings. He scrambled and almost missed the roof, but grabbed hold and vaulted up. The copter circled around to intercept him, fanning its light across the roof. Tony could make out weapon-launchers mounted on both sides of it, just above its landing gear.

The pilot's crackling voice filled the Command Center. "Visual confirmation, S.H.I.E.L.D.-TAC. I'm in position."

Hill stepped forward. "Roger that, Foxtrot-Four. Permission to use *tranquilizers* and *minimum force.*" She turned to Tony. "Satisfied?"

He didn't answer.

A hail of capsules and rubber bullets rained down on Patriot's running figure, ripping open the back of his jacket. He cried out, but kept moving.

"No injury, S.H.I.E.L.D.-TAC."

The agent turned to Hill, frowning. "This kid is bulletproof now?"

"Damn database," a second agent said. "I thought we had people updating this thing."

"Patience, people." Hill smiled again. "As Mister Stark says, we've been in this business for less than an hour."

"Where is he going?" Tony asked. "He's running out of island."

"According to our intel, the Young Avengers have a safe house right about..."

Still pursued by the helicopter, Patriot launched himself off the side of another building. But this time he wasn't aiming at a roof. He flailed in the air, then crashed straight into a plate glass window, shattering it. He let out a cry and tumbled inside the building.

"...there," Hill finished.

"Switching to copter view," the agent said.

The image became a shaky downshot on Patriot, standing just inside the shattered window. The room looked dark, abandoned; Tony couldn't make out any other figures.

"Guys!" Patriot yelled. "We gotta get out of here! I was...I was breaking up a *mugging* for God's sake, and now S.H.I.E.L.D.'s all over me!"

"He's in for a surprise," Hill said. "We picked up the rest of the Young Avengers half an hour ago."

"Actually, Wiccan's still in the wind," one of the agents said. "But local police have got a line on him."

"GUYS, THIS IS SERIOUS!" Patriot's figure wobbled as the copter circled around the gap in the building. "S.H.I.E.L.D. IS—THEY'RE NOT MESSING AROUND!"

"Tranqs ineffective, S.H.I.E.L.D.-TAC," the copter pilot said. "And now I can't get a bead on him."

Hill turned to an agent. "Is that building clear?"

"Yes, ma'am. No life signs."

"Foxtrot-Four, you are cleared to escalate."

Tony turned to her, alarmed. "What does that —"

The agent clicked back to a wide view. Twin incendiary missiles flashed out from the copter's weapon-launchers, headed straight toward the building.

The holo switched back to the copter's camera again—just in time to capture Patriot's terrified face. He stared straight at the camera, mouth open, as the missiles closed in on him.

Then the building exploded. The framework shattered and the top three floors erupted up into the air, glass and metal flying everywhere. A cloud of dark ash filled the screen, blotting out the devastation.

Tony grabbed Hill by the shoulders. "What are you doing? Are you *insane?*"

She winced under his metallic grip, then pulled angrily away.

"That kid is practically indestructible. What do you expect?"

"I *expect* you not to cause wanton property damage." He gestured at the dust-cloud on the screen. "The whole idea behind this is *not* to panic people!"

"I suppose our methods differ."

"If that kid is dead—"

"He's not." The agent stabbed at his controls, and the holo flickered from static to dust and back again. "I can't get a picture—NYPD cameras were knocked out by the blast. But Foxtrot-Four confirms: They've picked him up."

"This is wrong." Tony snapped on his helmet, and all his systems flashed to life. "This is—I'm going to speak to the president about this." He turned and strode toward the hatch.

"Stark."

Something in Hill's tone made him stop.

"We're on the same side here," she said.

He reached for the hatch, activated the airlock. The inner door hissed open.

"I know," he replied.

And off he flew, into the night.

TEN

AUNT May's house was very quiet. Old books, chotchkes; souvenirs from vacations taken back when air travel was far less casual. Framed pictures everywhere: Peter, Uncle Ben, and Peter's long-dead parents, posed proudly in their military uniforms. Sepia-toned photos from the early 20th century, maybe even the 19th. Smell of mothballs, of disinfectants manufactured decades ago.

Peter Parker sat on his bed, smoothed down the old checkered bedspread. Like everything else in the room, it had been here for decades. His old, clunky microscope; the analog-film camera he'd taken his first photos with. The science trophy with the dent in it, where Flash Thompson had knocked it to the ground back in high school.

All of it the same. *Preserved,* he realized, *but not obsessively. Proudly. There's a difference.*

So much of him, of Peter Parker, was here in this room. And yet a big slice, a big thread in the skein of his life, was missing.

He went to the closet, pulled back a loose board. Felt around for a moment, and closed a hand around his very first, cloth Spider-Man mask. It stared at him with oversized, white eyes, slightly discolored with age.

"Peter?"

At the sound of May's voice, he suddenly remembered why he'd come. A surge of panic ran through him. He wadded up the mask, stuffed it into his back pocket.

"In here, Aunt May."

Every time Peter came to visit, Aunt May made him wheatcakes, no matter what time of day or night. Fortunately, he was hungry.

"Goodness, Peter, you're awake early. The sun isn't even up yet."

She stood in the doorway. Wobbling a little, he noticed, but smiling for her nephew. Her hair was pulled back in a neat bun; her face showed a few more lines every year. Her hands were blue-veined, but steady.

Only one thing was odd: The tray in her hands held chocolate chip cookies, not wheatcakes.

"I couldn't sleep." Peter smiled hesitantly at the tray. "Cookies, Aunt May?"

She looked at the tray, as if seeing it for the first time. For a moment, she looked confused. Peter felt another stab of panic, of worry.

Then she shook her head. "I don't know, dear. Today seemed different."

"I'm not complaining." He took one, bit into it. Still hot. The chips melted onto his tongue, a pleasant, homey feeling.

May smiled and set down the tray. Peter finished his cookie, studying her in silence.

"How do you feel, Aunt May?"

"I'm fine, Peter. I'm always fine." She waved her hand, a dismissive motion. "But I worry about *you*."

"Me?"

She perched on the bed, motioning him to sit next to her. "Your luck with girls is...well, it's not stellar, dear. I'm sorry to have to say it."

"Aunt May—"

"I still think it's a shame about Anna Watson's niece. That's all I'm saying."

"Stop changing the subject, pretty girl. Are you taking your pills?"

"Who's changing the subject now?" She reached out, touched his knee. "Really, Peter, there's nothing wrong."

"Yes there is, Aunt May. There's plenty wrong." Then, at the fearful look on her face: "Oh no, not here. Not with you. It's just…there's a lot of stuff going on out in the world."

She nodded gravely. "The Stamford business."

"Yeah. People are really afraid right now."

"That is bad." She stood up, and a faraway look entered her eyes. "I was a little girl when Joseph McCarthy launched his big campaign against Communism. He managed to scare people into thinking there were Communists everywhere: in the Congress, in their backyards, waiting in the bushes to overthrow the government."

"Were there?"

"Oh, maybe a few. But most of them were too busy smoking marijuana to overthrow anything."

Peter laughed.

"This is a little different, Aunt May. People are afraid of superhumans, and there really are a lot of them running around. Flying, too."

"My point is, Peter: People make very bad decisions when they're afraid." He nodded.

"You're fidgeting, dear. What is it?"

"It's—I—I have to tell you something, Aunt May. And it's kind of, well, tricky."

Tricky? he thought. *That's an understatement. Get a hold of yourself, Parker.*

"Peter, listen to me." She put a hand under his chin, forced him to look into her eyes. "Whatever's going on out in the world, that's out *there*. It doesn't touch us. It doesn't come inside these walls. It's just you and me here, and you can tell me anything."

"Okay, but—this might be a shock."

Her eyes went wide. She stood up quickly, tottered once, then stared at him.

"So it's true."

"What?"

"It's—it's all right, Peter. I half-saw this coming. Mrs. Cardoman's boy just came out, and he's *so* much happier now. He's even talking about marrying his—partner, I guess you call it." She raised a hand to her chin. "Come to think of it, *he* used to date fashion models, too."

"What?" Peter jumped to his feet. "Aunt May, I'm not—wait, Jason Cardoman is gay? Oh, of course he is. But—"

"You have to understand, Peter. My generation didn't grow up with... we just didn't talk about such things." She reached out, touched his cheek. "But times have changed. And you...you have to be your own unique, wonderful self."

"Aunt May, I'm not gay."

"Oh."

For a moment, she looked confused again. Her eyes darted around the room, coming to rest back on Peter.

This is it, he thought. *This is the moment.*

But I can't. I can't do it.

Slowly she reached behind him. Her thin fingers closed on a small scrap of red fabric protruding from his back pocket. She tugged at it, tentatively, until a web pattern appeared. Then, in one quick motion, she yanked it free.

They stood together for a long moment, both staring at the blank-eyed mask of Spider-Man.

Then, to his shock, Aunt May smiled. A long, serene, wonderful smile.

"Peter," she said. "I've known about *this* for years."

He felt tears welling up.

"You're not so sneaky as you think, young man."

"Aunt May...oh, Aunt May..."

"But why today, Peter? Why now?"

"Because..."

He reached out with both arms, pulled her close. Buried his head on her shoulder, like when he was a little boy.

"...because something's going to happen," he whispered. "Something that *will* come inside these walls."

She reached up, patted his shoulders softly.

"But it's okay," he continued. "You'll be safe. I've made sure of that. No matter what, you'll be safe."

"Peter," she said, her voice a frail trill in his ear. "Dear Peter. I trust you. And whatever happens...I am so, so proud of you."

He hugged her tight, rocked her slowly side to side. Tears flowed down his cheeks.

For one moment, he felt utter peace.

Then the panic returned. Along with the thought:

That was the easy part.

ELEVEN

"MOBILE Bus One, we got him. The witch-kid's down."

At the sound of Director Hill's voice, Captain America's hands tightened on the steering wheel. He spoke quietly: "Location?"

"Brooklyn Bridge."

The badge on Cap's stolen S.H.I.E.L.D. uniform read: *Agent Lamont.* Thankfully, Maria Hill didn't seem to have recognized his voice.

Cap glanced over at the burly agent in the passenger seat—Axton, that was his name. He sat tense in his full armor, smiling, tapping a stun-truncheon against his hand.

"'At's the last one," Axton said.

"Hang on."

Cap wrenched the wheel around as hard as he could. S.H.I.E.L.D. Mobile Bus One—an eight-ton urban paddy wagon with Adamantium-reinforced holding walls—lit up in a blare of lights and sirens. It swung around in a U-turn through the crowded intersection, its bulk straining against the force, passenger-side wheels rising up off the pavement. Then it settled down with a low *crunch* and took off at full speed, heading south down West Street.

"S.H.I.E.L.D.-TAC, this is Bus One," Cap said carefully. "Moving in for pickup."

"Roger, Bus One. It's a mess down there, but we'll have the locals clear you a path."

"All right. This is what I'm talkin' about." Axton leaned forward, called up a dossier photo of the Young Avengers on the dashboard computer screen. "Patriot, Hulkling, Stature, Speed. Speed? That's a hero name?"

Cap blasted the siren again. A minivan skittered to the side of the road, making way.

"These kids," Axton continued. "They're what—sixteen years old? Seventeen, tops? And they're out there in their pantyhose laughing in our faces. Time somebody taught 'em a lesson."

A green sign appeared, big white arrow labeled: TO BROOKLYN BRIDGE. Cap pulled hard left, steering the bus onto Chambers Street.

Up ahead, he could see flashing lights. Echo of sirens in the night.

"It's not like we're banning 'em, man. Nobody's stopping these punks from doing their thing. Government's even *paying* these clowns to go official now. But you know something? They don't want that. They don't get a *buzz* off bein' legit. Freaks get off on the masks an' all that 'mystery man' crap."

To the right, a phalanx of lit-up cop cars blocked the ramp leading to the Brooklyn Bridge. Cap slowed, moving in. A gray-haired police captain signaled to his men, and the cars broke ranks, opening a lane.

Axton was still talking. "Gonna be one cold shower when they see the new pen they're building for these super-creeps. Frank in supplies says it messes with your head, makes it so you can't even *think* about escaping."

The bus lurched over a pothole, bumping between the line of police, up onto the bridge. The two lanes heading into Brooklyn had been cleared. Up ahead, Cap could just make out a small figure lying in the middle of the road, surrounded by another pair of police cars.

Wiccan. Last of the Young Avengers.

"Tranq'd," Axton said. "Hope it hurt the little creep. My sister used to date a super hero, you know. *Turbo*, he called himself. Thought he was pretty hot stuff."

The bus approached Wiccan, an unconscious teenage boy in gray. Tattered red cape around his neck. Cops stood in a semicircle around his body, their guns drawn and pointed.

"No real powers, though. Turbo, I mean. Always wanted to get him alone when he took off that power-suit—I woulda given him the swirly of his life. Hey man, shouldn't you slow down a little?"

"You know something, Axton?"

Cap pulled the wheel around again, and Axton slammed against the far door. Cap thumbed the door-lock open and kicked out sideways, aiming carefully for Axton's arm. The agent's elbow jabbed into the door-latch, clicking it open—and Axton tumbled out of the moving vehicle.

"You talk too much," Cap said.

Screaming, the S.H.I.E.L.D. agent rolled to the pavement, narrowly missing Wiccan's prone body. The row of cops drew back, startled.

Cap thumbed a hidden transceiver in his lapel to life. "Falc," he called. "Extraction. NOW!"

The Falcon's reply was drowned out by a flood of swearing on the S.H.I.E.L.D. frequency. "S.H.I.E.L.D.-TAC," Axton's voice yelled, "Mobile Bus One has been compromised!"

Should have hit him harder, Cap thought.

In the rearview mirror, Cap saw a blur of red and white flash down out of the night sky. Nine-foot wings spread wide, scattering the cops. The locals squeezed off a few quick shots, but Falcon was already airborne again, carrying the unconscious Wiccan in his arms.

"Got 'im," Falcon's voice said.

Cap frowned, jabbed at the S.H.I.E.L.D. radio. Silence. They'd changed frequencies, locking him out of the conversation.

The road ahead was clear—the cops had blocked it off from both ends. "Falc, where are you?"

"'Bout fifteen feet above your head."

Cap glanced in the rearview mirror. The cops were pointing and aiming their guns upward, trying to get a bead on the soaring, dodging Falcon.

Then another flash of lights caught his attention. Up ahead, on the Brooklyn side of the bridge, two more NYPD cars loomed into view, bearing down on him fast. Lights and sirens flashing.

"Stay with me, Falc."

Cap floored the accelerator, sending the bus shooting straight toward the two newcomers. Too late, the cop cars swerved, tried to get out of the way.

Cap gritted his teeth.

Mobile Bus One struck the first police car straight on, shattering its headlights. The cops flew out of each door, landing roughly on the pavement. They watched, horrified, as the Bus's huge wheels ground slowly up over the car's hood, smashing its windshield, crushing its engine clear down to the pavement. The Bus bumped, lurched, and squashed the cop car flat.

The other car skidded to a stop. The driver leaned out the window, fired off a few shots. They bounced harmlessly off the back of the Bus.

Cap was on his way.

"No sleep till Brooklyn," Falcon's voice said.

Cap frowned. "Is that a poem?"

Then he saw them, up ahead. Big flashing lights, bigger than the locals' cherrytop signals. S.H.I.E.L.D. vehicles, dropping down out of the sky to intercept.

He glanced in the mirror again. The NYPD cops, the ones who'd captured Wiccan, were on the move again. Closing in fast.

The new security state, Cap thought. *It's efficient, that's for sure.*

"Cap," Falcon said, "you got locals behind and S.H.I.E.L.D. up ahead. I dunno about you, but I only see two ends to this bridge."

Cap grimaced, thumbed the Bus's computer screen to life. Scrolled quickly through a series of dossier entries, then jabbed down on one:

```
Subject: William "Billy" Kaplan

Aliases: WICCAN

Group Affiliation: Young Avengers (unauthorized)

Powers: Probability-based magick; teleportation

Power Type: inborn

Current Location: New York, NY
```

Up ahead, the S.H.I.E.L.D. troops were setting down, right in the middle of the road. Three copters, another Bus, and—yes, that was Mobile Command Center 3A itself. Hovering just above the first exit in Brooklyn.

Maria Hill's voice filled the cabin. "Surrender, *Captain*. You've got nowhere to run."

They weren't even moving to intercept. There was no hurry; they knew they had him.

"Falc," Cap said. "Is that kid conscious?"

"Unfortunately. He just woke up, started screamin'."

"Change of plans. Rendezvous with me—NOW."

"With *you*?"

Cap glanced over at the passenger's side door. It still flopped loose, following Axton's ungraceful exit.

"Door's open."

Ground troops stood blocking the exit now, cocking and loading their weapons. They formed a full line, with the copters hovering right above. Rifles glinted from the copter doorways.

Cap's eyes flashed forward, then to the right; forward again, then right—and this time he saw the white flash of the Falcon's wings. The burly man grunted in midair, shifted the struggling Wiccan to his right arm, and reached out to grab the door handle.

"Hold 'er steady, will you?"

Then they were inside the cabin. Wiccan was whimpering and flailing around. Falcon glared at him, reached over to slam the door shut.

"Son," Cap said forcefully.

Wiccan looked up at him and shut up.

Falcon gasped for breath, folded his wings expertly behind his back. Then he grimaced, pointed at the road ahead. "That is one metric truckload of S.H.I.E.L.D. agents."

"Son," Captain America repeated. "We need an extraction. Do you know what that means?"

Wiccan just stared at him with terrified eyes.

"Your teammates are in the back of this vehicle," Cap continued. "All of them: Patriot, Hulkling, Stature, and Speed. I can't get them, or us, out of this alone. I need your help."

Cap pulled up a map of Manhattan on the cabin's video screen. He jabbed a finger in one particular spot, and a red circle appeared next to the word *Chelsea*.

They were drawing closer to the S.H.I.E.L.D. line. A dozen high-powered particle rifles flashed red laser-dots, zeroing straight in on the Bus.

"We need a teleportation spell," Cap said, pointing to the map. "And we need it now."

Falcon pulled the boy up, glaring straight at him. "*Understand?*"

"Y-yes, sir."

Wiccan started muttering to himself, eyes wide. He seemed thoroughly traumatized.

Up above, S.H.I.E.L.D. copters buzzed forward, filling the sky with noise. The sun was beginning to rise, the first glow of light showing on the horizon.

"It's got to be now, son," Cap said.

The first shot blasted out from a handheld S.H.I.E.L.D. cannon. It struck the Bus head-on, jolting the vehicle, slowing it just a tiny bit. A hairline crack appeared in the windshield.

"Somewhereelse," Wiccan was whispering. "Iwanttobesomewhereelse Iwanttobesomewhereelse I..."

"Captain." Maria Hill's voice was faint, crackly.

Then a bright blue glow seemed to rise within the cabin. Cap glanced right, and saw the kid—Wiccan—glowing with energy. Falcon shrank back, stunned. The blue glow expanded outward, filling the small compartment.

"I want to be *somewhere else.*" Wiccan's voice was clearer, louder now.

Cap leaned forward. The bridge, the road, the S.H.I.E.L.D. agents ahead...all seemed to glow, to flare bright with that same blue radiance. Everything flashed once, then faded from view.

For a long moment, all Cap could see was that blinding blue light. Pulsing, shining, so bright it burned the eyes. Then the light seemed to thin out into a dozen strands, all radiating outward from the central core. The dozen became a hundred, a thousand, and then a thousand

thousand beams of light, each pointed outward toward a different point in space.

Probabilities, he realized.

And then he was falling, tumbling outward away from the light-core, toward one of the strands. One single destination, out of millions.

"...somewhere else," Wiccan's faint voice said.

The Bus jolted, touched ground—and suddenly the acceleration slammed Cap back into his seat. He looked around in alarm. The truck barreled across a large indoor space, industrial and spare, half the size of a football field. Toward a brick wall. At 62 MPH.

"Frying pan, fire," Falcon said.

Cap slammed on the brakes, jerked the wheel sideways. The tires screamed, began to smoke. The Bus arced hard around, almost skidding to a stop before the wall. Almost, but not quite. Its rear end whipped around, crunching sideways against the brick wall with enormous force. The Bus strained hard and almost tipped over, then righted itself again.

Wiccan was still staring. "Somewhere else," he repeated, almost too quietly to hear.

Falcon smiled, slapped him on the back. "You did it, kid. We're here."

Cap wrenched open the door, dropped quickly to the floor. The back door of the Bus was dented, but its locking mechanism still held. He reached up with a handheld S.H.I.E.L.D. device, clicked it open.

"Come on out," he said.

Hesitantly, the four Young Avengers stumbled down the ramp. Stature, the young blonde size-changer, came first, followed by Patriot, Hulkling, and Speed. They all wore thick collars, glowing with power-inhibiting technology. Their wrists were cuffed behind their backs.

Falcon led Wiccan around to meet his friends. Wiccan's eyes met Hulkling's, and they both smiled. They clasped hands.

Cap reached toward Stature. Her red-and-black costume was bloody from a cut on her cheek; she flinched away. He clicked open her cuffs, and she stretched her arms, involuntarily growing a foot taller.

"What's happening?" she asked. "Where are we?"

"Congratulations, kids." Cap gestured to the far doorway. "You've just joined the Resistance."

A motley group marched toward them. Daredevil, grim in his all-red uniform. Goliath, eleven feet tall at present. Hawkeye the marksman, bow slung over his shoulder. Tigra the were-woman. And Luke Cage.

Falcon smiled. He strode up to Cage and clapped him on the shoulder. "Cage, my brother. Finally came to your senses."

"All good," Cage said. But he looked troubled.

Stature approached Goliath. "Doctor Foster. You're part of this?"

Goliath smiled, held out his arms. "Grow a little bigger so I can hug you."

One by one, the Young Avengers shrugged off their bonds. "What *is* this place?" Patriot asked.

"S.H.I.E.L.D. safe house number twenty-three," Cap replied. "Dates back to the Cold War. Existence known only to S.H.I.E.L.D. officials of clearance level Thirty-Four."

"How many of *them* are there?"

"Now that Nick Fury's gone? Zero. He told me about it, a long time ago."

Cap felt the adrenaline fading. A wave of sadness, of loss, washed over him. Suddenly he missed Fury—and Thor, too. Thor would have polished off those S.H.I.E.L.D. agents back on the bridge with one swing of his hammer. Then laughed about it.

Later, soldier. Cap straightened up, brushing dust off his shoulder. *There's a war on.*

The Resistance members were welcoming the newcomers. Wiccan, Hulkling, and Speed spoke excitedly with Daredevil and Hawkeye. The young girls seemed fascinated by Tigra, hesitantly touching her fur. Falcon told the story of his dramatic air rescue, gesturing with broad swoops of his arm, while Goliath, Cage, and Patriot listened.

"Cap?"

He turned. Wiccan stood before him, frowning, holding Hulkling's hand. Hulkling, a big green young man, was staring with worried eyes at Wiccan. Cap realized for the first time that they were a couple.

"Son," Cap said, "you did good work out there. You saved all our hides."

"Thanks. But, uh…what's the plan here? What do you intend to do, hiding out in this base?"

Cap straightened to his full height. The room seemed to grow quiet; all eyes turned in his direction.

"We intend to help people," he said, "just as we've always done. To do what's right."

Stature frowned. "But how can you—we—how can we do that? We're all outlaws, now. Wanted criminals."

"It's not going to be easy." He drew a deep breath. "Tony Stark holds all the cards: The law is on his side, S.H.I.E.L.D. is in his pocket, and he's got more money and technology at his disposal than most sovereign nations. Stark Enterprises has been raking in Homeland Security money for the past decade. Heaven knows what new weapons they've got waiting in their labs.

"So we've got to be smart. We've got to be sneaky. We've got to use every resource at our disposal. If we are to prevail—if we're going to live as *heroes*, free to operate in the public's best interest—then we're going to have to *win* our freedom. We're going to have to build the country we want to live in, one brick at a time. Just like our immigrant ancestors did."

There was a hushed moment. Then the Falcon whooped loudly, and the others began to clap and cheer. The huge room echoed with shouts and applause.

Cap turned away, fought back a tear. Later, he would think of this as the moment the Resistance was truly born.

Sadly, there would be plenty of sacrifice to come.

TWELVE

THE minute Tony Stark stepped up to the podium, his stomach jumped. He looked around, puzzled. He'd conducted dozens of press conferences here, in the main Stark Enterprises press room. Its white walls and wide picture window were almost as familiar to him as his home or his lab. Today the room was filled to overflowing, extra folding chairs crammed around the sides of the room, reporters milling and muttering in low tones.

Suddenly he realized: *That's it.* The last time the press hall had been this full was two years ago, when—unplanned, on impulse—he'd revealed to the world his secret life as Iron Man.

Tony cleared his throat and leaned in to the mike. "Have we been here before?"

A smattering of laughter rippled through the room. Tony glanced back at Pepper Potts, standing ramrod-straight just behind him, her expression professionally blank. Happy Hogan flanked her on one side, with the U.S. Secretary of Homeland Security on the other.

Pepper frowned at Tony, gave him a mock nudge forward.

Then Tony noticed another similarity to that other press conference. In the front row, her lovely legs crossed, sat Christine Everhart of Vanity Fair. When his eyes settled on her, she cocked her head and shot him a challenging look.

He flashed her a quick smile and looked down. He consulted his cue cards quickly, then tossed them onto the podium.

"Usually, when I stand up in front of a group of people, I begin with these words: 'My name is Tony. And I'm an alcoholic.'"

The crowd laughed again, a bit nervously. *At least they're not hostile.*

"This is different, of course. And yet, it's oddly similar." He paused for effect, took a quick sip of seltzer. "One of the first things you learn in recovery is that you have to come clean with people, on every level. I started that process two years ago. My identity as Iron Man is a matter of public record; so are my taxes, my family history, and a painfully detailed record of my personal failings. My life isn't just an open book; it's practically an open-source electronic text released under the Creative Commons license." More laughter.

"But there's something people who don't have my...problem...often fail to understand. An alcoholic doesn't seek help when things are going well for him. Some of us have to hit bottom. Others reach a point where the lifestyle, the cumulative effects on himself and on other people, become too much to bear. And still others experience a *moment of clarity*. A brief, vivid glimpse of his future, of the terrible fate that awaits him if changes aren't made.

"Ladies and gentlemen: Stamford was my moment of clarity.

"I have a lot in my life to feel ashamed of, but I'm very proud of my career as a super hero. I've saved thousands of lives, put hundreds of dangerous criminals behind bars, and stopped dozens of catastrophes before they could happen. I founded the Avengers, the world's foremost super hero team, whose long record of good works speaks for itself.

"No no, please don't clap. I don't want your applause today; that's not why I'm here. Because another lesson I've learned is that deciding not to take a drink is not the end of an alcoholic's journey toward the light. It's barely Step One.

"And for me—for the superhuman community I'm proud to be a part of—my decision to go public, to reveal the details of my life to you, was Step One. This, today, is the next step."

He paused, throat dry. Swept his gaze around the room, taking in the sea of reporters, scribbling and tapping furiously on note-taking devices.

"Superhumans, metahumans, heroes, villains. Whatever you call them, they have proliferated enormously in the past decade. Some of them are born with superior physical and mental abilities; others receive their powers through accidental means. Some, like me, have developed technological methods of enhancing our natural gifts. Some, having no actual powers, take their lives into their hands by donning costumes and taking to the streets. And still others are actual alien beings, either full-blooded or partly human.

"We live in a frightening, uncertain world. Wars rage in the Middle East and elsewhere; fear of terrorism has not abated. All over this country, families face the threat of economic ruin, of the loss of the American Dream that has always been this country's promise. The Dream that has been so very good to me, personally.

"So I stand here today, one man, to pledge to you: I will do what I can to make the world just a tiny bit less frightening. I can't solve the world economy, and I can't do much about suitcase nukes or biological attacks. But I can, and will, solve the problem of superhuman weapons of mass destruction.

"From this day forward, any man, woman, or alien being who takes to the streets or the skies, who seeks to use his or her natural or artificial gifts in a public setting, must perform the following steps. He must first register online with the Department of Homeland Security, a quick, painless process. Among the information required: The applicant's real name, address, twenty-four-hour contact information, level of experience, and the extent of his superhuman abilities, if any.

"That application will be swiftly evaluated by myself and the Homeland Secretary." The Secretary nodded once. "Depending on our evaluation, several things may happen next. The person may be approved for metahuman activity under the terms of the Superhuman Registration Act. She will be given a contract, apprised firmly of the guidelines of appropriate behavior, and issued a S.H.I.E.L.D. affiliate's badge. She will also receive a salary commensurate with her experience and skill, along with medical benefits, all under the oversight of the federal government and the international S.H.I.E.L.D. charter."

Tony took a breath. "If the applicant is less experienced, a conditional license may be issued instead. This will allow him to practice his abilities after, and only after, he has completed an intensive eight-week course at one of several training facilities being established by S.H.I.E.L.D. These facilities are top secret and located far from any major population centers, so there's no danger to civilians during the training process. Once the applicant has completed the course, he will be evaluated by a board of experienced super heroes. If he is deemed responsible and competent in the use of his powers, a full license will be issued. If not, he will have the option of retaking the training course or retiring from the process.

"Of course, there will be those applicants who pose a clear or potential danger to the public, either through recklessness, lack of moral character, or the sheer uncontrollable nature of their power. They will be denied the ability to practice their abilities. This, we believe, is only fair and just. A man may possess the knowledge of how to build an atomic bomb, but that doesn't give him the right to assemble one in the middle of Times Square." Tony paused. "Believe me, I learned that one at age nine."

The group laughed. *This is working,* Tony thought. *They're really with me.*

"I'm going to take a few questions now, and then I have a surprise for you. But before you ask anything, let me remind you that none of this is *my* decision. It's the law; it's been voted on duly by Congress and signed into law by the president. He has asked me, personally, to oversee implementation of the Superhuman Registration Act, and I have accepted. This is my privilege and my duty, in more ways than one.

"Yes, Gerry."

A stout man stood up. "What's the situation with super villains, Mister Stark?"

"Well, if they choose to register, they'll obviously fall into the third category—they'll be refused a license to operate. Unless, that is, they show both a desire to reform and a willingness to undergo training. Believe it or not, we have reached out to some high-profile offenders and are beginning a dialogue."

"Even if they're wanted for crimes?"

"There are...a few cases...that will receive special treatment. But that's, I want to stress that's a very rare situation. We fully expect most super villains to fail to register, which automatically places them in violation of the law. I can't go into details about our plans in that area without tipping off those very same criminals. But I will say this: We're developing radically new, stunningly effective methods both of capturing villains who refuse to register, and of holding them securely.

"Melissa?"

"What about super heroes—not villains, but those who are publicly known to have stopped dangerous criminals, to have saved lives in the past. What happens if *they* don't register? It sounds as though they'll be treated the same as the villains you've just described. Is that true?"

Tony stared straight ahead, for just a moment.

"It is," he said.

The room erupted in questions. Reporters leaned forward, hands raised, trying to outshout each other.

Then one voice cut through the clamor. Christine Everhart stood up, her dark eyes boring into Tony. He swallowed, suddenly nervous again.

"Mister Stark," she said slowly. "I think the public will want to know something. Why should a vigilante, a self-styled super hero, receive a salary and federal benefits when so many regular Americans are out of work?"

Tony nodded; he'd prepped for this question. "That's a very good question, Chris—Ms. Everhart. First off, only those heroes who are approved and agree to public oversight will receive such benefits. Second, you should know that the Senate debated this very point at length, and decided that the 'carrot' of salary and benefits was the most effective tool in recruiting a maximum number of superhumans to the program quickly.

"But on a larger point: I don't think we Americans are at our best when we ask 'Why should my neighbor receive this?' I think we're much better served to ask 'How can *more* Americans prosper the way my neighbor has?' That's how we build a better society. That's my goal here today, and every day I step through the doors of Stark Enterprises."

Applause. But Everhart remained standing, her mouth twisted into a frown.

"Follow-up." She gestured around her, at the STARK banner on the back wall. "Since you brought up Stark Enterprises: Isn't the new law going to bring in an enormous windfall of new government contracts to this company? A company that *you* own, a company that has already benefited enormously from the post-9/11 boom in homeland security spending?"

Tony could feel the eyes of the Homeland Security secretary on his back. Pepper shifted slightly, high heels clacking on the dais.

"Ms. Everhart," Tony said, "As you know, Stark Enterprises no longer manufactures munitions. That's another promise I made to the world, and one I intend to keep as we move forward.

"However, yes, we are of course a partner to the United States government in the war against terror, superhuman and otherwise. And I would be naive to deny that that connection, that partnership, is a major reason why the president has asked me to oversee this program. The safety and security of the American people: That's the top priority of the current administration, of Stark Enterprises, and of Anthony Stark himself. I see no conflict there."

The secretary stepped forward, clapped meaty hands together in applause. The reporters joined in, louder than ever.

Everhart sat down, glaring. *Guess I won't get another night with her,* Tony thought.

Then again, you never know.

"One more—yes, Dan."

A friendly man in a rumpled suit stood up. "How much does that suit cost, Tone?"

Laughter. Tony smiled, fingered his Armani jacket. "A lot." He gestured to Pepper, and she handed him a briefcase. "But not as much as this one."

He clicked open the latch and held out the briefcase, over the podium. The gleaming red-and-yellow helmet of Iron Man popped up, surrounded by the neatly folded metal mesh of the bodysuit. Gauntlets and boots tucked neatly in the corners.

"This is my job," Tony said. "This is what I do, who I am. I built this suit with my own two hands, over the course of a lot of years. That's why

I'm standing before you today, why I've agreed to administer this law: so that everyone in this country will have the same opportunity, the same freedom, the same security to work their tails off and build a bright shiny future, that I have been so privileged to enjoy.

"And on that note, I want to introduce you to a very important woman. Ms. Miriam Sharpe lost her son in the tragic Stamford incident, and it was she who made me aware of my own, complicit guilt in that event. I owe her reparations, and she's become my conscience in this whole endeavor, as well as the spokeswoman for civilian rights on this issue. Please give Ms. Sharpe a big hand."

Ms. Sharpe stepped out, confident and smiling. She'd undergone a subtle makeover since the funeral: Her suit was neatly tailored, her makeup meticulously applied. But she still looked like an ordinary housewife, the kindly mother next door.

The room rose to its feet, applauding wildly.

When Sharpe reached Tony, she burst into tears. "Thank you, Mister Stark. Thank you just, oh, just so much."

Tony took her by the shoulders, stared into her eyes. "No, Ms. Sharpe. Thank *you*."

A rustling overhead. Tony glanced up, then hastily positioned Ms. Sharpe next to him.

"And likewise..." Tony gestured toward the ceiling. "...I'm pretty sure *the amazing Spider-Man* needs no introduction."

Spider-Man swung down gracefully, trailing a webline behind, to land in a perfect three-point crouch. He wore his old costume, the red-and-blue cloth number. Tony had discussed it with him, and they'd agreed it would provide the maximum public recognition factor.

Tony stepped aside, and Spidey leapt forward, toward the applause. As soon as he stood at the podium, though, his demeanor changed. He seemed hesitant, almost shy.

"Umm, thanks. Really." Spidey scratched his neck nervously. "It's really...inspiring to hear Tony say all that, and to see how strongly his message resonates with you guys. It makes this all a lot easier. Well, a little easier."

Nervous laughter.

"See," Spider-Man continued, "the Registration Act gives us a choice: We can go the route Captain America advocates, and leave people with powers completely unchecked. Or we can go legitimate, and earn back a little public trust."

Come on, Peter, Tony thought. *Do it.*

"I'm proud of what I do. Of who I am. And I'm here to prove it."

Spider-Man reached up and whipped the mask off his face. The crowd gasped; cameras flashed, folding chairs clattered as reporters shot to their feet. The man in the spider-suit looked briefly panicked, then smiled shyly.

"My name is Peter Parker," he said. "And I've been Spider-Man since I was fifteen years old."

Tony Stark stepped forward again. He put an arm around Peter and exchanged a long, grateful glance with the young man.

Then Tony turned to face the crowd.

"Any questions?"

PART THREE

PIECES OF SILVER

THIRTEEN

"MORE coffee, Mister Hendrick?"

Captain America frowned, adjusted his tie. The fake mustache felt itchy on his lip.

"Mister Hendrick?"

Cap looked up, saw the young waitress holding out a glass coffee pot. He shook his head quickly; she rolled her eyes and walked away.

Goliath laughed. He leaned across the table, tweaked the nametag on Cap's work shirt.

"Better get some game, *Hendrick*."

Four of them sat at the table: Cap, Goliath, Daredevil, and Luke Cage, all in various types of disguise. Goliath wore a worn leather jacket; Daredevil was almost unrecognizable in short white shirt, vest, and tinted, trendy glasses.

Cap frowned. "My name is Brett Hendrick," he said for the fourth time, in a low voice. "I'm a security supervisor at a shopping mall in Queens."

"That's it," Daredevil said. "Now, my name is Cooper Peyton, and I'm an electrical engineer from Long Island."

"Victor Tegler," Goliath said. "Community Outreach Worker, based in Harlem. Man, I'm still not sure about that. I'm a West Coast kid."

Daredevil shrugged. "Bigger men than you have started out as community organizers."

"Cage?"

Luke Cage looked up from his notes. His massive, muscular frame was crammed into a black suit, and he seemed distinctly uncomfortable.

"What kind of name is *Rockwell Dodsworth?*" he asked. "And sweet Christmas—I.T. consultant for a major international finance corporation? I asked you to get me somethin' *cool*, like a race-car driver. Music producer, maybe."

Daredevil frowned. "This is what my contacts had available."

"Matt risked a lot to get us these new identities," Cap said. "He could be disbarred for this."

"Oh, yeah." Daredevil almost smiled. "*That's* what I'm worried about."

"Besides, the I.D.'s aren't important. They're just a place to go to ground when we aren't doing the important work."

"I'm actually getting into the new secret identity thing," Daredevil said. "I'm experimenting with new foods, new favorite movies. New bands."

Cap studied the blind adventurer for a moment. They'd been underground for almost three weeks now, a difficult time of adjustment. But the experience had apparently energized Daredevil. As long as Cap had known him, DD had been a dour, grim vigilante with a strong nihilistic streak. Now he seemed alert, purposeful.

Maybe change is good, sometimes.

"Ah, never mind." Cage stretched his arms, grimaced. "I'm just still sore from that beatdown we gave the Sinister Six yesterday."

"*You're* sore?" Goliath clapped him on the back. "Man, I had to grow to eighteen feet to trip up the Rhino."

"That was good work," Daredevil said. "And we're only just getting started. Right, Cap?"

"Hm? Sorry." Captain America looked up. "Just thinking about an appointment I had to break, with a kid from the Make-A-Wish Foundation. I told him we'd play baseball in his yard today, but the place is probably crawling with Tony's cape-killers."

"Sucks," Goliath said.

"It's the little things they've stolen from us," Cap said, "with this registration garbage. The little things that make us who we are."

"What you said." A sly smile crept across Cage's dark face. "Hendrick."

"Zip it, *Rockwell*."

The waitress arrived, bearing food. The four men set to it, as if they hadn't eaten in weeks.

"I still can't believe Spider-Man," Goliath said. "You think Tony Stark is *controlling* him or something? Through that new costume?"

"Tony wouldn't stoop to that," Cap said. "It wouldn't satisfy his ego. He wants everyone to agree with him, to see the pure light of reason behind his actions."

"And I know Peter. He's impressionable." Daredevil frowned. "That day in Stamford, I could already see he was under Tony's thumb."

"Strategically, it's a brilliant move. Nobody's guarded his secret identity more tightly than Spider-Man. His unmasking is a powerful message to all the costumes still sitting on the fence."

Cap's and Goliath's phones beeped simultaneously. Cap glanced at the screen, rose quickly to his feet.

"'Sup?" Cage asked.

Goliath read aloud: "Petrochemical plant on fire, over by the river. Base says there's three or four hundred people trapped inside."

Cap intercepted the startled waitress. "Keep the change, ma'am. And thanks for a wonderful meal."

She looked down at the hundred-dollar bill in her hand. "Wow. Thanks, Mister Hendrick."

"Call me Brett."

Cap gestured, and the rest of them followed him toward the back entrance. He thumbed a speed-dial number on his phone.

"Hawkeye, what's your sitch?"

"Just tryin' to train these kids. You want us on that call?"

"Yep. Bring everyone along." Cap hung up, dialed another number. "Falc?"

"On my way. Got Tigra, Cloak, and Dagger with me."

"Roger."

Cage slammed open the door to the restaurant's back alley. Strong smell of garbage and urine. Boarded-up windows on the houses behind.

"Emergency distress calls. Sneaking into alleys, changing into costume." Goliath smiled, shrugging off his leather jacket. "I hate to say it, but I'm starting to enjoy this."

GREEN smoke rose from the Geffen-Meyers petrochemical plant, dark and ominous in the twilight gloom. Cap could smell it from blocks away. The plant building faced the water, so details of the disaster were hard to make out from the street. A ring of local police cars surrounded the building, lights flashing.

Cap hastily arranged a rendezvous in a parking lot across the street. When everyone was assembled, he pulled Wiccan and Cloak aside. They both looked nervous, unsure.

"You two are our teleporters," Cap said. "People may be dying inside the plant, and we can't get past that line of cops any other way. Can you carry us all, between the two of you?"

Wiccan frowned. "I can get my crew in. Prob'ly two or three more."

"Cloak?"

Cloak looked around, scared. Dagger, his girlfriend, took his hand. "I'll do it, sir."

Cap, Tigra, Falcon, Wiccan, and the Young Avengers materialized inside first. The plant's roof had been ripped off, and several explosions had apparently torn up the floor. Small fires raged, water spouted from severed pipes. Walls lay half-toppled, obscuring parts of the complex; one whole side of the building had been blasted open to the pier, where a loading dock lay splintered and destroyed, its stump falling off into the water. Green smoke wafted through the air, forming toxic patches all over.

"Man." Tigra held a furry finger to her sensitive nose. "This place *stinks*."

In the middle of the room, a dark shroud swirled into being. Cap tensed—and watched as Hawkeye, Daredevil, Cage, Goliath, and Dagger all tumbled out, shivering with intense cold.

"It's okay," Dagger said. "The chill will wear off soon."

The shadow swirled about, resolved itself into the dark form of Cloak himself. He staggered, dazed for a moment. Dagger walked up before him, glowing, and held out her hands. Light blazed from her into Cloak's tired form, vanishing into the darkness of his being. Revitalizing him.

Cap shook his head. Those two had nothing but each other; Cloak relied on Dagger for his very survival. How could you ask two young people like that to register, to turn over their entire lives to the government?

"All present," Falcon said.

Daredevil bent down, picked up something from the floor. Cap turned to him.

"Silver dollar," Daredevil said.

"Something's wrong." Cap's eyes narrowed. "How many workers did the report say?"

"Three or four hundred." Goliath frowned at a handheld analyzer. "But I'm not getting any radio signals out of this place at all—"

Goliath stopped dead, staring down at the floor.

Falcon fluttered up behind him, Cap close by. "What is it?"

Then they all saw it. A fallen wall-stone with the chiseled words:

GEFFEN-MEYERS
A DIVISION OF
STARK ENTERPRISES

"Emergency evac!" Cap yelled. "It's a *trap*—"

Too late. Tranquilizer darts rained down out of the sky. Tigra leapt away, Falcon took to the air. Hawkeye notched an arrow in his bow, quicker than the eye could see.

But the tranquilizers only struck two members: Wiccan and Cloak.

"Tyrone!" Dagger screamed. She ran to Cloak, reached for his falling figure.

Cap whipped his head upward. Thirty feet up, silhouetted against the clouds, at least six heavy S.H.I.E.L.D. copters hung in the sky, their engines muffled by Stark stealth technology. One of the copters pivoted, and a gunman loomed into view on its side, moonlight flashing against his weapon's nozzle.

"Of course it's a trap. How else were we going to get you all in one place?"

Cap whirled, raising his shield. The gleaming figure of Iron Man wafted up over a shattered half-wall, his repulsor rays glowing with power.

Then Spider-Man was behind Tony, leaping and flashing his webs. "Don't do it, Flags."

Cap grimaced, motioned his people back. They fell in behind him and shrank back toward the open, river-facing side of the plant.

The rest of Tony Stark's forces marched up behind their leader, looming into view through the slowly clearing green haze. Ms. Marvel. The massive She-Hulk. Three-quarters of the Fantastic Four: Reed and Sue Richards, and Ben Grimm, the Thing. Black Widow.

Dagger looked up from Cloak's unmoving body. "What have you *done* to him?"

Spider-Man held up a hand. "Just a little tranquilizer, kid. To make sure nobody gets teleported away." Spidey cocked his head, looked upward. "Skybird One, you got us covered?"

A gruff, filtered voice filled the air. "Oh yeah. Just give the word. *Please* give the word."

Cap grimaced. He recognized the voice: his former "partner," S.H.I.E.L.D. Agent Axton.

Then Maria Hill's voice cut in. "Mister Stark. We are in position and ready to end this—"

"We do this *my* way, Commander," Tony said. "Or you can abort right now."

Hill's sigh was audible. "Director Hill to all airborne units. Hold your fire. Repeat, hold your fire and await further orders."

All eyes were on Iron Man and Captain America now. Cap squared his shoulders and marched straight up to Tony Stark.

"Going soft, Tony?"

"We didn't come here to arrest you, Cap." Tony gestured upward, at the copters. "I've talked S.H.I.E.L.D. into offering you one final chance at amnesty."

"You mean surrender. *No thanks.*"

"C'mon, Cap." Spider-Man leapt up next to Tony. "When we fight each other, the only people who win are the bad guys. This goes against every principle you ever believed in."

Cap stared at Spider-Man. The new costume, with its gleaming metal eyes, gave him a much less human countenance than ever before. Cap could almost picture the young man inside transforming, like an insect in a cocoon, into a new version of Iron Man.

"Don't talk to me about principles, Spider-Man. I saw your little stunt on TV. Is your Aunt May happy that the Vulture has her zip code now?"

Spider-Man clenched his fists. "Why don't you ask the mommies and daddies in Stamford if they think *Captain America's* still fighting the good fight?"

Spidey took a step toward Cap. Cap tensed, and the two men stared at each other for a long moment. Then Tony moved between them, slowly lifting his helmet up to reveal his face.

He looked very tired.

"Cap, please. I know you're angry, and I know this is an enormous change from the way we've always worked. But we aren't living in 1945 anymore." Tony gestured behind Cap, addressing the assembled Resistance. "The public doesn't want masks and secret identities. They want to feel *safe* when we're around. We've lost their confidence, their respect. This is the only way to win it back.

"You've known me half my adult life, Cap. You know I wouldn't do this unless I believed in it with all my heart. I don't want to fight you— none of us does. All I ask...just let me tell you my grand plan for the twenty-first century."

Reed Richards' elongated head snaked through the air. "It really is extraordinary."

Sue Richards, Cap noticed, was staring at her husband. She didn't look happy. Neither did Ben Grimm.

"Five minutes." Tony held out his metal-gauntleted hand. "Will you give me that?"

Cap turned to survey his troops. Cage looked very grim. Tigra's eyes were wide, almost feral. Goliath had eased up to eight feet in height, but he was hanging back. Dagger still knelt over her fallen partner, and the Young Avengers had gathered around Wiccan's limp form.

Daredevil leaned against a wall, alone. Flipping his newfound coin up and down, up and down.

Cap's two closest lieutenants, Hawkeye and the Falcon, stood together. They both cocked their heads at him: *Your play.*

He turned back toward Tony. "Five minutes."

"That's all I need."

Slowly, Cap reached out and clasped Tony's hand. Tony's gauntlet felt cold through Cap's glove.

Spider-Man's smile was almost visible through his mask. "All right! Way to go, Wings! Didn't I tell you this was all gonna work out?"

Then Tony yanked his hand back, stared at it. "What the hell?"

Blue lightning shot out of Tony's hand, arcing up and around his metallic form. His limbs began to jerk, uncontrollably, and he screamed in pain.

Cap took a step back. "Old-line S.H.I.E.L.D. electron scrambler," he said, pointing at a small device on Tony's gauntlet. "Another thing Fury gave me, years ago."

"Wh-why?"

"In case you ever went over to the wrong side."

Spider-Man moved in. But again Tony motioned him back, grimacing in agony. The other power fighters on Tony's team—She-Hulk, the Thing, Ms. Marvel—stood their ground, waiting for a signal.

The Resistance moved in, flanking their leader.

Iron Man writhed on the ground, struggling to regain control of his armor. Cap glared down at him. "Your *grand plan* sounds more like 1940s Germany to me. What exactly do you plan to do with people who refuse to register?"

"You don't—understand," Tony gasped. His face was still visible, his helmet sparking blue above his forehead. He struggled to rise.

"I understand one thing. *You took down two of my boys.*"

Cap punched him in the jaw, a massive blow. The blow he'd always wanted to deliver to Hitler, to Mussolini, to Stalin. Tony's head whipped back, blood trailing through the air.

The plant exploded into violence. Ms. Marvel rose up into the air, firing off power-blasts; the Falcon soared up to meet her, wings flapping wildly. Hawkeye notched his bow, urging the Young Avengers forward—but the Thing and She-Hulk formed a linebacker-style barricade, blocking their way. Goliath grew to nine feet, then twelve, raising his arms menacingly against all comers. Powerful light-knives shot out from Dagger's hands, sparking on contact with Spider-Man's metal suit.

Daredevil and the Black Widow circled each other, scuttling up and down half-walls in a dark ballet. Daredevil fired off his billy club, narrowly missing her head.

Cap kicked down hard on Tony's back, heard a power relay snap. Tony's eye-lenses flashed bright as a final short-circuit disabled his armor. Then he was still.

A whirring noise above. "Watch the skies, people!" But when Cap looked up, the S.H.I.E.L.D. copters were hovering higher, arcing up and away.

Cap frowned, then jumped back just as Tigra landed in front of him, slashing and cutting at the muscular form of She-Hulk. The two women grappled fiercely. Tigra was all speed and fury, but She-Hulk's powerful blows were taking their toll. Tigra reached out, slashing claws across her

enemy's green face. She-Hulk howled, jumped on top of Tigra. They
rolled away—

—and Cap found himself face-to-face with Reed Richards.

"Cap." Reed held out an elongated hand. "Please..."

Something caught Cap's eye. He reached out and snatched a tiny
transceiver out of Reed's ear. Reed grabbed for it, but was too slow.

Cap sprinted toward the far side of the plant building, ignoring
Reed's calls. He held the stolen transceiver up to his ear and heard Maria
Hill's voice:

"—all airborne units: Do not engage. Repeat, do not move in unless
perimeter is breached. Prepare to activate Niflhel Protocol, at my—strike
that, at *Iron Man's* command. Until then, hold your positions."

The Thing pasted Hulkling across the jaw, hard. "I don't wanna fight
you guys!" the Thing said. "Why can't you just do like you're told?"

Chaos all around. Falcon and Ms. Marvel continued their aerial battle; Daredevil crouched down now, staggering under the Widow's sting-
blasts. Luke Cage had joined Tigra's fight, grappling hand-to-hand with
She-Hulk.

Hawkeye made his way over to Cap, firing off arrows with every step.
"We outnumber 'em, Cap," he said. "But they got a lot more muscle on
their side. And copters."

Cap nodded grimly, backing toward the wall of the chemical plant.
He gestured upward to Goliath, who now stood fifteen feet tall. Goliath
nodded, and shouted out "EVERYBODY! HEAD FOR THE WATER!"

Then the Thing assaulted one of Goliath's legs, while She-Hulk
body-rammed the other. Goliath toppled and fell, letting out a pained
cry. When he struck the concrete floor, the whole building shook.

Patriot stumbled over to Cap, flinging his throwing-star weapons behind him at Spider-Man. The web-slinger followed right on Patriot's tail,

moving swiftly on those metallic tentacles, furious and uncharacteristically silent. The stars bounced harmlessly off his red-and-gold uniform with a skittering sound.

Cap raised his shield—and Spider-Man vanished.

"Wh-wh—" Patriot turned to Cap. "Where'd he go?"

"Spider-Man's wearing a new suit designed by Stark." Cap's eyes scanned the air furiously. "It's bulletproof, equipped with glide-function and stealth mode..."

"You forgot *butt-kicking*."

Before Cap could react, Spidey was there—suddenly, silently, appearing in the air just inches from him. Cap dodged to the side, narrowly avoiding a burst of spider-webbing. But Spidey's tentacles flashed through the air, wrenching Cap's shield out of his hands. Spider-Man kicked, hard, and Cap fell backward toward the jagged floor.

Cap landed, rolled onto his back, and looked up for Spider-Man. But all he saw, far above, was the Falcon swooping down:

"Cap! *Look out!*"

And then Iron Man was on him again. Helmet down, red eyes blazing with power, every inch the unstoppable Avenger. Tony grabbed Cap by the shoulders, lifted him up into the air. "Been improving the reboot time on my armor, Cap. You impressed?"

Tony lifted Cap over his head and slammed him clear through a wall.

"UGGGHHHHH!"

Bright phosphenes swam before Cap's eyes. Dimly, he heard the sounds of combat all around. He raised his arms like a boxer, shielding his bloody face. But a servo-enhanced roundhouse blow from Iron Man blasted into his stomach, doubling him over. He dropped to the ground, kicked out blindly. Missed.

"You're wasting your time," Tony continued. "This armor has recorded every punch you've ever thrown. It knows your next move before *you* do."

He punched Cap again, in the face. Once, twice. Cap heard a sickening crunch, tasted blood where a tooth used to be.

The world was slipping away. A voice—Hawkeye?—said: "He's *killing* him!"

There was a weird crackling in Cap's ear, followed by a flurry of voices. At first he thought he was hallucinating, but then he remembered: *The S.H.I.E.L.D. transceiver.*

"Situation spiraling out of control."

"Three dozen more cape-killer units surrounding the perimeter."

And then Maria Hill: "Hold them on standby. Signal coming in from Stark: Activate Niflhel Protocol."

The gleaming face of Iron Man filled Cap's vision, wavering and shimmering. "I'm sorry, Cap," Tony said. "Really, I am."

Then, behind Tony, the heavens seemed to light up. A massive bolt of lightning stabbed down from the sky with a deafening crack, sending the Falcon and Ms. Marvel spinning through the air. It struck down right in the center of the chemical plant, splintering concrete, knocking Cage and Hawkeye off their feet.

Cap shielded his eyes from the blinding light. When his vision cleared, the sight he saw shocked him to his core.

A column of light rose from the floor of the chemical plant, lightning flashing out from it in all directions. And at the center of the lightning, hammer held high, stood the angry, imperious form of the mighty Thor.

FOURTEEN

WHEN the fighting broke out, Sue Richards fell back on her usual opening gambit. She became invisible.

She'd been reluctant to come to the chemical plant at all. Reed had assured her, several times, that Tony had everything planned, that nothing could go wrong. He said it was important they all be there, to show support, to prove to Captain America that most heroes believed in the Registration Act. He asked her to think of their children, of the kind of world she wanted Franklin and Valeria to grow up in.

Then Reed had vanished, spirited up to the S.H.I.E.L.D. Helicarrier in the company of Tony Stark. *I'll meet you on-site,* he'd said. And then, too quickly as always: *Love you.*

Now Sue stood, backed up against a cracked concrete wall, watching a reborn thunder god call down lightning from the heavens. Thor's hammer cracked and flashed, and rain began to sheet down onto the ruined factory. Up above, S.H.I.E.L.D. copters wheeled about, swerving to avoid the un-earthly lightning bolts.

Sue was still invisible.

Tony's metallic voice crackled in her earpiece: "Everyone stay back."

She watched through driving rain as She-Hulk, Ms. Marvel, and Spider-Man backed away from the source of the lightning. She couldn't see Cap, but some of his Resistance—Luke Cage, Dagger, Patriot and Hulkling of the Young Avengers—moved in slowly toward the thunder god.

Falcon dropped down out of the sky. "Thor?" he said.

Thor turned dark, flashing eyes toward him.

There's something different about Thor, Sue thought. *He looks…bigger than before. Massive, coiled with power. Malevolent.*

"Thor, what are you doing? It's me, man. Falcon."

Hawkeye frowned, swept rain out of his eyes. "We all thought you were *dead*, big guy—"

Thor didn't speak. Just narrowed his eyes in anger, in godlike distaste. A drop of spittle formed on his curled lip, then vanished into the flood of rain.

He raised his hammer again and hurled it, incredibly fast, into the assembled Resistance members. It struck Falcon in the stomach, knocking him off his feet, straight into Hawkeye. Tigra leapt away just in time to avoid their flying bodies.

The hammer soared on, arcing upward as if nothing had interrupted its flight. It grazed Goliath's cheek, drawing blood. Stature, the size-changer of the Young Avengers, shrank down just in time to avoid its path; but Dagger wasn't so lucky. The hammer struck her straight-on, sending her flying into Speed and Patriot.

Luke Cage stepped forward, yelling "I got this!"

Cage's skin, Sue remembered, was steel-hard. But not hard enough. Cage gritted his teeth, puffed out his chest toward the flying hammer. It struck him with tremendous force—and he flew backward, clear out of the factory. He soared out over the water, massive arms flailing, and came down with a distant splash.

Sue looked around frantically, searching for Reed. There he was: on the far side of the chemical plant, a blur of stretching blue. Eyeing every move, like a biologist watching a new type of microorganism being born.

Sometimes Sue hated his scientific curiosity.

She allowed herself to become visible, and waved to him. Reed caught her eye, tried to smile, and motioned her toward him. She grimaced, nodded, and willed herself invisible again.

She started toward him, skirting around the action, keeping a careful distance from Thor. The thunder god just stood, sneering, his brutish eyes following the long arc of his hammer through the air.

As she circled the edge of the factory, Sue caught glimpses of several mini-dramas, each illuminated by a series of lightning flashes:

Flash: On the edge of the plant, Daredevil and the Black Widow chased each other up jagged walls, through shattered windows, looming in and out of view through the sheeting rain. At the top of a disused chemical urn, Daredevil stopped and looked back down at the Widow, disappointment etched in the set of his mouth.

Sue thought his mouth formed the words: *You don't know what freedom is.*

The Widow took careful aim with her stingers, firing off several bolts. Daredevil tried to dodge, but he was too slow. The bolts struck him; he arched in pain, then fell from his perch.

When she caught him, the Widow's expression was a mixture of contempt and regret.

Flash: A bolt of lightning lanced down, over in the corner where Wiccan and Cloak lay drugged and unconscious. Hulkling—the Young Avengers' resident strongman—leapt up and took the bolt before it could reach Wiccan. Hulkling screamed as the bolt burned through his chest. Then he fell on top of Wiccan's unmoving form.

He's got a healing factor, Sue remembered. *I think.*

Flash: Dagger pulled herself up off the floor, grimacing in pain, her tiny frame dripping wet. "Oh my god," she said, her high voice barely audible over the storm. "This is wrong. We've got to get out of here. This is *really really wrong*—"

Thor reached out a meaty hand and clasped it around his hammer, halting its flight. Lightning flashed from it again, like a further warning from the gods.

Dagger's right, Sue thought. Something was very, very wrong. She looked up and around, searching for Reed again.

When did the world turn into this?

The Resistance was beginning to regroup. Patriot, Speed, and Stature formed a line, protecting their fallen comrades. Hawkeye and Falcon exchanged frantic words, pointing at Thor.

Thor just hissed, raised his hammer slowly into the air.

Tony, Sue thought suddenly. *Where is the all-powerful Tony Stark?*

Then Thor seemed to lurch forward, throwing all his weight against his hammer. It slammed into the ground like a pile driver. The floor seemed to explode upward in a blinding flash of light.

Chaos, screams. The Resistance members were closest, so they were hardest hit; but Sue saw Reed's coiled, flailing body whip up into the air, too. Her force field kicked on almost by instinct, blunting the worst of the impact, but she too found herself knocked off her feet. She landed hard against a wall, grunted in pain—

—and saw, not eight feet away, Captain America. Bloody, battered, his face twisted in pain. Lying propped against the wall, rain puddling around his body, with the powerful form of Iron Man standing over him. Spider-Man stood, half-crouched, just behind Tony.

"Cap," Tony said, "*Please* don't get up. I don't want to hit you again."

Cap grunted, moved a hand to his back to brace himself. Tried to rise, and failed.

"Your jaw's practically hanging off," Tony continued. "Just surrender and I'll get you medical attention. S.H.I.E.L.D. has medics standing by."

"S.H.I.E.L.D.," Cap said. It sounded like a curse.

He grimaced, rose to his feet with great difficulty. Raised rheumy, furious eyes toward his red-and-gold enemy.

"You really think I'm going down," he hissed, "to some pampered playboy *punk* like you?"

I should say something, Sue thought. *I should stop this.* But she felt helpless, almost paralyzed.

This, she realized, was what it had come to: an irreconcilable battle between Iron Man and Captain America, each of them absolutely convinced his cause was just. Nothing could stop them, not gods, not villains, not even their fellow heroes. This battle would continue until one of them was dead.

Spider-Man stepped forward. "I got this, Tony." He moved in toward Cap again, gleaming like a newborn insect.

But Tony shook his head, backed up a step. Pressed a stud on his glove.

"Iron Man to all points." His voice was loud, now, in Sue's ear transceiver. "Activate your audio blocks."

Then he turned back to Cap and said: "This is going to hurt."

A horrible, screeching wail filled the air, seeming to stab right through Sue's inner ear. Scorching, unspeakable agony. She fell to her knees, clutching her head.

She smelled Reed before she saw him, felt his long, winding fingers dance across her face. He reached into her ear, flipped a switch on her transceiver. The noise subsided to a low, barely audible whine.

"Sorry," he said. "Didn't have time to brief you on that part of the plan. Good thing you became visible, when the frequency-wave hit." He smiled, a very tired smile. "I'm glad you're okay."

She stared at him for a moment. His familiar sheepish smile, his winding, elongated neck. His cheek touching hers.

Then she heard the screams. The Resistance members writhed on the ground, moaning in agony. They had no protection against Tony's aural assault.

Captain America rose to his knees, his mouth wide open in a silent scream.

"You're a tough old bird," Tony said, "I'll give you that. This frequency puts the human brain into shutdown. But look at you, still trying to get up."

Cap looked down, spat through his pain.

"I'll make this quick," Tony continued. "Just close your eyes and you'll wake up in our new detention center."

"This is horrible," Sue whispered.

"I don't like it either," Reed said. "But at least this way there's no broken bones."

Another bolt of lightning cracked down. Reed turned to look at Thor, standing majestic and cruel in the center of the carnage. Rain dripped off his long golden locks, barely touching him.

"Thor," Reed said. "Stand down. The S.H.I.E.L.D. cleanup squad can handle things from here."

"Peter," Tony said. "Take charge of the prisoners. We need to inventory them before—"

"LOOK OUT!"

Tony whipped his head up—too late. Goliath loomed over them, at least 20 feet high—taller than Sue had ever seen him before. His roar of pain filled the air; he had no protection against the frequency-wave. But he held above his head a massive, severed chemical vat, dripping with green liquid.

With a howl of agony, he dropped his burden straight on top of Iron Man.

Dagger—her eyes wide in agony—fired off a volley of blinding light-bolts. The vat hit Iron Man; the bolts struck the vat; and the vat exploded in a massive fireball.

She-Hulk, caught on the edge of the fireball, screamed and ran, her costume flaming bright. The Black Widow rushed to help her.

The flames flared high, grazing the cabin of a hovering S.H.I.E.L.D. copter. It lurched, rolled through the sky—and slammed into the airborne Ms. Marvel. She cried out, stunned, and tumbled to the ground.

Good god, Sue thought. *Have they killed Tony?*

Slowly the fireball subsided. And at its center, crouched on one knee, the silhouetted form of Iron Man faded into view.

"I'm okay," said Tony's voice, through Sue's transceiver. "Little singed."

And then she noticed: The whining in her ears was gone.

The fireball hadn't killed Tony, but it had deactivated his frequency-wave. The Resistance were climbing to their feet: Hawkeye, Falcon, Tigra. Dagger and the Young Avengers.

Captain America raised an arm and yelled, *"Attack!"*

Then he slumped forward and fell to the ground.

Once again, the world exploded into flashing costumes and power blasts. Spider-Man faced off against Speed, snapping tentacles struggling to catch the fast-moving teenager. Falcon took to the air, dive-bombing the Thing. Hawkeye struggled to draw a bead on the Black Widow, who shot stinger-blasts back at his dodging form.

Ms. Marvel rose slowly from the floor of the plant, winced as she put weight on an injured arm. Her eyes were red with rage.

Captain America lay still, facedown on the concrete floor. Falcon called down to Hawkeye: "Hawk! Get to Cap. We've gotta get him out of here!"

Sue turned urgently to Reed. "Reed. We have to stop this."

Sue thought she saw a flicker of fear in his eyes. "I've already deactivated Thor."

"What do you mean *deactivated?*"

Tony Stark staggered forward, his armor audibly creaking. The explosion had done him some damage.

"Regroup," Tony said. "We've got to—"

But Goliath had turned his huge body toward the assembled Avengers. He crouched down, grabbed at the jagged floor beneath their feet, and *pulled*. They toppled and flew up into the air. Force-blasts went wild; Ms. Marvel tumbled through the air. Spider-Man shot out with his webbing, grabbed on to a half-collapsed support beam.

Thor turned to watch the chaos. Lightning sparked.

Falcon swooped out of the sky, carrying Hawkeye in his arms. Hawkeye pointed down toward Cap's prone body.

Slowly, the thunder god reached out with his hammer.

Goliath turned to him. "Get ready for the shortest comeback in history, Thor."

No, Sue thought. *Oh, no—*

Thor's hammer glowed bright, brighter than ever before. With a deafening crack, lightning flashed forth from it, plowed straight through the air—

—and punched a hole straight through Goliath's chest.

Then there was blood and lightning and rain, and Goliath's twenty-foot body toppled back into the far wall of the chemical plant. Landed with a crash, shattering plastic and metal and concrete.

Still invisible, Sue crept up to him. She didn't care what Reed thought. She didn't care if S.H.I.E.L.D. grabbed her. She didn't even care if Thor's lightning flashed out again, claiming her as another victim.

She touched Goliath's cold, meter-long hand, saw the smoke rising from the hole where his heart had been. And she knew: He was dead.

Rain continued to pound down all around. But the battles had stopped. Ms. Marvel held her arm, wincing in pain. She-Hulk was down, burns covering half of her body. Iron Man still knelt unsteadily, rebooting critically damaged systems.

S.H.I.E.L.D. hovered above, watching with cold, mechanical eyes.

Everyone else just stood very still, staring at the 20-foot corpse of a hero who had dared to defy the Superhuman Registration Act.

Sue felt nothing. She felt cold. All she could think of, the only thing that came to mind, was a phrase Tony Stark had uttered during his famous press conference: "Stamford was my moment of clarity."

This, she realized, *is mine.*

The Resistance were scrambling around, traumatized. Falcon and Hawkeye had made their way to Captain America, scooped him up. The Young Avengers moved to join them, with Dagger close behind. "Fall back—regroup," Falcon said. "We've got to get out of here or we're all—"

Thor turned toward him, raised his hammer again. His eyes narrowed with inhuman cruelty, and lightning shot forth again. The same force that had killed Goliath, aimed now at the entire, assembled Resistance.

Iron Man flew forward, his damaged armor wobbling in the air. "Thor!" he cried. "NO—"

—Reed started toward them, but shrank back from the godlike assault—

—and then Susan Richards, the Invisible Woman, founding member of the Fantastic Four, leapt over to join the Resistance. She gritted her teeth, raised her arms, and erected the largest force field of her career.

Thor's lightning flashed, sputtered against the field, and stopped short.

Iron Man and Spider-Man darted eyes and sensors around, searching for some new enemy. Behind the force field, the Resistance members were equally puzzled. The Falcon held Cap's limp form in his hands.

Sue stepped outside her own force field, facing Thor, Iron Man, and Spider-Man directly. She willed the field, behind her, to full strength.

And became visible.

Ben Grimm, the Thing, lurched forward. He stared at her, astonished. "Suzie? What are ya *doin'?*"

Tony Stark swiveled his eye-lenses from Reed to Sue, then back to Reed.

Thor fixed her with a murderous glare. Began to raise his hammer.

Reed coiled his way forward, snaked his head in front of the thunder god. "Emergency shutdown code!" he said. "Authorization Richard Wagner, 1833-1883."

Thor's eyes went blank; for the first time, his expression softened. The lightning-energy faded, and the hammer slipped from his limp fingers, clattering to the floor.

Sue gritted her teeth; the strain of maintaining this huge force field was enormous. She turned, glanced back at the Resistance. "Get out of here," she said. *"Now."*

Patriot gestured across the floor, at the limp bodies of Wiccan, Hulkling, and Cloak. "What about them? Our wounded?" They lay across the room, out of range of the force field.

"She's right," Falcon said. "We have to leave."

Sue turned, reached out her hands...and the Resistance began to disappear. First Hawkeye and Tigra, then Patriot, Stature, Speed, and Dagger. At last there was only the Falcon, still carrying their fallen leader's unconscious body.

"Susan," Falcon said. "Thank you."

Then they too were gone.

Sue's power was invisibility, not teleportation. The Resistance would have to make their own escape. But at least she'd given them a head start.

To Sue's surprise, no one made a move toward the rebels. Black Widow was busy bandaging up She-Hulk and Ms. Marvel. S.H.I.E.L.D. seemed confused, conflicted; their copters wheeled up and about, surveying the landscape but not moving to pursue. Tony's movements were still jerky, uncoordinated. Thor stood stock still, a statue in the rain.

Ben and Reed, Sue's teammates and family, just stared at her. They seemed stunned, shell-shocked.

Spider-Man sat crouched on a wall, staring at the smoking body of Goliath.

Reed snaked an arm toward Sue's waist. "Darling—"

She flinched away, whipped her head around. "Don't even speak to me. Not one damn word."

And then, one more time, Sue Richards vanished from sight.

FIFTEEN

DATA assaulted Tony Stark from all sides. Medical reports. Routing checks on the new prisoners. Statements from Congressmen. Maria Hill's voice, like sandpaper, requesting a strategy session. Reports on the Initiative training camps being constructed in Arizona and elsewhere. Funeral arrangements. Hundreds of emails from reporters, mostly asking what the hell had gone down today on the west side of Manhattan.

Beside Tony, in the elevator, Reed Richards snaked his head up and down absently, muttering to himself.

Tony flipped his helmet up off his face, cutting off the data flow. "Reed? You all right?"

Reed's head was up by the ceiling now. He stared at a light fixture, his lips moving almost soundlessly.

"Reed."

"Mm? Sorry, Tony." Reed's head snapped back down onto his body, like a turtle retreating into its shell. "I was running those Negative Zone calculations in my head."

His eyes looked wide, haggard.

"She'll come back, Reed."

"Mmm? Oh, I suppose so. Yes." Reed twitched, a facial tic Tony hadn't seen before. "I'm mostly concerned about the procedures we've got in place for the new prisoners. Wiccan is powerful, and Daredevil can be quite devious."

"I know."

"You've got the transfer scheduled for later today, yes? Perhaps I should head straight for the Baxter Building and make sure the portal's ready."

"Soon, Reed. I need you here first."

"Ah."

Twitch.

He's haunted, Tony thought. *But not by problems with the detention center, and not by abstract calculations. Not even by his wife's betrayal, though that'll hit him soon enough.*

No. He keeps seeing the same thing I do, in my mind's eye: Bill Foster, Goliath, struck dead by a lightning bolt through his chest.

The doors hissed open, straight into the Avengers Tower biolab. High ceilings, bright lights, screens and monitors and medical tables everywhere. And superhumans. Black Widow, Spider-Man, and Ms. Marvel, her arm in a sling. Ben Grimm stood in back, uncharacteristically quiet.

In the center of the room, the massive figure of Thor lay on a slab. His clear blue eyes stared straight up; no trace of intelligence showed in them. His hammer lay askew next to him.

Dr. Hank Pym leaned over an incision in Thor's head, frowning. He raised a scalpel, and his hand shook slightly.

"Tony?" Spider-Man approached, in full costume. "What happened out there?"

Tony grimaced. Sympathetically, he hoped.

"I thought we were doing this so no one else got hurt," Spider-Man said.

Tony held up a hand to him, turned toward the prone figure of Thor. "Hank? Any news?"

Hank Pym glanced up from his work. His white lab coat stood out against the bright-colored costumes filling the room. He looked like he'd been crying.

"News?"

Hank laid down the scalpel, crossed to a TV monitor, and clicked it to life. An aerial view of the chemical plant appeared. Copters buzzed in and out of sight; below, the various heroes scampered around like ants. Then, inevitably, Thor raised his hammer and blew a hole through Goliath.

"S.H.I.E.L.D. footage," Black Widow said. She gestured at Hank. "He's been watching it compulsively."

Tony frowned. Hank Pym had been a super hero himself, first as Ant-Man, then Giant-Man and Yellowjacket. He was the first of the size-changing heroes, but in recent years he'd hung up his tights, preferring to concentrate on scientific research. Including the Niflhel Protocol.

Goliath, Tony recalled, had once been Hank's lab assistant.

"Hank," Tony said, "it's a tragedy. I'm sorry. I know you and Bill were friends."

"Friends. Yes." Hank turned to Tony, accusation in his eyes. "And I just watched a superhuman I helped *create* blow a hole straight through my friend."

Reed studied Thor. "I wonder why he—Thor, I mean—behaved like that. Is he missing a human conscience? Does he need a human host to fuse with?"

"Why? *Why?*" Hank whirled on Reed. "Maybe the problem is we weren't meant to *clone a god!*"

Spider-Man leapt through the air. "Clone?" He landed on the wall, just above the prone thunder god. "Thor is a *clone?*"

Tony grimaced. He cast his gaze across the assembled heroes, watching them as the revelation sank in. Ms. Marvel whipped her head toward him, an unfamiliar note of doubt in her eyes. Black Widow seemed rattled. Ben Grimm stood staring, his huge rocky jaw gaping wide.

Hank Pym shivered, as if trying to shake off his own guilt.

"Tony?" Spider-Man continued. "How in the five boroughs do you clone a god, anyway?"

Hank sat down, lowered his head. "Very first meeting of the Avengers, Tony set it up. Had me grab a lock of hair from Thor." He laughed humorlessly. "I was Ant-Man, then. Shrank down so small, I was almost microscopic. Thor thought he had fleas."

"So this..." Spider-Man reached out to pick up Thor's hammer. "This isn't really Mjolnir? It's some copy...the Hammer of Clor?"

Tony looked at him, puzzled.

"Clor," Spider-Man repeated. "Clone-Thor. Get it?"

"Not funny, Peter."

Spider-Man snapped to attention. Still holding the hammer, he shot his hand out toward Tony, in a Nazi salute.

Then, immediately, he lowered the hammer. "Sorry."

Tony surveyed the group. They all looked to him for guidance, for assurance that they were on the right path. But they were all shellshocked. Even Spider-Man, gleaming and kinetic in his metallic suit.

This is a crucial moment, Tony realized. *The whole Registration movement could fall apart, right here and now. Everything depends on what I do in the next few minutes.*

"Peter," Tony said. "Show me your face? I'm asking, not ordering."

Slowly, Spider-Man pulled off his mask. He too looked tired, sunkeneyed, and a bit ashamed.

"Thank you. Now." Tony paced the room, stopping just before Ms.

Marvel. "I know this isn't exactly what any of you signed up for. Carol, how's your arm?"

"Some people got it much worse," she said. "She-Hulk is still in intensive care. She's recovering, though."

"Good. I'm glad to hear that. Now, we're all thinking about the same thing: Bill Foster. His death was a tragedy, a horrible accident. The kind of thing that should never, ever happen, especially on our watch.

"But. BUT. We all knew this wasn't going to be easy, and we knew there'd be battles along the way. I'll be blunt: Anyone who didn't expect a casualty here and there, was deluding himself. We're talking about a major change in the lives of every metahuman on Earth.

"And that's what we have to remember. Bill Foster shouldn't have died. But his death is the price of what we're doing. If this process means another nine hundred civilians *don't* die as collateral damage in a super-battle, then—I hate to say it, but—I can live with Bill's death. Not easily, and I won't sleep well tonight. But I can live with it."

Ms. Marvel nodded gravely. Black Widow cocked her eyebrow. Ben Grimm just leaned against a table, his expression even stonier than normal.

Hank Pym stared at clone-Thor, shaking his head.

"The math," Reed Richards said softly. "The math works out."

"Thank you, Reed."

"Tony, I..." Peter Parker looked around nervously. "I want to believe you. I know your intentions are good. But is this—" He gestured at the screen, which still showed the frozen image of Goliath's dead body. "Is *that* what's gonna happen? Every time someone doesn't register, doesn't follow the rules?"

"Of course not. That's what the detention center's for."

"Yeah. The detention center." Peter nodded, looked Tony straight in the eye. "Think I could see that place, Tony?"

Something shifted in the room, in the air. Some balance of power, of authority.

"You wanted my sharp mind," Peter continued. "Right, boss?"

Tony stared back at Peter for a moment. Then he smiled, a warm, fatherly smile.

"Sure, Peter. Reed and I are headed over there now. Want to join?"

Peter pulled down his mask, red-and-gold lenses popping into place over his eyes. Again, he nodded.

"Hank," Tony said. "You've done enough here. Your registration is on file—why don't you take a week off. 'Clor' can wait on ice till you get back."

Reed stretched out an arm, touched Hank Pym on the back. Hank nodded, stood up, and trudged toward the door. He looked defeated, a shell of a man.

"The rest of you, take what time you need," Tony continued. "But check in at regular intervals. Things are only going to heat up from here, and I'm going to need every one of you."

Murmured assent. For now, it would have to do.

"Right." Tony slapped his helmet down over his face, motioned for Reed and Spider-Man to follow him. "Let's move, gentlemen. Project 42 awaits."

SIXTEEN

SOMETHING dark was growing inside Captain America. Something hard and angry, deep in his gut. Something he'd never felt before; something he didn't like at all.

It wasn't the death of Goliath...not exactly. Cap had lost men before, in war and in civilian battles. It always hurt, but it was a part of life. The life he'd chosen, decades ago, when a scrawny orphan kid first volunteered for the wartime super-soldier program.

Falcon wrapped a thick bandage around Cap's forehead. "Hold still," Falc said.

No, Cap realized, it wasn't the death. It was the *way* Bill Foster had died. Men and women under Cap's command had perished defending their country, saving innocents, or so that their fellow warriors could survive. Once in a while, you even lost a man by sheer, tragic accident. When that happened, you drank a sad toast, punched a few walls, and carried on.

This was different. Goliath had died as a direct result of Tony's actions. Tony Stark, the man Cap had called friend for years.

Cap coughed, then winced. Everything hurt: his face, his arms, his legs. Tony had really done a number on him.

Falcon fastened the last bandage, took a step back. "You look like the mummy half-escaped from his tomb," the winged man said. "But you got a few teeth left."

"I plan to use 'em," Cap said.

He tugged at the electrodes fastened to his bandaged chest. The medical wing of Resistance headquarters was remarkably well-outfitted with diagnostic equipment. A technician in a white coat stood at the monitors; like everyone they'd hired, she'd been personally vetted by at least two Resistance members.

Hawkeye entered the room, followed by Dagger, Stature, Speed, and Patriot. The kids looked shaken, unsure. So did Hawk.

"How's the man?" Hawkeye asked.

"Hawk, I need your help." Cap stood and pulled off the electrodes, ignoring the technician's protests. "We're gonna have to abandon this location. Tony's about to step up all his efforts to find us; even an off-the-books S.H.I.E.L.D. base is just too risky."

"Stop, Wings," Hawkeye said. "Don't say another word."

Cap frowned. Falcon fell in behind him.

Hawkeye looked down, shifted his quiver from one shoulder to the other. "Cap, I think we should appeal for amnesty."

"Amnesty? Are you insane?" Cap gestured around the room, winced as his arm slipped briefly out of joint. "We just picked up another fourteen supporters. Valkyrie, Nighthawk, Photon...Tony's losing allies by the minute."

"And how many people did *we* lose? Hulkling, Wiccan, Daredevil, Cloak..." Hawkeye turned to Dagger, who winced at her partner's name. "Sorry, doll."

"Hawk," Falcon began.

"No no, listen to me. Those guys are all on their way to whatever super-gulag Reed Richards has been building."

Cap chose his words carefully. "And you're willing to let them get away with that?"

Dagger grimaced. "They can do anything they want, now. They've got Thor on their side."

"That wasn't Thor," Cap snapped. "That was some Frankenstein's monster they grew for their super hero army. You didn't know Thor, girl. Don't think for a moment—not one moment—that he would have *murdered* a good man like Bill Foster."

Dagger shrank back. Stature put a hand on her shoulder.

Cap immediately felt remorse. *Snapping at a young girl. What's wrong with me?*

"Cap," Hawkeye said, "I've been on the wrong side of the law before. Spent a lot of my life there. It sucks. You helped pull me out of that life… hell, for a while, you and me practically *were* the Avengers.

"And you once said to me: When the law outnumbers and outguns you twenty-to-one, there comes a time when you gotta stop fighting."

"That's true, when you're in the wrong." Cap stared at him. "When you're right, you plant your feet in the ground and *hold the damn hill.*"

"I'm real sorry about Bill Foster. But he was dead the moment he thought he was bigger than the law."

"Hawkeye."

"Stop, Cap. I'm leavin'. So whatever you do, *don't* tell me where you're planning on movin' this base to."

"I wouldn't tell you the time of day."

"Good. 'Cause you oughta be thinkin' about something else. The more people join your little underground club, the bigger the possibility you might have a mole in the ranks."

Cap said nothing. The idea had occurred to him. Tony had managed to lure them to the chemical plant a little too easily.

Hawkeye turned, started to leave.

"What you gonna do, Clint?" Falcon's fists were clenched in fury. "Pull on those little jackboots and smack whoever they tell you to?"

"No." Hawkeye's voice was soft now. "I'm gonna be a Good Guy."

Everyone stood quiet. Patriot cast a questioning glance at Speed, who smiled nervously and shrugged. Speed looked at Stature, who looked away.

Then Stature turned and started after Hawkeye.

Patriot reached out, grabbed her arm. "Cassie?"

"Sorry, Eli. But I don't want to wind up in some super-jail, like Wiccan and Hulkling. I got into this to fight villains, not cops or other super heroes."

Speed circled around her, touched her shoulder. "C'mon, Cass—"

"Tommy, you know how this is gonna end." Stature glanced briefly at Cap. "He's just another old man scared of the future."

"Go." Cap's voice was a low growl now. "If your freedom means so little to you."

Stature grimaced, hugged her teammates quickly. Then she ran to join Hawkeye.

"Eli, Tommy? What about you?"

Patriot glanced at his teammate; Speed grinned back. "We're in."

"Dagger?"

Dagger's hands flared bright, light-knives flashing into the air. Her eyes shone with inner light, with determination.

"I want my partner back," she said.

Cap nodded in approval. "Good."

They gathered around him then: Falcon, Patriot, Speed, and Dagger. All looking to him for guidance, for leadership. For just a moment, the dark thing in Cap's gut relaxed, lightened.

He hoped he could be worthy of them.

"We've got a lot of work to do. Falc, notify all troops: We're bugging out. I think Cage has a Harlem safe house we can use for a while. Dagger, see if anybody has any special knowledge regarding Stark Enterprises security systems. Patriot, Speed, you talk to the new recruits. Make a list of their special powers."

As they scattered, Cap took a step. His leg exploded in agony; he almost fell. "And somebody get me a Midol?"

SEVENTEEN

TWELVE days had passed since the press conference. Twelve days that turned Peter Parker's life inside out.

Aunt May had been hounded by reporters, forced to hole up inside her house. People shouted "traitor" at Peter in the streets. The Daily Bugle filed suit against him for misrepresentation and breach of contract, citing the amount he'd been paid for Spider-Man action photos over the years.

And a visit to Peter's old high school turned into a nightmare when Doctor Octopus crashed his guest lecture on physics. Thankfully, no students or faculty were hurt. But Principal Dillon had made it very clear that no further alumni lectures would be welcome.

Since then, sleep hadn't come easily. Peter kept waking up, several times a night, with a low noise rumbling in his head. He'd never had migraines before, but he wondered if this might be the first symptom.

Then came Goliath. And that horrible moment, delivered in HD through the lenses in Peter's new costume, that he couldn't get out of his mind.

So Spider-Man practically sleepwalked through the trip with Tony and Reed. S.H.I.E.L.D. had cordoned off several midtown blocks with trucks and paddy wagons, isolating the Baxter Building. When Spidey asked Tony why, the billionaire replied, "Prisoner transfer."

Spider-Man webbed his way above the cleared street and landed on the side of the Baxter Building. Tony and Reed stood below, deactivating the main door's defense systems. Four or five S.H.I.E.L.D. copters hovered above, along with that flying command post Maria Hill used.

Briefly, Spider-Man thought: *How many agents does S.H.I.E.L.D. have, anyway?*

"Stark to Commander Hill." Tony's metallic voice rang in Spidey's ear. "I have an errand upstairs, Maria. Can your boys handle the transfer?"

"I think we got it. *Mister* Stark."

Spider-Man frowned. He liked Tony, felt genuine gratitude toward him; and he believed in Tony's cause, in the need to safeguard innocent people against powerful metahumans. Superhuman battles had grown more deadly, more vicious over the years, with a corresponding rise in civilian casualties. If Tony could reverse that trend, Spidey would follow him anywhere.

But Tony hadn't told him everything. Like the fact that he'd had scientists busy cloning a dead god. Did Tony have locks of *everyone's* hair squirreled away on ice, just in case?

Things were happening very, very fast. Spider-Man barely had time to process one shock before another one slammed him off his feet.

Off his feet.

Like Goliath.

"Peter," Tony called. "You coming in or not?"

THE Negative Zone portal hummed with life, lights dancing along its metallic edge. Inside, an unearthly nebula blazed, haloed all around by stars and asteroids. A display screen read: PROJECT 42 GATEWAY / ACTIVE.

"Your costume will protect you," Tony said. "Just strap on this grav-pack for maneuvering."

Spider-Man shrugged on the metallic backpack. It was surprisingly light. He pointed into the portal: "That's where the prison is?"

"Detention center," Tony said. "Reed, the access code please?"

No answer. Spidey glanced over at Reed, saw him hunched over a control console, staring blankly. One elongated arm stretched out behind him, idly manipulating a console all the way across the room.

"Reed?"

"Mm?" Reed looked up, bleary. "Oh, yes. Of course." He typed quickly, extending and retracting his fingers to reach the keys. "Sending the code to your armor, Tony."

"Got it. You know what to do when S.H.I.E.L.D. arrives, right?"

Again, no answer.

Reed had been very quiet on the trip over. *Marital troubles,* Spider-Man thought. *Wonder what that's like.*

"The fabulous Negative Zone," Spidey said. "We just...walk through?"

"Follow me."

Tony's boot-jets flared. He arced upward, pivoted his body to horizontal position, and flew straight through.

Spider-Man stared, shrugged, and leapt.

Passing through the portal was like nothing he'd ever felt before. First his arms, then his head, then his torso and legs—all of them felt *inverted* somehow. The process wasn't painful, but he found it disturbing.

Then he was inside, and the portal was gone. All around him stretched Negative Zone space, vast and bright, filled with objects of all sizes and shapes—stars, jagged asteroids, distant planets. It looked like deep space, if someone had pumped deep space full of extra matter and lined it with hidden funhouse mirrors to distort the distances involved.

"Weird, right?" Tony hovered just before him. "You get used to it."

"It felt like I was...being turned inside-out," Spider-Man said.

"That's pretty close to what happens."

"How can that be? How does that possibly, conceivably *not kill us?*"

"I asked Reed that, once," Tony replied. "He launched into some elaborate quantum-physics explanation I couldn't follow. Then he stopped in mid-sentence, and this funny little grin crept over his face."

"He didn't know either."

"He didn't know."

Tony gestured toward a cluster of asteroids, took off toward them. Spider-Man followed, activating the grav-pack via his costume's mental controls.

"S.H.I.E.L.D. is preparing to transfer prisoners," Spidey said. "I guess that means the guys we captured at the chemical plant?"

"Correct."

"So that's how this is gonna work? Anybody who doesn't register, gets brought to the Baxter Building and shipped in here?"

"Only temporarily. Reed Richards first discovered the Negative Zone; right now, the only portal on Earth is the one we just came through, in his laboratory. But Stark Enterprises is already building portals in major prisons all over the country. Once those are operational, violators of the Super-human Registration Act will be dealt with like any other criminals: processed by the proper authorities, then transferred here."

Spider-Man frowned. "You forgot 'given a fair trial.'"

"There are no trial provisions in the SRA, Peter."

"What?"

"You don't give an atomic bomb a fair trial. Or an enemy combatant on the field of battle." Tony pointed up ahead. "Altering course. Follow my lead."

An asteroid loomed closer, one jagged rock among many. Buildings gleamed on its surface, reflecting the starlight. Spider-Man peered at it for a moment, and began to feel queasy.

"Follow me down, Peter. And don't deviate from the flight pla—Peter?"

The structures on the asteroid's surface were clearly visible now, jutting up like manmade building blocks. But something about them seemed very odd. Their configuration seemed to shift, flashing frighteningly from one arrangement to another. Spider-Man stared at them, felt a twinge of panic with every shift. His gut, his hindbrain screamed: This architecture is inhuman. Twisted, fearful. *Wrong.*

Tony's voice sounded distant in his ear. "...sorry. Set your lenses to Filter 18, strength level one notch below maximum."

Spidey could barely process the words. He stared, eyes wide, twitching. "What?"

"Never mind, I'll do it for you."

Spider-Man's vision blurred, went blank for a second. He blinked, disoriented, and then the scene became clear again.

The buildings had stopped shifting. They rose like a futuristic city now, gleaming and majestic against the bare rock of the asteroid. Far below, guards in full armor patrolled the perimeter of the land and soared around the highest spires.

"Security protocol Reed worked out," Tony said. "It uses a specially designed architectural configuration, in combination with the unique properties of the Negative Zone, to create a virtually escape-proof environment."

Spider-Man hovered, stared down at the cluster of spires. He remembered the effect they'd had on him, just seconds ago, and shivered. *"Rogue Moon,"* he whispered.

"One of Reed's favorite sci-fi novels. I think it was an inspiration."

"The guards are protected?"

"Actually, most of them are robots."

Tony led him down to a landing pad, out where the gleaming metal of the complex petered out onto bare rock. Three robot-guards approached, pulse-rifles protruding from their arms.

"GUARD POST BRAVO RECOGNIZING ANTHONY STARK. IDENTIFY SECOND HUMANOID."

"Spider-Man, real name Peter Parker," Tony said. "Guest of Anthony Stark."

"CONFIRMED. REGISTRATION ON FILE." The lead guard's face was blank, lights dancing behind its black-glass plating. "PRESENT ACCESS CODE PLEASE."

"Tango Sierra Lloyd Bridges."

"ACCESS CODE CONFIRMED."

The guards moved aside. Tony led Spider-Man, on foot, toward a seemingly featureless silver wall. A door irised open, twenty feet high and almost as wide.

"'Lloyd Bridges'?" Spidey asked.

"A custom-designed app randomly generates new passwords every half-hour. The app has an unanticipated fondness for the names of 1960s TV actors—yesterday it was 'Charlie Foxtrot Adam West.'" Tony laughed. "When it gets to Sebastian Cabot, I'm pulling the plug."

They passed through a large corridor, into a courtyard where baby plants sprouted from transplanted Earth soil. Spider-Man craned his neck, looked up at the featureless skyscrapers all around. The scope of the place was incredible; ceilings, buildings, everything seemed larger than life. And very new, very metallic, totally antiseptic.

"You said most of the guards are robots?"

"There are some human medical personnel and administrators, to make sure nothing goes wrong. But Reed and I discussed the matter at length. We decided the more we minimized the possibility of human error, the better this place would work."

Tony led him into a smaller, tighter corridor. Held up his gauntleted hand, and a heavy door swooshed open.

"Here are the apartments."

"You mean the cells?"

"Semantics."

The hallway was lined with thick, angular metal doors, each with a small slit of one-way glass embedded at eye level. Spider-Man jumped up onto the wall, crept along it to the first door. He lifted a hand to raise his mask off.

"Careful," Tony warned. "You take off your lenses, the disorientation effect will hit you again. It works everywhere inside the prison, except within the cells themselves."

"Gotcha." Spidey turned back toward the cell, leaned over to peer through the glass.

The inside looked like any sparely appointed living room, anywhere. Sofa, flatscreen TV, desk with a built-in computer monitor. A small fold-up bunk sat mounted against one wall, and Spider-Man could see the edge of a kitchen alcove in the background. The only oddity: a large armchair with wrist-restraints and a helmet hanging above it.

"Gotta admit, it looks nicer than my first Manhattan apartment. Bigger, too." Spidey shrugged. "What's that chair-thingy?"

"Virtual reality system. Lets them take little mind-vacations, even when they're trapped in here. We may have to modify it, of course, for villains with tech-manipulation abilities."

"I don't see anybody inside."

"The facility has only just become operational. Very few of the cells are occupied." Tony cocked his head, consulting some internal data file. "Ah. Try this one."

Spider-Man leapt down, crossed to the next cell. Peered through the glass.

A waterfall of sand dropped down before his eyes, landing on a heaped pile of clothing on the floor of the cell. The sand gathered, began to form, and rose up from the floor. Filled out a muscle shirt and jeans, forming into the unmistakable form of Spider-Man's old foe: The Sandman.

"We caught him a couple weeks ago," Spidey said. "With the Sinister Six."

"*You* caught him," Tony replied. "That was good work."

Inside, Sandman flipped through a magazine, frowned at it. He picked up a remote control and plopped down on the sofa, sending grains of sand flying all around.

"He looks kinda sad," Spider-Man said.

"Sad? He's in prison." Tony turned to Spidey. "People like Sandman are too dangerous to be allowed to walk around. You know that."

"I'm not arguing about him, but...a lot of my friends, our friends, are gonna wind up here too. They'll be locked up, same as him."

"All their needs will be seen to. They'll be comfortable."

"But they can't leave."

"Of course they can. The minute they agree to register, to go public with their identities and follow the laws of the United States of America. To follow the courageous example *you* showed, back at the press conference."

Once again, Spider-Man felt the low rumble in his head. The ache that had kept him awake, these past several nights.

"Come on," Tony said. "The S.H.I.E.L.D. shuttle should be arriving about now."

Spidey followed him back, through the corridors and the courtyard and the huge metal doors. His head was swimming. Those buildings rose up a hundred, maybe a hundred and fifty stories. How many people would this place hold, ultimately? How long would they stay here? How much had it cost to *build*?

Outside, the S.H.I.E.L.D. shuttle was just arcing in to a landing. It looked like an airborne version of the Mobile Buses, thick and heavy, with rocket-tubes mounted on all four corners of its stern.

A hatch hissed open. A pair of S.H.I.E.L.D. agents strode out, in full riot gear and protective goggles. The robot guard moved to intercept them.

"PRESENT ACCESS CODE PLEASE."

"Echo Delta Julie Newmar," the agent said.

"ACCESS CODE CONFIRMED."

Tony turned to Spider-Man. "Codes are getting better."

The S.H.I.E.L.D. agent gestured inside the vehicle. Two more agents led Cloak out onto the landing pad. The young man wore his full costume, but with manacles at his wrists and ankles. A thick helmet was clamped on his head, stretching down to cover his eyes.

"Power dampener," Tony explained. "It also shields them from the distortion effect."

Wiccan and Hulkling stumbled out next, similar helmets covering their eyes.

"They've been assigned a double apartment, together." Tony gestured to Spider-Man. "We're not trying to punish anyone, Peter. This is about containment."

A tall, thickly built agent brought up the rear, escorting the red-garbed figure of Daredevil. DD walked easily, confidently, despite his fetters. When he reached Tony and Spidey's position, he stopped and turned straight toward them, despite the helmet covering his eyes.

His radar sense, Spider-Man thought. *The dampener must not be stopping it completely.*

"Tony Stark himself," Daredevil said. "Here to admire your handiwork?"

Tony said nothing.

"Impressive." Daredevil gestured up at the towering spires. "Built by Stark Enterprises, right? The government's really been handing out those no-bid contracts. How many millions have you made this month?"

Spider-Man turned to Tony. "Millions?"

Tony hesitated. With a jolt, Spidey realized: *It's a lot more than millions. Billions, maybe.*

The S.H.I.E.L.D. agent prodded Daredevil forward. But Tony held up a hand. "It's all right, agent. I'd like to talk to Daredevil while you bring him in."

Daredevil turned blind, hooded eyes to Tony and Spider-Man in turn. Then he marched toward the door. Tony fell in beside him, and Spidey followed.

"Daredevil—is it Matt? Never mind." Tony held up a hand, opened the door. "I want you to understand why we're doing this. I assure you, I don't take any pleasure in hunting down my friends."

Daredevil's lip curled in distaste.

"I sat there in Washington, on Capitol Hill," Tony continued, "and I watched them debate this issue from every side. In the end, it came down to two choices. Registration, or a total ban on all super hero activity. I think you'd agree: none of us wants that.

"You've heard of the Fifty State Initiative? It's real. It's happening. Eventually there will be fifty super-teams, one in each state. Every member trained, licensed, and accountable to the U.S. taxpayer. It's the next stage in superhuman evolution. We're already training new super heroes, and working to find a place for anyone who wants to join us.

"Daredevil: If you're interested—if you want to come clean, to register and go public right now—you'd be at the top of my list. You could even have your own team, call the shots. What do you say?"

They'd reached the cellblock. The S.H.I.E.L.D. agent lifted an access card and said a few words into the cell door. It whooshed open. The cell inside looked just like Sandman's—a bit neater, Spider-Man noticed.

"Otherwise," Tony continued, "this is the alternative. And nobody wants that, either."

Daredevil stood in the doorway, silent and grim. At length, he turned to the big S.H.I.E.L.D. agent.

"Agent Chiang," Daredevil said. "Would you give it to him, please?"

Tony turned to the agent. "Give it to me?"

"Ah, yeah." Agent Chiang reached into a pocket-compartment, pulled out a small disk. "When we processed him, we found this under his tongue. We tested it, it's harmless. But he said he was savin' it for you."

Tony took the object in his hand. Spider-Man peered in and saw what it was: an ordinary silver dollar.

"I...I don't understand," Tony said.

Daredevil half turned toward him. "That's thirty-*one* pieces of silver you've got now, Judas."

Then he turned and strode into the cell. The door swooshed shut behind him.

The agent secured the door and started back through the corridor.

"Come on," Tony said.

Spider-Man lingered for a moment, gazing at the cell that held his longtime friend. The rumbling in his head seemed louder now, pulsing, filling his mind.

He turned to follow Tony back through the prison. Past rows of cells soon to be filled, exercise rooms and courtyards waiting to be used. Tony seemed to have talked himself out; he was quiet now, thoughtful.

And slowly, Spider-Man realized what the ache in his mind was. *Spi-*

der-sense. Not like he'd known it before, a sharp shock warning him of imminent danger. This was lower, steadier, more constant. A different kind of alarm entirely.

He followed Tony Stark out and up, off the surface of the asteroid, away from the prison called Project 42. But he couldn't escape the buzzing in his head. The nagging feeling that things had gone very wrong, and were about to get even worse.

EIGHTEEN

My Darling Reed,

First off, I wanted to let you know that Johnny's doing better. The stitches came out yesterday, and he's been happily recuperating at the penthouse apartment of someone named "Marika."

Same old Johnny. I know I should be happy, but I'm not.

I'm so ashamed of you right now, Reed. And I'm ashamed of myself for going along, for passively supporting your fascistic plans.

That's why I'm leaving.

The suitcase lay on the bed, half packed. It was small, carry-on size, with little wheels: barely enough space inside for a change of clothes, some toiletries, and a well-worn blue super hero costume. Somehow the costume still fit, even after two children and dozens of super villain battles.

Sue smiled. *Must be the unstable molecules.*

She'd had to sneak into her own home, past the S.H.I.E.L.D. blockade. If Reed were to check the entry logs, he'd see that she'd entered her passcode—and, of course, the security cameras would record the outer door opening briefly, then swishing shut. It wouldn't show anyone entering, of course, because no one had. At least, no one visible.

But Reed was distracted. Very, very distracted, even more so than usual. Right now, one floor above, he and Tony Stark were overseeing the transfer of the captured "Resistance" members to that horror show they'd built in the Negative Zone.

Once Sue was inside the building, she hadn't felt the need to stay invisible. Reed would never notice her. These days he had no time for anyone, except Tony.

Sue flung open the top bureau drawer, felt around for her old, disused communicator. Found it: a bulky walky-talkie device with a "4" etched onto it. She tossed it into the bed, next to the suitcase—and then her eyes stopped on something else, lying in the back of the drawer. She pulled it out, held it up to the light.

A model rocket ship. And not just any rocket: a replica of the privately built ship that Ben Grimm had piloted out of the desert that fateful night. The night that Sue, Reed, Ben, and Johnny braved the cosmic ray belt at the edge of Earth's atmosphere, and were transformed into the Fantastic Four.

She'd almost forgotten this model. Reed had built it for her on their first wedding anniversary. The paint job was meticulous, down to the silver detailing on the old-style rocket tubes. The tinted cockpit even showed four little silhouettes inside.

She remembered thinking it was possibly the worst anniversary gift in history. And that had made her love Reed even more.

She wiped away a tear. Turned to the baby monitor on the night table and switched it on. Listened, for just a minute, to the voices of Franklin and Valeria arguing with HERBIE, their robot babysitter, about who was allowed to pick a DVD to watch.

Then she heard a noise, just past the doorway. She snapped off the monitor and willed herself invisible—then thought better of it, and faded back into view. It was pointless to hide. If Reed didn't already know she was here, the half-packed suitcase would be a dead giveaway.

"Suzie?"

The figure in the doorway was bigger, bulkier than Reed. Ben Grimm's rocky frame stood slumped, almost in defeat. Sue let out a relieved breath—which caught in her throat when she saw what he was holding.

Another suitcase. Fully packed.

Please understand, darling: This is not a cry for attention. This is not me trying to distract you from your all-important work.

This is because your hands, both our hands, are soaked in Bill Foster's blood. And you're so blinded by your graphs and projections and doomsday scenarios that you can't even see it.

Today I broke the law. I helped a team of wanted felons escape duly deputized federal forces. Those felons happened to be some of our closest friends, who fell into those forces' clutches out of a pure desire to help innocent people. But that doesn't seem to matter.

Tony and his goon squad have their hands busy right now, licking their wounds and locking up prisoners and setting up their super hero training squads all over the country. If there's a scrap of decency left in them, I hope they're putting together a funeral for poor Bill Foster, too.

Sooner or later, though, they'll come after me for what I've done. They'll probably offer me amnesty, because of your importance to Tony's plans. I don't want to put you in that position—but more importantly, I don't <u>want</u> their amnesty.

I want to do what's right.

They stood together awkwardly for a moment. Each staring at the other. "You're leaving?" Sue said.

Ben pointed at her suitcase. *"You're* leavin'?"

"I have to, Ben. After today." She grimaced, felt tears rising again. "But what about you? I don't—are you going to join Captain America's group too?"

"Naw." He dropped the suitcase; it landed with a loud THUNK. *What does he have in there?* Sue wondered. *Spare rocks?*

"Suzie, I took a long look around after the battle was over. At that chemical plant. There was toxic goo all over the floor, jagged glass an' metal, not a wall left standing. Now, Tony had wrecked the place pretty good to start with, as part'a the trap. But I saw what we did, all of us, fightin' like starved rats in that little space.

"An' I couldn't stop thinkin': What if there'd been people around? What if one single civilian had sneaked past the barricades, a reporter maybe, an' got himself crushed in between me an' Luke Cage? Or under that big acid vat Falcon dropped?"

"I know." Sue crossed to him. "Listen. I have a rendezvous scheduled for—"

"No no no! I don't wanna know. I ain't pickin' sides here. Far as I can tell, Cap's as guilty in all this as Tony Stark."

Sue frowned. "What are you saying?"

"I'm sayin' the registration law is wrong, an' I can't uphold a law I don't believe in."

"That's what I'm—"

"But I'm still a patriot, Suzie. I love my country. I ain't gonna fight the government, or let that government brand me like a criminal. So the way I see it, I only got one choice.

"I'm leavin' the country."

She stopped, took a step back. "Oh."

"France, I figger. At least till this is over." He glanced at the night table, and his big blue eyes grew misty. "Aw, hey. Look at that."

Sue followed his gaze over to the model rocket. She picked it up, handed it to him. They stood together for a minute, staring at it.

"We were the first," she whispered.

"Yeah." He turned to her, an odd look in his eyes. "You ever regret it all, Suzie?"

"What?"

"All of it. The rocket flight, the powers. Followin' Big Brain all over creation: into space, other dimensions, the freakin' Negative Zone. The fights, the drama...you had a few other guys after ya there, for a while."

She frowned. "Ben..."

"You ever regret marryin' him? Settling down?"

She smiled sadly. "I'm not sure I'd call this 'settled down.'"

"That ain't an answer."

A harsh buzzing rose from the communicator, lying on the bed. Sue snatched it up quickly.

Ben raised a massive eyebrow. "I ain't seen one'a those for a while."

She held up a finger, motioned him to wait. "Johnny?"

Her brother's voice crackled through static. "You there, sis?"

"Hang on one minute, Johnny." She turned back. "Ben—"

"I gotta go, Suzie. Good luck."

"You—oh, you too, you big goof."

"Just do me one favor, okay?" Ben's face was very serious. "Stay away from Atlantis."

"Sis? I can barely hear you."

"Johnny, hold on—"

But when she turned back toward the door, Ben was gone.

You won't hear from Johnny for a while either, Reed. I'll take care of him, the way I've always done.

But where we're going, I can't take Franklin and Valeria. So I'm leaving them in your care. And I beg you, darling: Please find time for them, the time you've so often denied them in the past.

I also didn't want your last memory of me to be tainted with all the fights we've had in the past few weeks. I'm glad we made love last night, and I want you to know it was amazing. It was always amazing.

Fantastic, even.

"Sis, we haven't used these communicators in years. Where'd you even find them?"

"I couldn't risk cell phones, Johnny. Tony Stark can see through satellites, these days." She grimaced. "But I don't think anyone uses this frequency anymore."

"You always were the brains of the family. Well, *our* family." Static rose again, then subsided. "...next move?"

"Where are you? Still at Marika's?"

"Martika. Yeah, it's—"

"Mar*tika*. No, don't even tell me. Let's meet in half an hour—say, outside the Blazer Club. Nobody'll expect to see us there again."

"Scene of the crime. I like it."

"Be inconspicuous. But no stupid disguises. Leave the fake nose and glasses at home."

"Aw, sis. The ladies love that one."

"I gotta go, Johnny. See you soon. I love you."

"You're such a girl."

The communicator went dead.

Sue turned back to the baby monitor. *I should go see the kids,* she thought. *One last time. This is going to be hard on them.*

But she knew: *If I do that, I won't leave.*

She picked up the rocket model, hefted it in her hand. Held it over the suitcase, then turned away and placed it, carefully, back in the bureau drawer.

I'll be back, she thought. *I hope.*

Then she zipped up the suitcase and turned invisible.

I hope I don't look like a coward for leaving this way. I hope you don't think I'm a bad wife or, even worse, a bad mother.

I'm doing this for the best of reasons. Tony Stark's crusade was born out of noble intentions, I know that. But I also know, deep in my heart, that it will not lead anywhere good.

You're the smartest person I know, Reed. And I hope, I pray, that your genius can resolve this situation before one side ends up slaughtering the other.

I love you, darling. More than anything in the world. Fix this.

-Susan

NINETEEN

"PETER, I tell you I'm fine. Nobody has threatened me, nobody's—Peter, *where* are we *going*?"

Peter Parker glanced at the map on his phone, then leaned forward. "Take the next right," he told the cabbie.

"It's not that I love having policemen outside the house all the time," Aunt May continued. "But they've been very nice."

"They're not policemen, Aunt May. They're S.H.I.E.L.D. agents."

"Either way, Mister Smarty. That doesn't explain why I had to pack up my things and sneak out past them." She looked out the window, grimacing in distaste. "And what are we doing in *Brooklyn*?"

The cabbie half turned toward them. "This block, sir?"

"I think so. Slow down."

Like many New York neighborhoods, Fort Greene had come up a lot over the past decade. Rows of old brownstone buildings had been cleaned, refaced, and restored to their 19th-century splendor.

"Peter—"

"Just a minute, Aunt May. Please." He frowned, peered out the window. "Should be the next one on the…whoa."

The cab lurched to a halt.

"Whoa it is," the driver said.

Aunt May clutched at Peter's shoulder now, afraid. He turned to smile at her, gently removed her fingers. Then he opened the door and stared.

Most of the block was lined with concrete sidewalks and plain iron railings. But in front of one particular building, the sidewalk had been replaced with elegant, old-fashioned flagstones. Plants grew everywhere: Inside the fence, along the sidewalk, lining the steps leading to the main entrance. A young maple tree sprouted from a square cut into the walk, dirt still mounded around its base.

He frowned, double-checked the address. No mistake.

"Peter." Aunt May struggled with her suitcase. "Didn't I teach you to help a lady with her bag?"

He hefted the suitcase easily, paid the cab driver, and led Aunt May up the steps—all in a daze. His heart was pounding. This wasn't going to be easy, and the appearance of the house made him feel like he'd stepped into some mirror-world.

Maybe she won't be home, he thought. And then: *No. She has to be.*

She answered the door in jeans spotted with dirt and grass stains, a casual shirt tied up at her lovely waist. Her long red hair was tousled, hint of sweat on her brow. She held a trowel in one hand.

Her eyes went wide with shock. "Oh my God."

"Mary Jane," Peter said.

They stood together for an awkward moment, staring at each other. The thought flickered through Peter's mind: *Is she gonna stab me with the trowel?*

Then Aunt May pushed past him, her arms wide. "Dear," she said. "It's been too long."

Still stunned, Mary Jane reached out and hugged the older woman. But her gaze stayed on Peter.

"Good to see you, Aunt May," MJ said slowly. "Why don't you sit down and have some tea. I think your nephew and I need to talk."

MJ'S backyard was, if anything, even more impressive than the front. It was vast, covered with green: bushes, tomato plants, neatly tended rows of flowers. A carriage house stood beyond, with an arched glass-tiled roof; she'd converted it into a greenhouse.

Peter looked around, amazed. "This place is...it's really something, MJ."

She stooped down, hastily tamped down a hole she'd been digging. "It's largely self-sustaining, Tiger. The walls are insulated with recycled denim, there's solar panels on the roof. The roof garden helps keep the place warm in the winter, and prevents toxic water runoff. I'm thinking about drilling a geothermal well, but that takes a lot of permits."

"Don't take this the wrong way, MJ. But this doesn't sound like you."

"An actor friend did something similar in Clinton Hill, told me about it. But I guess, really, I just needed a project. Something that was really mine. After..."

She trailed off.

"After I left you at the altar," he finished.

"You mean, Spider-Man did." Her lip curled up in a sad half-smile. "Guess that's a secret I don't have to keep anymore."

"I would have married you," he said, his voice faltering. "I mean, that thug had me unconscious during our *scheduled* wedding. But afterward. Any day, any time."

After the wedding debacle, she'd fled town, refused to speak to him for two weeks. He tried everything to make it right: flowers, gifts, hand-written notes, tearful video apologies. When she'd finally agreed to talk, he assumed she'd finally forgiven him. But her answer was clear and definite: She would never marry Spider-Man.

And Spider-Man, he'd discovered, wasn't something he could give up.

She waved him off now, a bit of the old smirk creeping onto her face. She crossed to a long bench made out of a single log and plopped down on it, stretching out her long legs. Her shirt rode up a bit more, revealing that incredible stomach. No wonder she was still getting gigs at Vogue and on VH-1.

She looks amazing, he thought. *Is she getting* younger?

"So, Tiger. You couldn't call first? Too busy making headlines?"

He perched awkwardly on the edge of the bench. "I don't really trust the phones right now."

"Sounds good and paranoid." Then she leaned forward, suddenly serious. "Hang on. All this publicity…has somebody threatened Aunt May? Is that why you brought her here?"

"No. Not yet."

"I saw the Doc Ock thing, on the news. Tiger, didn't you think about this stuff before you revealed your identity on national freaking TV?"

"I did! Really, I did." He turned away. "And somebody promised to keep her safe. But…"

"But?"

"But I'm not sure I trust that person anymore."

"We're not kids anymore, Peter. Knock off the guessing games."

"Tony. It's Tony Stark."

"Tony Stark." She raised a hand to her lovely lips. "The richest man we know, the guy who's now basically in charge of all super hero activity in the country. Don't you think he can handle keeping your aunt safe?"

"It's not a question of *handle*. It's just…" He got up, started to pace.

"Watch those geraniums," MJ said. "They're just starting to bloom."

"There's a lot of weird stuff going on, MJ. Did you hear about the hero who died yesterday? Bill Foster?"

"Goliath, right?" She frowned. "The news reported it, but they didn't give too many details."

"That's because Tony doesn't want to tell people how it happened. That Bill got impaled by a lightning bolt, shot off by a defective clone of Thor that Tony's guys grew as part of their new hero team."

MJ stared. "I think I just had a little stroke," she said.

"I keep seeing it," Peter continued. "Blood spurting out Bill's back, his huge body tumbling like an oak. And that's not all. It's only the beginning. Tony's also got a prison for metahumans...this weird, antiseptic fortress run by robots. It's not even on Earth, it's in some weird dimension called the Negative Zone."

He paused, gasped for breath. He could feel himself starting to break down, the barriers falling. Something about this place, about seeing MJ again. He'd never been as close to anyone as he'd been to her, and now that she was with him again, he found he couldn't stop talking.

"There's supposed to be...Tony wants fifty super-teams, one for every state. It's all top secret right now, but I've seen some of the names he's trying to recruit. You can't fill out fifty teams without signing up some pretty unstable people."

"Peter—"

"And Captain America! There's no better man in the world, but I stood there and watched Tony just pound the crap out of him, beat him to a bloody pulp. I'm not squeamish, MJ, you know that, I've seen things. But this was just *wrong*. It was...oh dammit..."

He wiped away a tear, tried to smile.

"Stupid pollen. You got too many plants out here, you know that?"

And then she was there, directly in front of him, her lovely dark eyes boring into his. Challenging him, just as she'd done when they were kids. She smelled of skin and earth and strawberry perfume. Her lips were slightly parted.

He moved forward to kiss her, driven by a deep, unconscious need. But she held out a hand, pushed him away.

"What are you going to do?" she asked.

Peter looked down, embarrassed. "Tony's a good man. He's done so much for me, for a lot of people."

"But you think he's gone too far."

"I'm just gonna talk to him. He and me, we think alike. He said so."

"You don't sound sure."

"I'm not sure of anything. Well, one thing. Just one."

He pulled her close, hugged her like a sister. Buried his head in her shoulder.

"You're the only person." He felt tears rising again. "The only person in the, in the world that I really, truly trust."

She said nothing. Raised lithe hands to his shoulder blades, held him tight.

"I need you to take her away," he said. "To keep her safe."

"Safe from what?"

"From—from nothing, hopefully. But if this doesn't go the way I hope—if *he* doesn't see—"

"Dammit. Dammit, Petey." MJ broke away, stalked across to a clutch of sunflowers. "You expect me to uproot my whole life and—"

"I know. I know, but it's—"

"—and leave my *house* that I just *finally* got the way I want it, after *everything* that's..."

She buried her head in her hands, started to cry.

Peter stood, helpless.

"I can't let her be hurt," he whispered. "Not because of…"

MJ turned hard, tear-stained eyes toward him. "Because of Spider-Man."

He nodded.

"Is everything all right out here?" Aunt May poked her head out the back door, then grimaced. "Oh, I see. More of the old drama. Well, don't mind little me. Oh, my, Mary Jane. What lovely posies you have."

AUNT May sputtered and protested. She jabbed her finger at Peter, repeatedly, and for a terrible moment he expected her to explode into a full-on tantrum, the kind she hadn't allowed herself since Uncle Ben's death. But in the end she nodded, set her mouth, and allowed Mary Jane to lead her to the car.

In the end, as she'd said, she trusted him.

Peter stood on the sidewalk, watching Mary Jane's Mini Cooper recede down the street. MJ had barely said a word to him while packing. But he knew that she, too, understood.

He let out a long breath, collapsed back against the young maple tree. Closed his eyes, inhaled the thick nature-smell. He thought of the two women he loved most in the world, crammed together in that tiny car, headed for parts unknown. *Don't tell me where you're going,* he'd begged Mary Jane. *It's better that way.*

He wondered when he'd see them again.

PART FOUR
THE DECIDERS

TWENTY

WAS it all sliding off a cliff? Tony Stark couldn't tell. Public opinion had turned against Registration somewhat, after the chemical plant debacle; the latest polls were split pretty evenly. The defection of Susan Richards was a problem, too, one that he'd have to deal with eventually.

And the international community wasn't happy. European Union leaders had been making speeches nonstop against the new policy, happy to have something to take attention off their own failing economies. Wakanda, the African nation that supplied Stark Enterprises with the valuable element Vibranium, was considering cutting off all diplomatic relations with the United States.

The sunken nation of Atlantis was another potential problem, since one of the dead New Warriors had been a daughter of their royal family. Prince Namor, ruler of Atlantis, had once staged a full-scale invasion of the surface world. Not much had been seen of Namor, or of the enigmatic blue-skinned Atlanteans, in recent years. Tony hoped Namor's legendary temper had cooled with time.

The X-Men had practically walled themselves up in their school. Maria Hill was ready to assault the gates full-on with S.H.I.E.L.D. shock troops, arrest and detain everyone inside. Tony had persuaded her to hold off. The X-Men's relationship with the larger hero community had always been uneasy; they wouldn't give in easily to an invasion. The result would be a bloodbath all around.

But Hill was right about one thing: Every holdout added to the overall problem. For Registration to work, a critical mass of heroes had to comply. Otherwise the whole process would backfire. Instead of taking control of the problem, Tony and S.H.I.E.L.D. would seem helpless, ineffectual—and *that* would pave the way for more repressive, hostile forces to step in.

On the positive side, the training camps were really coming together. Intel continued to stream in from inside Cap's Resistance. Project Thunderbolt had entered its alpha-test phase. And slowly but surely, more heroes *were* registering. Just this morning, Doc Samson and the Sentry had signed up.

Registration is the law, Tony reminded himself. *In time, everyone will fall in line.*

"Just over this hill, Happy." Tony ducked farther under Happy Hogan's big umbrella, stepping carefully around a mud puddle. Rain sheeted down all around, painting the cemetery in grays and browns.

"Whoa," Happy said.

The hole was eleven feet wide by thirty feet long, and at least twenty feet deep. Six large industrial cranes whirred and strained, slowly lowering the wrapped, manacled body of Goliath down toward the ground.

People stood watching, grouped uncomfortably in twos and threes. Ms. Marvel and the Black Widow stood together; Carol looked tall and elegant in a gray suit, while Natasha wore a black trenchcoat. Reed Richards wore a corduroy jacket and tie, but his arms were stretched out protectively around Franklin and Valeria, his two children. They looked puzzled and uncomfortable in formal clothes.

"Reed brought the kids?" Happy asked.

"He didn't want to leave them with the robots all day." Tony sighed. "And there's nobody else left at the Baxter Building."

An older black couple held each other. The woman met Tony's eyes for a moment, glaring at him. He looked away.

"Bill's parents," Tony said.

"This must be rough for 'em," Happy replied. "Especially since you couldn't shrink the body down again."

"Hank Pym's on leave right now. But I called him, he said it couldn't be done. Something about electrical brain activity and organic tissue decay."

"I wonder how much the family had to shell out for...what? Thirty-eight burial plots?"

"Nothing. I took care of the expenses. Least I could do."

A crane lurched slightly. Goliath's body slipped, and his arm banged against the edge of the hole. Tony grimaced.

"God, Happy. Is this all worth it? Do I have the...the right to do this?"

Happy said nothing. Just stood, holding up the umbrella, shielding Tony from the deluge.

"Stark?"

Maria Hill's voice, in his Bluetooth earpiece, made Tony jump. He turned away from the grave, clicked it. "What?"

"Got a few people for you to meet."

"Dammit, Maria. Let me get Bill Foster into the ground first."

He cut off the call before she could speak again. That woman was really becoming a problem. If she had her way, all the capes, all the heroes would be shut down for good.

Tony looked around. "Where the hell is Peter Parker?"

Reed approached, towing the kids behind him. He looked like he'd been dragged through the sewer. "Tony."

"Reed. Thanks for coming. Hey Franklin, Valeria."

Happy crouched down, tried to ruffle Franklin's hair. The boy turned away, hid behind his father's leg.

Reed held a wet slip of paper, clenching and unclenching his fist around it. "What's that?" Tony asked.

"Nothing," Reed said, and hurriedly stashed the paper in a pocket. But Tony caught a quick glimpse of the signature at the bottom: *Susan*.

"Reed." Tony reached out a hand, clasped it on Reed's shoulder. "This is a rough patch. We'll get through it. We're doing the right thing."

"Daddy," Val said, "my shoes are growing sodden."

Reed patted her on the back and turned away. The kids followed.

"See you at the Baxter Building tonight," Tony said. "S.H.I.E.L.D. has a new batch of prisoners."

"Of course," Reed said. He sounded old, defeated.

With a dull mechanical noise, the cranes released their burden. The enormous body of Goliath settled to rest in its deep, muddy grave.

A speaker came on, and the Eurythmics song "Hey Hey, I Saved the World Today" filled the air. It sounded sad, dirge-like. A childhood memory sprang, unbidden, to Tony's mind: Annie Lennox in a music video, dressed in a crisp man's business suit, her hands waving and conjuring over a globe of the Earth. She looked like a machine, powerful and sexual, cradling the world like it was her own personal toy.

"Tone?"

Tony looked up. The cranes had moved back. Steam shovels groaned and creaked, lifting wet earth to dump into the grave. People scattered, shuffling slowly away.

Ms. Marvel and the Black Widow approached. Natasha had an odd look in her eye. "Everybody's happy now," she said, "the bad guy's gone away."

"What does that mean?" Tony snapped.

She waved a hand in the air, gave him her Stupid-American look. "The song," she said.

"Mister Stark?"

Tony turned. Miriam Sharpe, the woman from Stamford, stood under a small umbrella. Happy tensed at the sight of her, but Tony held out a hand.

"Mrs. Sharpe. I'm sorry I haven't had time to—"

"No no, don't worry about it. I just came by because—I know you guys lost a lot of support in the super hero community, after..." She gestured at the gravesite.

Tony frowned. Behind him, Ms. Marvel and the Widow were listening, too.

"I wanted to say my piece," Sharpe continued. "Goliath knew what he was doing, and what he was doing was breaking a law designed to save people's lives. If he'd only gone legitimate, he'd still be alive." She smiled at Tony, a tear starting to form in her eye. "This isn't your fault. No more than, than a cop could be blamed for shooting a punk who pulls a gun on him."

"Mrs. Sharpe..."

"Shh. I also wanted to give you this." She reached into her purse. "It was my son Damien's favorite toy since he was three years old."

He took the toy, stared at it through the rain. A six-inch Iron Man action figure, its joints stiff, red-and-gold paint worn with age. He rolled the toy between his thumb and forefinger. Pushed at the arm; it swiveled upward.

Still works.

Tony looked up at Mrs. Sharpe, completely lost for words.

"Just to remind you why you're doing this," she said.

He touched her shoulder once, a wordless thank-you. Then he turned away, still clutching the toy figure. It felt warm in his hand.

Tony jabbed a finger at his earpiece. "Maria? Talk to me."

Brief pause. "About time, Stark. Meet me at the west entrance. But be prepared…your little funeral has stirred up some of the natives."

NIGHT was just falling as Tony ducked his head and trotted through the cemetery gate, passing between two lines of demonstrators. From his right, a chorus of groans and boos erupted, punctuated with cries of "Fascist" and "Cape killer!" To the left, a smaller ripple of cheers rose up. "Keep us safe!" someone yelled.

Tony took a moment to study the two groups. Both sides were a mix of college students under rain ponchos, ordinary working people, and some grieving women he recognized from Stamford. *If you were to pull out a random member of the protest,* Tony realized, *I couldn't identify which side she belonged on.*

One side hates me because I'm a super hero. The other side is cheering because I'm an authority figure.

State troopers had erected sawhorses to keep both groups back. But the cops looked nervous. Tony stopped to ask a trooper, "You have enough men here?"

"National Guard's on the way." The trooper grimaced. "We can hold out till then."

"Stark," Maria Hill's voice said again, in his ear.

The S.H.I.E.L.D. Mobile Command Center sat parked along the street, jutting out into the first lane of traffic. A line of guards surrounded it, parting quickly when Tony and Happy approached.

Inside the War Room, two newcomers waited. Hawkeye stood grimacing, in full purple costume, his bow lying on a table nearby. With him was a tall blonde girl in red and black, wearing a domino mask. Tony frowned for a moment, not recognizing her.

"Stature," Maria Hill said. "Formerly of the Young Avengers."

"Of course." Tony held out his hand. "And Hawkeye. Good to have you back, Clint. I know it can't have been an easy decision."

Hawkeye rubbed his neck. "Hardest I've ever made, Tony."

"I know. Your head knows the right thing to do, but your heart just wants things to stay the way they've always been."

"Yeah, but...we're livin' in a different world now. Guess it took Goliath dying to make me realize that."

Tony studied the bowman for a minute, then turned to face Stature.

"What about you...Cassie, right? This is a huge step you're taking here."

"I know that." She looked him straight in the eye. "My teammates don't understand."

"But you do."

"People want us to be properly trained, sir. It's not the 1940s anymore."

"That's the truth," Happy said.

"All I want is to do my job, to the best of my abilities."

Tony nodded, slowly. This was good news; two more recruits. And yet, something nagged at him. Something wasn't right here.

Hill stepped forward. "We've got a lot to go over, Stark. Starting with Project Thunder—"

Tony raised a hand to his neck, made a slicing motion. Hill followed his gaze over to Hawkeye, then nodded.

Hawk smiled. "You don't trust me, Tone?"

"Believe me, Hawk. There's parts of this operation I don't tell *myself* about."

Stature's eyes followed them, like a ping-pong game.

Hill gestured to a pair of agents. "Stathis, Roeberg. Take the new recruits back to the city by limo. You can fill 'em in on procedures along the way."

"Roger."

Hawkeye shouldered his bow and followed the agent to the door. He paused, shot Tony a last glance.

Pissed off at me? Tony wondered. *Or is he pulling a scam, and wondering if I've seen through it?*

Hill came up next to him. "You think Cap's trying to put a mole in your operation."

"We've got one in his, don't we? And Hawkeye owes a lot to Captain America." Tony frowned suddenly. "Any sightings of Spider-Man today?"

Hill gestured to the remaining S.H.I.E.L.D. agent. "Ellis, run the CapeSearch protocol. Subject: Peter Parker."

The agent's hands flashed over his controls. A dizzying number of surveillance-camera images flickered across his screens, blurring into a brightly colored super hero montage. The display halted on an aerial shot of Spider-Man, in his red-and-gold armored costume, swinging across the night skyline of midtown.

"Last sighting, yesterday 1834 Hours. Outside the Baxter Building."

"1834 Hours. That's right after I left him." Tony frowned. "Nothing after that?"

"Not in costume, sir. The civilian-ID subroutines aren't up and running yet."

Tony turned to Happy. "Hap, you've got the suit, right?"

Happy held up Tony's briefcase.

"Good. Maria, I hope you won't mind me changing in front of you."

"I've seen it before."

Agent Ellis's head snapped up in surprise. "Back to work, mister,"

Hill barked.

"What's up, Mister Stark?"

"I think I've got a big problem, Hap." Tony snapped open the brief-case, stared at the Iron Man costume. "And it's time I took care of it."

TWENTY-ONE

"GOT it. Okay, thanks. Be there in half an hour."

Sue Richards hung up the pay phone, turned back to her brother. Johnny was dressed in jeans and a jacket. A large bandage poked out from under his baseball cap, but he looked much healthier than the last time she'd seen him.

"Falcon gave me the address," she said. "It's in Harlem."

Flames started to rise from Johnny's head and shoulders. "I can fly us—"

"Put that out! S.H.I.E.L.D.'s got eyes everywhere." She looked around, suddenly paranoid. "We'll just hoof it."

"Yes, big sister. At least the rain's stopped."

Sue started off up Eleventh Avenue. She and Johnny had gone straight to the Resistance's former headquarters, only to find it boarded up and abandoned. For a terrible moment, Sue had thought: *Did Tony round them all up?* But no—they'd just relocated.

They walked in silence for a moment, past gas stations and low-profile nightclubs and auto parts stores closed for the night. Over here, on the far west side, new things hid among the old. A trendy restaurant was likely to open right next to an ancient bodega, then close up again one night, leaving no trace.

"How's Reed doing?" Johnny asked.

Sue hesitated. "You know that thing he does when he gets totally wrapped up in a project?"

"No. No idea what you're talking about."

She laughed. "This is like that, times ten. He and Tony Stark are… they're like two kids in a candy store. No, more like two kids building their own, giant candy store. With every kind of candy in the world under their absolute control."

"Are we still talking about candy? 'Cause you're making me hungry."

She stopped under a streetlamp, turned to look at Johnny. Since she was fifteen, Sue had taken care of him. Now he was all grown up, a handsome young man, living his own life. And yet…

"Johnny, I have to do this. I made my choice when I helped the Resistance escape from Tony's thugs. But…"

"Don't, sis."

"…but you don't. You can still come in from the cold." She rubbed both hands on his broad shoulders. "Go turn yourself in."

Johnny gestured toward a large, blocky factory building. She followed him into a dark alcove next to the outer door. When they were hidden from the street, he held up a flaming finger to the brick wall. He traced the letter "A" in the air, leaving an afterimage trail before Sue's eyes.

"A," he said, "Registration, so far, has gotten me nothing but a fractured headbone. B, Tony Stark is a rich jerk."

Sue giggled. "Well, go ahead. What's C?"

"C?" Slowly, he traced the flaming letter in the air. "C is that my sister and I have always faced tough situations together, and I would never abandon her. Never."

She felt tears rising. She hugged him, hard.

Then they heard the cry.

"You—"

"Yeah," he said. "Inside the building."

He lit his whole hand on fire and ran it across the wall like a flashlight. The windows were boarded, the bricks chipped with decay and neglect. But the door...

Johnny pushed lightly at the door. It creaked inward. A big padlock on a chain lay on the ground, picked and discarded.

Again, they heard it. A distant call for help.

"Douse your light," Sue whispered. Then she reached out, turning them both invisible. Stepped past him and started inside, holding up her hand to generate a protective force field in front of them.

They felt their way down a dark, dusty corridor. No power was on, not even emergency lights. But twice more, they heard the faint cries: "Help me!" and "What are you *doing*?"

The corridor opened onto a disused loading bay. High ceilings, smell of gunpowder and old newspapers. A single light shone from a portable electric lantern, placed right in the center of the floor.

On a large support beam, stretching from floor to ceiling, a man had been strung up tight with heavy cord. The lantern illuminated him from below, casting giant, rapidly jerking shadows on the ceiling. He struggled in panic, cried out: "Why? What do you *want*?"

The man's briefcase lay open on the floor, papers spilling out in a fan pattern. Tablet computer, too, a long crack along its screen.

A few feet away, his tormentor crouched down, cleaning a big hunting knife. Muscular arms, thick legs, a fierce brow. Skull pattern on his shirt.

"That's the Punisher," Johnny whispered.

"Yeah," Sue replied.

"Is *he* registered?"

"I sincerely doubt it."

The Punisher's head whipped up. For a moment, he stared straight at the door. Sue shivered; his cold eyes seemed to bore into her.

Even more quietly, Johnny said, "We're still invisible, right?"

Sue nodded sharply, raised a finger to her lips.

The Punisher frowned, swept the room with his eyes. Then he turned back to his work, pulled a fresh whetstone out of his bag.

Sue motioned Johnny forward, and they crept silently into the room. The Punisher was a vigilante, a killer known for taking down mafia bosses in a very permanent way. After his family had been murdered in a mob hit, he'd sworn revenge against all organized crime.

The man on the beam was whimpering now, struggling against his bonds. Sue studied him: He wore a white button-down shirt, crisply pressed slacks, and a loosened tie. His shoes, dangling and flailing, looked neatly shined and expensive.

This was no mob boss, not even one who'd gone legit. This was a businessman.

The Punisher held up the knife, studied its blade against the lantern light. Without facing his victim, he said, "Wilton Bainbridge Junior. They call you 'Wilt,' don't they?"

The man frowned. "Y-yeah."

"Wilt." Punisher turned to him, held up the blade. "We need to have a conversation."

"A conversation? Oh. Y-yeah! I'm, I'm not going anywhere."

Punisher smiled, a bloodless smile.

"You're a banker. Right, Wilt?"

"Y-yeah."

"And you sit on a lot of boards of directors, too."

"I guess."

"Like Roxxon International."

The man nodded. He still seemed frantic, but curious now, too. Looking for an opening.

"Roxxon's developing a lot of tech for the government these days," Punisher continued. "Oh, not as much as Stark is. But there's plenty of contracts to go around. And some of those involve technology that could be used to interfere with my business."

"Your business."

"That's right." Punisher held up the knife an inch from the squirming man, running it through the air from his stomach down to his crotch. "So I need you to tell me everything you know about something called the CapeSearch protocol."

"The CapeSearch—oh yeah! Sure." Wilt eyed the knife. "That's easy. It's pattern-recognition software, used to cross-check thousands of sources to locate any super hero, or, or, or villain, in the world. It's not really new, it's an adaptation of Homeland Security software already used in airport spot-checks. The only wrinkle is, it also detects use of metahuman powers. You know, like, like freezing rays or gamma radiation."

"Metahuman powers." Punisher turned away, nodding. "Thanks, Wilt."

"This is weird," Johnny whispered. "The Punisher doesn't kidnap civilians. I've certainly never heard of him extorting information from them."

Sue nodded, motioned him again to be quiet.

"What about Project Thunderbolt?" Punisher asked.

"Wh-what?"

"I thought at first it was a code name for that thunder-god monster that ran amok yesterday. But my sources tell me it's something different, something very dangerous. What's Project Thunderbolt, Wilt?"

"I, I don't know."

Punisher turned murderous eyes on him. Held up the knife, pricked his own finger with it. Didn't even flinch as blood flowed from the tiny cut.

"I don't know!" Wilt flailed, struggling against his bonds. "I've heard the name, but we didn't have anything to do with it. It's top top secret, developed solely by S.H.I.E.L.D. and Stark Enterprises."

"You don't know anything."

"I don't! I swear!"

Punisher turned back to his bag. He reached inside and pulled out a high-powered assault rifle.

"Then I guess you're no more use to me, Wilt."

Johnny's grip tensed on Sue's shoulder.

But Wilt shook his head, summoning up a last bit of bravado. "So you're gonna kill me?"

Punisher didn't answer. Pulled out a box of shells, emptied them into his hand.

"I don't think you're gonna kill me." Wilt was sweating, Sue noticed, but he seemed more confident now. "I know you, I know your rep. You don't just murder ordinary people in cold blood. You kill *criminals*, period."

Meticulously, Punisher loaded the shells into the rifle barrel. "That's right. I kill criminals.

"Let me break it down for you, Wilt." Punisher turned toward him. "Eight years ago, while in the employ of Terriman Gaston and Associates, you sold mortgages to Chase, Bank of America, and several other major national banks."

"Yeah. So?"

"You sold the *same* mortgages, in several hundred cases, to three or more different banks. Very, very lucrative."

"You're gonna kill me for *that*?" Wilt stared, incredulous. "Everyone was doing it."

"Among the mortgages you triple-dipped were a clutch of houses in a single development, in Hialeah, Florida. Just outside Miami. Ring any bells?"

Wilt shook his head. Fear had crept back into his eyes now.

Punisher looked down the length of the rifle, frowned. He pulled out a swab, started cleaning the barrel. "Two different banks came in to foreclose on those houses. The residents were all first- and second-generation immigrants from Cuba, come here to start a new life. Suddenly, white guys in suits are at their doors, repo-ing their rightly purchased homes with police backup. The Cubans were in no position to argue.

"Desperate, homeless, and starving, these immigrants banded together and began selling heroin. They faced some stiff competition at first, but they quickly learned to become ruthless, and established a toehold in the greater Miami area." Punisher turned back to his captive. "Do you know what you were doing at the time, Wilt?"

"I, I don't recall."

"I'll jog your memory. You spent a chunk of your newfound profits on something called the Aphrodite Cruise, a seafaring orgy where high-priced prostitutes service wealthy businessmen against a background of decadent Greek architecture. Nice work if you can get it, I suppose.

"Meanwhile—while you were snorting coke off the stomach of a stripper called 'Mnemosyne'—our Cuban friends enlisted a regular customer named Enrique. Enrique's habit made him erratic and unreliable, which caused him to lose his job. When his money dried up, the Cubans cut off his heroin supply. So Enrique decided to rob a Taco Bell. The manager tried to be a hero, and mowed down Enrique with a .30-06 But not before Enrique shot three random patrons in the head.

"One of those patrons was an African-American construction worker named James Victor Johnson."

Wilt stared, incredulous. "What in the world are you talking about?"

"James Victor Johnson died three hours after the robbery. His sister tracked me down. Told me the whole story." Punisher paused. "Well, half of it. Took some research to trace it all back to you."

"And—and *that's* why you grabbed me?"

"That's why."

"What about all the other stuff? About S.H.I.E.L.D. and the Cape tech?"

Punisher shrugged. "You're a resource, Wilt."

"And you're crazy. You're *totally insane!*" Wilt strained wildly now, tugging hard against the cords. "You actually blame me for that guy's death? That's not my fault."

The Punisher cocked the rifle, a sharp snapping sound that echoed through the empty room.

"Oh no," Sue whispered.

"You don't want me." Wilt trembled. "You should be going after the creep who shot that guy. Or, or the drug dealers. The thugs, the, the low-lifes who do that stuff!"

"Oh, I will." Punisher leveled the rifle up at his victim, peered through the site. "But I like to start at the top."

Sue felt a blast of heat. A tattered, charred baseball cap fell onto her, little flames still dancing on its surface. She flinched, batted it away, and looked up—

—to see Johnny Storm, the Human Torch, arrowing through the air toward the Punisher. Fire blazed from every inch of Johnny's body; he'd destroyed his outer clothing, incinerating it in one fierce, sudden flare-up.

The Punisher looked up. Not quite in time.

A fireball burst free from Johnny's hands, striking the Punisher's rifle. Punisher swore, shook his hand in pain, and the gun flew free. It clattered to the ground.

Johnny circled around, came in for a landing between the Punisher and his victim. He allowed his fire to fade away, revealing his Fantastic Four uniform.

The Punisher dropped to a crouch. He sneered up at Johnny. "The Human Torch. Working for Stark now, I see."

Johnny frowned. "What?"

"You're not gonna take me in."

"I'm not here to—I'm *here* to stop you from killing people!"

"He's crazy," Wilt yelled. "Lock him up!"

"Johnny!" Sue called. "Don't let your guard down—"

But she was too late. The Punisher reached into his boot, pulled out a second knife, and threw it at Johnny point-blank. It struck his cheek, drawing blood. Johnny cried out and fell backward, instinctively flaming on again.

Then the Punisher's boot was on his neck, incredibly fast, pinning him down to the floor. Flames rose up from Johnny's struggling form, licking harmlessly at the Punisher's clothes. "Flameproof Kevlar," the vigilante hissed. "Douse the fire, kid. *Now.*"

Johnny made a strangled, gurgling noise. His flame died down.

Sue grimaced. Still unseen, she started to creep forward.

"Your invisible sister's here, too, isn't she?" Punisher looked around. "Are you working with S.H.I.E.L.D.? How far away are they?"

An enormous blast rang out. Sue looked up and saw the ceiling cave in, falling in huge fragments toward them. Dust, whirring, and lights up above. Instinctively, she activated her force field.

Wilt, strung up higher than the others, screamed. A huge chunk of granite struck the top of his support beam, severing it from the ceiling. Wilt fell, screaming, still lashed to the beam, heading straight toward Johnny and the Punisher.

Sue reached out, extended her force field to cover her brother. Wilt bounced lightly off the field, wriggling free of his bonds, then dropped a few feet to the floor. Sue flashed the field off for a split-second to let him inside, then raised it again over all four of them.

Wood and plaster fell all around, clouding the air. The Punisher hadn't moved an inch—he still stood with his foot on Johnny's throat. Slowly he turned toward Sue, and she realized that, in the confusion, she'd let herself become visible.

The Punisher bared his teeth.

Wilt wriggled loose of his bonds. He scrambled around the inside of the force field, trying to get away, but bounced off its edge with a cry of pain.

Then a huge searchlight stabbed down through the hole in the roof. Sue flinched.

"CAPESEARCH RESULTS: FRANCIS CASTLE, THE PUNISHER." The voice was deafening. "JONATHAN STORM, THE HUMAN TORCH."

Up above, four heavy-duty S.H.I.E.L.D. copters hovered, buzzing and swooping through the concrete dust.

"SUSAN RICHARDS, THE INVISIBLE WOMAN."

The Punisher leaned down to speak to Johnny, who was still writhing on the ground. "You're *not* with them?" he asked.

"Nrrggh!"

"THIS IS S.H.I.E.L.D. TEAM FOUR. STAND DOWN AND PREPARE TO BE APPREHENDED."

The Punisher turned to Sue. "Enemy of my enemy?"

"What?" she asked.

"Temporary truce."

"*Yrrsss!*" Johnny cried.

The Punisher raised his foot. Johnny coughed, grabbed his throat. Punisher reached down for him, helped him to his feet.

"FINAL WARNING. DROP ALL WEAPONS, CEASE ALL UN-AUTHORIZED USE OF POWERS."

Sue ran to Johnny, making sure the force field stayed intact. Wilt cowered in a corner of the invisible, dome-shaped energy barrier.

The Punisher waved a rifle to indicate the copters, tilting and hovering just above the blasted-open roof. "They're not gonna go away," he said.

Sue nodded, grim. She shrugged off her outer clothes, revealing her FF uniform below. Then, all at once, she lowered her force field.

"Get us out of here," she said.

Johnny nodded, burst into flame. He grabbed her under the arms, by her flameproof uniform, and took off toward the sky.

A sharp *rat-a-tat* noise made Sue glance down. Wilt was making a dash for the door, away from the Punisher—who stood his ground, firing off two automatic rifles at once. At the walls, not the copters; randomly kicking up dust to cover his escape.

He must have a hell of a weapons bag, she thought.

"METAHUMANS ATTEMPTING ESCAPE. FIREFOX-TEN AND -TWELVE, MOVE TO INTERCEPT."

Sue and Johnny sliced upward through the air, straight toward one of the copters. A ferocious antiaircraft barrel protruded from its side, slowly swiveling to take a bead on them.

"Johnny!" she cried.

"Hang on, sis."

He zigzagged through the air, up past the roof opening, then turned almost horizontal, soaring under the lead copter and past the other two. Bullets whizzed past, filling the air; Sue ducked her feet up, dodging them. She struggled to maintain a force field, but it was almost impossible to concentrate under these circumstances.

Then Johnny made a U-turn, sickeningly fast, straight into the on-coming fire. He reached out a hand, melting the bullets to slag in midair.

Sue could barely look.

Johnny shifted, still holding her beneath him, and began to soar up-ward. The copters buzzed behind, turning and climbing to follow.

"ALL UNITS STAY IN PURSUIT. METAHUMANS HEADING UPTOWN, STRAIGHT TOWARD TEAMS NINE AND ELEVEN."

Sue looked ahead, gulped. Past the night spires of New York, above the green sprawl of Central Park, she could see a second batch of copter lights heading straight toward them.

We're sitting ducks up here, she thought. *Like a comet, flaming through the night—*

"Sue," Johnny said. "Make us invisible. *Now!*"

She nodded, closed her eyes tight. *Trust him,* she thought. *Trust your brother.* Slowly, Sue's invisibility power kicked in. Johnny's flame faded from view. She signaled him it was done, and he began to drop toward the street below.

"TEAM NINE, THIS IS TEAM FOUR. HAVE LOST VISUAL ON METAHUMANS. DO YOU HAVE VISUAL?"

"NEGATIVE, TEAM FOUR."

"ENGAGE POWER SENSORS..."

The amplified voices faded as the street rose to meet them. Johnny gradually doused his flame, and they landed softly on a quiet corner of Central Park West. He gasped, coughed, and leaned against a lamppost, breathing hard.

A pair of joggers trotted by, oblivious to the invisible duo. One jogger cocked his head at the gasping noise, shrugged, and continued on.

Sue examined Johnny's cut face, his bruised throat. "You all right?"

"Y-yeah."

"Your head wound is bleeding again. That'll have to be looked at."

"Great."

She glanced up at the sky. The copters were veering off now, buzzing angrily toward the south. They'd done it—lost S.H.I.E.L.D., for now at least.

"Better not...use my powers again," Johnny said. "I think that's how they tracked us."

"Come on." Sue took her brother by the arm, steered him into the wooded, patchily lit park. When they were hidden from view, she dropped her invisibility shield. "Let's get to the Resistance. They'll fix you up."

"Blasted Punisher." Johnny coughed again. "Think they got him?

"I doubt it. But that is *so* not our problem."

They walked down a paved walkway, the traffic noises dwindling in the distance. The park was quiet; just a few clutches of people talking quietly or laughing.

"Not such a bad night," Sue said. "We saved a man from being killed."

"Maybe he deserved it."

"Maybe." She smiled at him, took a deep breath of night air. "But that's not for us to decide, is it?"

TWENTY-TWO

TONY, *I need you to understand. I just don't know if I can...*
Spider-Man shook his head. *No. Not strong enough.*

He sat perched like a mantis in Tony Stark's workshop, on the edge of the main computer bench. Before him, an array of screens blinked with a constant flow of information, including S.H.I.E.L.D. updates, superhuman dossier reports, population projections, and statuses of known alien races. The floor beyond was strewn with Tony's half-built projects: mini-reactors, engines, fuel supplies, what looked like half a flying car, and prototype Iron Man suits of every possible color and shape—torsos, helmets, gloves, gauntlets, rocket-boots, even a lower-body unit with tank-tread wheels on it.

I know you're in a hurry, Tone. Tony. You're always in a hurry. Maybe that's part of the...

The computers had been on when Spider-Man arrived; in his haste, Tony hadn't even activated a password lock. Spidey reached out a metallic tentacle and tapped an icon on a screen.

Above him, in the air, a holographic image shimmered into being. Tony—in one of his earliest Iron Man suits, solid yellow, blocky and thick—was standing alert on a city street. A ten-foot-tall Hank Pym lumbered up to join him. *Hank was the first Goliath,* Spidey recalled. *Or was it Giant-Man, then?*

A flash of red and black, and the Wasp—Janet Van Dyne, Hank's future wife—flitted onto the scene, no more than a foot long, her headgear pointed like a stinger. And then: Thor. He dropped from the clouds, hammer whirling, smiling a smile that said: What a wondrous thing to be here today, among the mortals.

It's just, it's all moving too fast. Tony, can you just listen to me for a...

Spider-Man stared at the hologram. These were the very first Avengers, newly formed; even Captain America hadn't yet been found, floating in suspended animation. The Holo-Avengers fanned out, turning to watch as their enemy appeared out of thin air. A purple-suited man with devil's-horn hair and a murderous look in his eyes.

Spidey frowned, tapped the display to stop playback. He double-clicked on the purple figure and a label appeared: THE SPACE PHANTOM.

The Space Phantom.

Things used to be simpler, didn't they?

The file he'd accessed seemed to be a chronological record of the Avengers' cases. Next to it, on the screen, a second icon read: P PARKER. He reached out a finger and tapped it.

The Avengers scene vanished, replaced by footage of the recent press conference. Spider-Man watched as his own image yanked off his mask, flinching at a thousand camera flashes. Holo-Tony put a protective arm on Holo-Peter's shoulders, nodded at him warmly.

Spidey scrolled back through the file. He found himself watching a record of his own career, in reverse order. His appearance at the Stamford disaster, wearing his new costume. Tony asking him to join the Avengers. Clearing himself, at long last, with the New York City Police Department.

Confronting J. Jonah Jameson, in Jameson's office, about the publisher's libelous editorials. Fighting Venom, Hammerhead, Silvermane, Kraven, the Vulture.

Tony's records were impressively thorough. A strange sensation ran through Spidey's stomach; he felt flattered, but also somehow violated.

There was one final image in the file. A still picture, two-dimensional and faded. A little boy with thick glasses smiled up as a man hung a medal around his neck. The medal read LITTLE SCIENCE WHIZ FAIR—FIRST PLACE. The man had gray hair, a meticulously tailored suit over his strong frame, and a stern look on his face.

Spider-Man leaned forward, frowning. The boy was himself, at age six or so. But the man...? He double-clicked the figure.

HOWARD ANTHONY WALTER STARK.

Behind the blank lenses, Spider-Man's eyes went wide. *Tony's father.*

Spider-Man had forgotten that award, the very first he'd ever won for science. And he'd certainly forgotten the man who gave it to him.

But Tony hadn't.

"Peter? Your tentacle is tapping a hole in my chair."

Spider-Man leapt up, startled. He reached out and touched the computer screen. The hologram vanished.

Tony stood, in full Iron Man gear, at the entrance to the workshop. A curved ramp led up and out, allowing him to make quick aerial entrances and exits.

"Didn't see you there, boss."

Iron Man took two cautious, almost mechanical steps into the room. "I don't remember inviting you into my workshop, Peter."

"Sorry. I had to see you."

Iron Man stopped, spread his arms. "Here I am."

His chestplate glowed with power.

Spider-Man walked up to him, held up a hand. "Look—"

"Why don't you sit back down and say what you came to say." It wasn't a question.

Spidey felt a flash of anger. *He's doing that thing with his voice. The volume's turned up, and the frequency bites into your brain. Makes you want to obey him.*

"It won't take long," he said. "I just wanted to tell you I'm leaving the Avengers."

Tony's eyes flared red. "I see."

"I'm really grateful to you for, for everything. But locking heroes up in the Negative Zone? Killing Bill Foster?"

"Thor reacted like a police officer, Peter. He was threatened, he responded with deadly force. But Bill Foster was a friend of mine...do you really think I'm going to let something like that happen again?"

"No! No, not if you can help it. But you're in over your head, Tony."

"What do you suggest we do with the unregistered super-people? Lock them up with regular prisoners? They'd be out again in fifteen minutes."

"No, of course not. But...do we have to lock them up at all?"

"Here's what you need to understand, Peter." Tony whirled on him, fists clenched. "There are forces within S.H.I.E.L.D., and more importantly within the federal government, who want nothing more than to outlaw superhumans. Absolutely and completely."

"Get—"

"The compromise we offered them was regulating our behavior. Voluntarily, and according to a plan *I* would administer. Because there's no going back to the old days, Peter. That was never on the table."

"Get out of my way, Tony."

"What are you planning to do, Peter?" Tony stood before him now, tall and imposing, all weapons systems glowing. "Go on TV again, recant your support for Registration? Maybe join Captain America's band of traitors?"

"I'm not sure yet."

"You little idiot." Even through the armor, Spidey could hear the heat in Tony's voice. "Do you really think you can just quit all this, go back to your old life? Everyone knows who you are now. What will you do for money? What about *Aunt May?*"

Rage boiled up inside Peter Parker. He *punched* Tony with all his strength, a superhuman blow that dented the armored figure's chestplate. Tony flew through the air, shattering a computer console, and slammed into the wall.

"Aunt May," Spider-Man snarled, "is far, far away from you."

Tony raised his hand and fired a repulsor ray. Spider-sense flared in Spidey's brain, but too late. The ray slammed into him, knocking him to the ground and taking his breath away.

"I trusted you, Peter." Tony's voice was quieter now. "I took you under my wing. I gave you everything. This is how you repay me?"

A second repulsor ray blasted out, then a third. But Spider-Man was on his feet now, leaping and dodging, twisting his arms backward to propel himself down the wall. "Nope," he said. "*This* is."

Spider-Man leapt straight toward Tony—

"Emergency passcode: Delta Delta Epsilon," Tony said.

—and Spider-Man froze in midair. All his joints felt suddenly paralyzed, unresponsive. He clattered painfully to the floor, crashing down hard on one shoulder.

He looked around, dazed. He'd landed among an array of Iron Man helmets: red, gold, silver, white, some with fins or extra weapon mounts. When he looked up, Tony loomed over him like Zeus looking down from Olympus.

"Peter," he said. "What kind of an engineer would I be to hand over a suit as powerful as yours without building in a safeguard? To make sure it couldn't be used against *me*, its creator?"

Spidey struggled for breath.

"Listen," Tony continued. "You don't have to do this. You don't have to run. You're already registered; the hard part is finished. I'm willing to forget about this little tantrum."

Spider-Man gasped, then spoke five words aloud. Too quietly to be heard, he realized.

"What was that?"

"I said...passcode: Whatever A Spider Can."

Spider-Man whirled on his side, almost too fast to see. Raised an arm and shot webbing up into Tony's face, blocking his lenses.

"What kind of a *science whiz* would I be not to figure out and nullify your override—*boss?*"

Again, Spidey reached out and slammed both fists into Tony's startled figure. A killing blow, the kind he would never use against an ordinary foe. *But this,* he realized grimly, *is one of the most powerful men on Earth. In more ways than one.*

Tony crashed backwards, clawing at the webbing on his faceplate. Reached out with both repulsors, firing wildly. Spider-Man weaved and dodged, scuttling along the wall, past a freestanding equipment shelf. Making his way toward the ramp that led to the emergency exit.

Then the inner door burst open with an explosive crash. Spider-Man turned to look, momentarily startled.

A platoon of S.H.I.E.L.D. shock troops, in full-body armor, dashed into the room, their faces hidden by bulletproof, opaque visors. Their leader turned his head toward Tony, who struggled to his feet, slowly burning the webbing off his face with a low-power repulsor ray.

Spider-Man leapt toward the ramp that led to freedom. The S.H.I.E.L.D. leader pointed to him and yelled, "Down, Mister Stark! We got him!"

A hail of gunfire drowned out Tony's response. Spider-Man had no time to dodge; the bullets struck him head-on. His armored costume kept them from entering his flesh, but they stabbed against his arms, legs, torso, knocking the breath out of him. He leapt through the air, twisted wildly, and fired off both web-shooters at random.

Then he was running up the ramp, jumping and bouncing off the corridor walls. Bullets continued to lance into his back and calves, knocking him off-balance, punching little holes in his suit. Every joint, every muscle, every inch of his skin stung. He stumbled once and slammed his shoulder painfully against the wall.

But he kept moving. It was the only way to survive.

Slowly his consciousness receded, leaving only instinct. As if from a long distance away, he heard Tony Stark's metallic voice yell, "Stop! *Hold your fire!*"

Then he came to a large hatch, left slightly ajar after Tony's entrance. Spider-Man wrenched it open and launched himself outside. The cold night air wafted over him, shocking him awake. He hung in midair for an instant, then reached out to cling to the outside wall of the building. He breathed hard, letting the noise of the city wash over him.

Inside, footsteps clomped up the ramp. Spidey slammed the hatch shut and webbed up the seams, sealing it tight. Then he started down the side of the building, toward the street far below.

Get to a manhole, he told himself. *Just stay conscious till then. If you can reach the sewers, you'll be safe.*

But he knew, deep inside, that he was kidding himself.

Peter would never be safe again.

TWENTY-THREE

TONY Stark raised both hands, aimed repulsor rays at the hatch, and blasted it open. Bolts splintered, webbing flew apart. The door exploded open, hanging loose on one hinge.

Tony thrust his head outside, looked downward. Something was climbing down the wall, dodging and scuttling from side to side, moving closer to the sidewalk far below. Light from a streetlamp glinted off of its metallic, inhuman form. Only then did Tony recognize it as Peter.

What have I done to him? Tony thought. *What have I done to all of them?*

He issued a mental command: MAGNIFY IMAGE. His armor hesitated—no more than a microsecond, but worrisome nonetheless. Then his vision zoomed out and down, centering automatically on Spider-Man. The wall-crawler's mask was torn, his mesh suit dotted with dents; blood dripped from his chin. He touched down unsteadily on the sidewalk, ducked low, then sprinted toward a manhole.

Tony tensed to leap, issued a warm-up command to his boot-jets. A dozen alerts flashed before his eyes: BOOT-JET EFFICIENCY 56%. ARMOR INTEGRITY COMPROMISED. VISION SYSTEMS 72%. JOINT/MOTIVE SYSTEMS COMPROMISED BY

FOREIGN LIQUID.

Spider-Man's webbing. It had spread all through his armor, gumming up all the mechanical systems. Tony swore quietly. *If only I'd redesigned the damn webbing when I built the rest of his suit.*

He'd have to change to a spare Iron Man suit before going after Peter. If there was still a suit left intact in the workshop.

He turned, trudged back down the ramp. Dust hovered everywhere, and the cordite smell of spent shells covered the dull odor of burning electronics.

The workshop was a disaster. Shattered computers, broken Iron Man suits, workbenches and power packs cracked and dented everywhere. *Hundreds of thousands' worth of damage,* Tony thought. *Maybe millions.*

Maria Hill stood speaking to the S.H.I.E.L.D. platoon leader. She wore tight black fatigues, body armor, and sunglasses, but no helmet. She turned toward Tony, her mouth twisted in disdain.

"So. Your pet insect has abandoned the hive."

"Arachnid," Tony said.

"What?"

"Not insect, arachnid. Nothing. Never mind." Tony crossed to a cabinet riddled with bullet holes. "I'm going after him. Assuming your men haven't destroyed all my equipment."

"Excuse us for trying to save your life."

He bent down to touch a cabinet lock—and stumbled. Nearly fell.

"I don't think you're going anywhere," Hill said. "Sergeant?"

A burly S.H.I.E.L.D. agent bent down to catch him. Tony waved him off, angry. "I'm all right."

"I think you've got a busted knee. Maybe worse."

She was right, he realized. The armor was holding him up, preventing him from realizing the extent of the damage. Spider-Man had a rep as one of the most powerful superhumans on Earth; that was one reason Tony had recruited him in the first place. Now he had firsthand proof.

Hill touched a comm-button on her shoulder. "Director Hill, authorization alpha," she said. "Activate Project Thunderbolt."

"No," Tony said.

"Operatives Four and Six. Sending coordinates now. Target: Spider-Man."

"No! I've got this—" He stumbled, slumped into a chair.

"With respect, Stark: You do *not* have this." Hill loomed over him, her lip curled in contempt. "Nor do you command S.H.I.E.L.D. This is my call."

Tony slumped in defeat. He lifted his helmet, looked up at her with his naked eyes. "Don't hurt him."

"Don't worry, I won't put another death on your bleeding-heart conscience. If I can help it."

"You won't put another death on *our* conscience. At all." He rose to his feet, glared at her. "The Registration movement does not need that kind of publicity."

"I'm sorry your little *arachnid* disappointed you, Stark. Mentoring is a bitch."

She snapped her fingers. A S.H.I.E.L.D. agent appeared at her side, holding a comm device with a USB cord hanging off it. "Now. Shall we watch the show? There's got to be a video screen still working, somewhere in this mess."

FIVE minutes later, the dust had thinned and an area of the floor had been cleared of debris. The workshop's holoprojectors were trashed, but a S.H.I.E.L.D. agent stood tuning in a blurry picture on a flatscreen. Another agent set out folding chairs around the screen. Tony sat in shorts and a work shirt while a S.H.I.E.L.D. medic taped up his knee.

The agent looked up from the flatscreen. "We're go."

Hill touched her shoulder-comm. "This is a sixty-minute trial only," she said. "Invisible mode essential. Operation Thunderbolt is still top secret. Are all nanosanctions in effect?"

"Yes, Director."

"Location trace active."

On the screen, a map appeared, showing the winding maze of Manhattan's underground sewer system. Two blips labeled 4 and 6 moved swiftly along the tunnels.

"I've got the T-bolts locked," the agent said, "but Spider-Man's deactivated the GPS tracker in his suit. Pulling up a best guess now." A red-and-gold blip began to flash, showing Spidey's approximate location, several twists and turns ahead of the other blips.

Hill smiled. "I knew we couldn't trust that guy."

"Don't sound so happy about it." Tony glared. "I don't need to remind you what the Thunderbolts are, Hill. Super villains."

"Former super villains. Who have been duly registered with the government and trained in an intensive crash course. They've been chipped, tagged, and injected with nanomachines that allow us to control their behavior absolutely."

Tony frowned. "Like dogs."

"*Wild* dogs." She gestured at the screen, at the moving dot that indicated Spider-Man's position. "And I don't see a lot of difference between them and him."

No, Tony thought. *You wouldn't.*

The screen shifted to a jerky video image of the sewer pipe's interior. Dark lighting and old incandescent bulbs were spaced far apart along the walls. Steeply curved walls slid past as the camera moved; water splashed up from the floor.

"Both operatives have cameras mounted on their uniforms," Hill explained. "That's Operative Six's camera. Agent, punch up the dossier on him."

A still image appeared in the corner of the screen: a fearsome figure in spandex and metal mesh, with a flaming pumpkin-head and a terrible grin. Lettering beneath it read:

```
Subject: Steven Mark Levins

Aliases: JACK O'LANTERN

Group Affiliation: none

Powers: body armor, 360-degree vision, wrist
blasters, assorted grenades

Power Type: artificial

Current Location: New York, NY
```

On the main video, the sewer pipe opened up onto a long, straight tunnel. Up ahead, in the distance, something splashed in the water.

"Operative Six?" Hill said.

"I hear you, sexy." Jack O'Lantern's voice was low, cruel, and not a bit winded by his long trip through the sewers. "I think we got 'im."

"Roger, Thunderbolts. You are clear to engage."

Tony tensed. Leaned forward, staring at the screen.

The camera lurched to the right, and a second figure swung into view. A lanky man in purple boots and a pointed hood, with blue mask and sharp pointed teeth.

"Operative Four." Hill gestured to the agent, and another profile appeared in the corner of the screen.

    Subject: Jody Putt

    Aliases: THE JESTER

    Group Affiliation: none

    Powers: assorted toy and "joke" gimmicks (po-
    tentially lethal)

    Power Type: artificial

    Current Location: New York, NY

Jester turned toward the camera and grinned. "I got this one," he said. He reached into a satchel and pulled out a small plastic doll with a comically angry expression on its face. Wound its crank twice, three times, and set it down in the water.

The toy took off down the tunnel on tiny rockets, skimming across the sewer water.

"Switch to Jester's camera," Hill said.

The image shifted to a view of Jack O'Lantern, crouched and danger-ous atop a flying disk, hovering just above the water. He reached out and grabbed Jester, pulling him aboard the disk, and together they sped off down the sewer tunnel after the windup toy.

Jester's camera view shifted forward. The figure of Spider-Man zoomed into view, frantically splashing his way away from them, through the murky water. His suit was torn, the tentacles hung useless now. Part of his face showed through the torn remains of his mask.

The toy whizzed into view, heading straight toward Spider-Man. He turned, startled.

"What the—"

Then the toy exploded. A huge fireball filled the screen.

Tony whirled toward Hill. "You said he wouldn't be killed!"

"You think that could kill him?" She rolled her eyes. "Back to Operative Six camera."

On screen, the dust slowly cleared. Spider-Man sat crouching in filthy water now, coughing. Above him, the tall figure of the Jester gloated wildly.

"Well, if it isn't Little Peter Spider-Man." Jester laughed. "How does it feel to be on the wrong side of the law, *Parker*? You like seeing the *Jester* wear a sheriff's badge?"

The image swung about, as Jack O'Lantern circled Spider-Man from above. "You oughta see who we're hangin' with now, Petey. Bullseye, Venom, Lady Deathstrike...me an' Jester are finally on the villains' A-list."

"And it's legit, too."

Spider-Man shook his head, struggled to focus on the circling villains.

"Oh, baby." Jester pulled out a yo-yo, hurled it at Spider-Man. "This is too awesome for words."

The yo-yo struck Spider-Man in the chest, exploding like a small concussion grenade. He cried out, fell backwards, and splashed down into the water.

Jack O'Lantern moved in fast. His hand shot out into the frame, grabbed Spider-Man and slammed him against the tunnel wall.

"You know," he hissed. "This gig seemed like a bum deal at first. Working for S.H.I.E.L.D....but then word from the top says kick the crap outta Spider-Man." He reached out, smacked Spider-Man's head hard. "What can we do, right?"

"We're only obeying orders," Jester said.

Jester reached out and tore off another chunk of Spider-Man's mask.

One eye showed clearly now, bruised and swollen partway shut. Spidey's head lolled to the side, unmoving.

"Hill," Tony said.

She frowned into her shoulder comm. "He's down, Thunderbolts. Drop him and wait for cleanup crew."

"Aww, S.H.I.E.L.D.—"

"Lay one more finger on that guy, Jack, and I shoot five thousand volts through your system. You know I'm not bluffing."

On the screen, Jack O'Lantern's fingers relaxed around Spider-Man's neck. The wall-crawler dropped to the tunnel floor, landing with a splash.

"S.H.I.E.L.D. support is on their way. Just cuff him and sit tight."

Tony exhaled in relief.

The screen shifted back to Jester's camera. He turned to Jack O'Lantern, whose blazing orange pumpkin head filled the screen. "Spoilsport," Jack said.

Then Jack's head blew apart, shattering into bits of brain and pumpkin. The villain's death-scream rang out, shrill and filtered over the comm system.

"*What the hell!*" Jester screamed. His camera swung around wildly, searching the tunnel walls. "S.H.I.E.L.D.! S.H.I.E.L.D., do you read? *There's somebody else down here—*"

Another shot rang out, deafening in the enclosed space. Jester's camera lurched, tottered, and tipped upward to show the roof of the tunnel. The view twitched again, then stopped moving.

"He's down too." The S.H.I.E.L.D. agent worked his laptop frantically. "Jack's camera is not transmitting. Still got Jester's—"

On the screen, a heavy black boot loomed into view, blotting out the tunnel roof. It paused, almost dramatically, then stomped down hard.

The screen went to static.

Hill jumped to her feet. "Get me a visual. Any visual!"

The agent tapped his keyboard, hissing breath between his teeth. He looked up and spread his arms helplessly.

Hill pounded her fist down on a table. "What the hell just happened down there?"

"Transmission's cut off, Director. We're deaf and blind."

"Dammit." She touched her shoulder-comm again. "All S.H.I.E.L.D. units in vicinity of Fourth Street and Broadway. Proceed immediately underground, to sewer pipes at coordinates on feed 24-J. Patrol all streets within a five-block radius; report anyone or anything trying to surface through manhole or other egress point. We may have a Resistance operation in progress, or—"

"Acting Director Hill."

Wincing in pain, Tony moved to block her way. She frowned at him, but held her ground.

"I'm not impressed by your methods," he said. "You failed to capture your quarry, and you lost two agents from your pilot program on their very first assignment."

She frowned. "Big loss."

"Nonetheless. I asked you to handle this my way, and you refused."

"You can barely walk. And this problem is largely of your making. No one told you to invite Spider-Man, a notorious loner with antiauthoritarian tendencies, into your inner circle."

Tony stood seething for a moment. He looked around at the wreckage of his work, the smashed equipment. The many helmets of Iron Man, dented and smashed and riddled with S.H.I.E.L.D. bullets.

"Get off my property," he said.

She glared at him, then gestured to the S.H.I.E.L.D. agents. They began holstering weapons, stowing away equipment, zipping up carry-packs.

Efficient as always, Tony thought. *Military to the end.*

"Snap it up, boys. We've got a spider to catch."

"You won't catch him," Tony said.

"Wishful thinking, Stark?" Hill turned, gave him one last glare. "We *will* catch him."

Then S.H.I.E.L.D. was gone.

Tony stood alone for a long time. Tested his knee, tried putting weight on it. It stung, but he could walk. That was enough.

It took him three tries to find a cell phone that worked.

"Pepper, I need a cleanup crew." He looked around at the wreckage. "And see if you can get the president of the United States on the line, will you?"

TWENTY-FOUR

A smell of fresh ink rose up from the brand-new driver's license. Captain America handed it to Sue Richards. "Barbara Landau," he said.

"Ryan Landau." Johnny Storm looked up from his own license. "We're supposed to be *married?*"

Cap looked up from the paper-strewn conference table. Fluorescent lights glared down, painting the group in unflattering, washed-out hues.

"We're running low on cover identities," he said. "With Daredevil incarcerated, our source has dried up."

"Married." Sue glanced over at her brother. "That's got to be the creepiest thing we've ever done."

"How do you think I feel, sis? You look like my last date's grandmother. *Ow!*"

Cap sighed. Moving to the new headquarters had been difficult; transporting the monitoring and medical equipment across town had seemed impossible until Sue showed up. Her invisibility had saved them from detection several times.

But the Resistance, Cap knew, was still on shaky ground. He couldn't forget Hawkeye's parting warning, about a traitor in the group. And his own injuries were still slowing him down. His left arm still hung in a sling; it stabbed with pain every time he stood up.

Take it slow, he told himself. *Remember what you told the others: Step by step. Brick by brick.*

Tigra walked in, frowning. "Still no cover ID for me?"

"We've gone over this, Tigra." He indicated her bikini-clad body, covered head to toe with striped orange fur. "You're not exactly inconspicuous."

"Yeah." Johnny smiled. "Must be tough looking as hot as you."

Tigra purred and rubbed her back up against Johnny's shoulder. She turned, flashed him a flirty smile.

Sue rolled her eyes.

"Sorry, Mrs. Landau," Johnny said.

"I used to pass for normal all the time," Tigra said. "All it took was an image inducer."

"Which is Stark Enterprises technology," Cap said. "We can't have any of that here; Tony's probably got everything they've made in the past ten years tagged with location tracers." He turned back to Sue and Johnny. "As for you two, the important thing is: These cover identities get you out in public again. Which lets you help people. That's what we're here for, right?"

Tigra smiled again, turned toward Johnny. "He's always so righteous," she said, gesturing at Cap. "Takes all the fun out of arguing with him."

Luke Cage strode in, leading the others. "Say it loud, Cap. You like the new crib?"

"It'll do. Spartan, but that's a plus." Cap rose, gave Cage a half-hug. "What was this place again?"

"African-American Employment Specialists, Inc. Helping the hard-working black man compete in a white man's world. Fell victim to the economy, an' it's been empty more'n a year."

"No love for the hard-working black man," Falcon said.

Cage nodded. "Mmmm-hm."

One by one, they filed in and took seats around the big table. Cage, Falcon, Tigra. Dagger, Photon, the newly arrived Stingray in bright red and white. Sue and Johnny, Patriot and Speed.

The Resistance.

"Okay, let's get to it." Cap scanned a handwritten agenda. "Anyone been captured lately?"

Photon was a relative newcomer, a young African-American woman with light-based powers. "Nighthawk and Valkyrie," she said, "busted in Queens. Which cuts our aerial team down to Falcon and yours truly."

Stingray spread his wings. "And me," he said.

Falcon frowned. "Glidin' ain't flyin', son. No worries, Cap. We got it covered."

"Damn S.H.I.E.L.D. units." Cap clenched his wounded hand into a fist, felt the pain stab through his arm. "For every man we've gained these past few days, we've lost one too."

"And they're all in that prison."

"Maybe we can do something about that," Cap said. "Does anyone know the status of their prisoner transfer plans?"

Sue cleared her throat. "Tony and Reed are setting up Negative Zone portals at major prisons around the country, including Rykers. But none of them are operational yet. So far, everyone's still being shunted through the Baxter Building."

"The Baxter Building." Cap raised an eyebrow. "Susan, can you get us in there?"

"Normally, yes. But I...I'm sure Reed will have changed the security codes. I might even be a liability...the computers would detect my presence immediately."

"Just as well. I've got another urgent mission for you."

Cap turned to Johnny, who shook his head. "Don't look at me. If Suzie can't get in, I don't stand a chance. Reed's been making notes on how to nullify my powers since...since before I *had* powers."

"Dammit. There *is* a window of opportunity here." Cap swept his eyes around the group. "If we can take down the portal in the Baxter Building, that'll leave them without anywhere to send our guys. In a week, that won't be a problem for them. We've got to strike soon."

"Cut the cord," Cage said, "and the whole thing unravels."

"If we're lucky."

"What we need is to get some guys *back*," Falcon said. "Make this a fair fight again."

"What do they call that place?" Patriot asked. "Number 42?"

"Nobody knows why."

"Knowing Tony Stark, it prob'ly has something to do with his dad—"

They all heard it at once: heavy footsteps, boots clomping on the outer hallway floor. All eleven Resistance members shot to their feet at once, turned toward the doorway—

—and saw the Punisher, lit stark black and white by the glaring lights. Filthy water dripped from him; he smelled like old trash. In his hands he held a limp, bloody form, its costume ripped and shot open in a hundred places.

Spider-Man.

"Get me a medic," the Punisher said. "NOW!"

THE infirmary had been hastily adapted from an open office area, cots and diagnostic machines crammed in where cubicles had stood before. Two medics lifted Spider-Man onto a bed, casting wary glances at the Punisher.

"Doesn't weigh much," the first medic said.

Punisher grunted. "Try carrying him three miles."

Cap and the others stood back, leaving a wide area free for the medics to work. But Cap's eyes never strayed from the Punisher.

"What happened?" Cap asked.

"Multiple fractures and serious blood loss," the Punisher replied.

"I mean—"

"Tony Stark and his buddies. I think there was some kind of hallucinogen in the bombs they attacked him with, too."

"And you rescued him." Cap crossed to the Punisher, confronted him directly. "What happened to his attackers?"

Punisher shrugged.

The medics looked up from Spider-Man's limp form. "This costume is fused to his skin in places."

"Remove every inch and burn it," Cap said. "It's Stark issue—they could be tracking him right now."

"You know," Tigra said, "this might all be a setup."

Punisher smiled. "You think *I'm* working with Tony Stark?"

"I don't understand any of this." Speed shook his head. "You all saw the press conference. Spider-Man is so far up Iron Man's butt you can't see his feet anymore."

"Maybe he was, kid," the Punisher said. "But he's on our side now."

"*Our* side?"

"Falc—"

"No no, Cap, give me a minute." Falcon pushed past Captain America, pointed a finger at the skull emblem on Punisher's chest. "You're a wanted murderer, Punisher. You've capped more men than most of the guys we fight. Since when are you on *our side?*"

Punisher stared him down. "Since the other side started enlisting super villains."

Tigra smiled grimly. "Am I the only one seeing the irony here?"

"The way I see it," Punisher continued, "you people need all the help you can get."

"Great," Johnny Storm said. "Why don't we call up Hannibal Lecter and see if he's available, too?"

"Because Hannibal Lecter doesn't have the black-ops training to get you into the Baxter Building."

Falcon stared. "You can do that?"

"I got in *here*."

Falcon opened his mouth, started to reply. But he stopped, as the implications sank in.

Sue Richards looked around. "Please tell me this group isn't so far gone that we're signing up the *Punisher*?"

On the medical table, Spider-Man stirred. He let out a faint moan.

Cage turned to Cap. "Your call, boss. Do we hand Skull-Man over to the cops, or do we hear him out?"

Cap turned away, frowning. He'd run up against the Punisher once before; it had been one of the toughest fights of his life. Punisher could be a formidable ally, for either side.

On the table, Spider-Man lay, frail and writhing. Fighting for his life.

I'm trapped, Cap realized. Whichever way he chose, whichever path he took, something terrible was going to happen. He could sense it, deep in his war-hardened bones.

And they're all depending on me. To lead them; to help their lives make sense again. To build this tattered Resistance into a permanent force for good.

Step by step. Brick by brick.

He turned back to the Punisher.

"Talk," Cap said.

TWENTY-FIVE

"TAKE a breath of that air, Hank." Tony Stark spread his arms. "Lot healthier than New York, am I right?"

Initiative Training Camp 09AZ, in Arizona, bustled with activity under the bright Southwestern sun. Newly registered recruits, in brightly colored training uniforms, flew and ran and sparred and lifted Sherman tanks for practice, all across the sprawling yard. S.H.I.E.L.D. officers and men in clipboards followed them like mother hens, nodding, frowning, and jotting down notes on each recruit's performance.

Fully half the yard was cordoned off for new construction. S.H.I.E.L.D. troops mingled with government workers in backhoes and steam shovels, shouting instructions back and forth. They'd been laboring round the clock, knocking down old buildings and laying down new foundations, converting the former Marine base into a facility resilient enough to house superhumans. Like everything else in the Registration plan, the camp was coming together on the fly—and very, very fast.

Hank Pym flashed Tony an unsure smile. He squinted up at the sun, shaded his eyes from the glare.

"I'm just not sure, Tony. I'm a bioresearcher, not a drill sergeant."

"You don't have to be the guy in the yard with the megaphone, Hank. I just want you running things."

A blurry figure whizzed by, too fast to see clearly. Hank frowned. "Who's that?"

Tony consulted his tablet computer. "Hermes. Greek god, newly arrived on Earth. If *he's* willing to register..."

"What kind of speed is he hitting?"

"Mach One, if he hasn't eaten. But we'll have him at Mach Three by the time we go public." Tony smiled. "Hey, I keep forgetting to ask. How's Jan?"

"We're not really, uh, talking right now."

Hank's attention turned to a group of young people in trainee costumes, standing and laughing. He looked sad, lost.

He needs this, Tony thought. *And I need him.*

Tony felt impatient, hot and out of place in his Armani suit. The tablet computer in his hand seemed slow; he'd become accustomed, he realized, to controlling machines with his mind rather than his fingers. He hated taking the armor off these days. It made him feel like a fish stranded on land, flailing around for data.

But the main Iron Man suit still needed a couple hours of repair, time Tony just hadn't been able to find. Besides, he'd wanted to appeal to Hank as a man, as an old friend. Iron Man was becoming too much of a public authority figure.

"'Scuse me, guys." A burly construction foreman gestured to a huge crane, lumbering toward them. A massive, one-piece building frame swung from its main cable. "Need to get this down on the foundation."

Tony and Hank hurried out of the way. "Holographic Combat Simulator building," Tony said. "When it's operational, it'll let you train the recruits in hundreds of different simulated environments."

Hank smiled. "You don't give up, do you?"

"There's no *time* to give up, Hank. We're setting up the Champions in California, those new Mormon heroes in Utah, and I've assigned the Spaceknights to Chicago."

"I heard Force Works is going to...Iowa?"

"Pending background checks and the local authorities giving their absolute approval." Tony paused. "The public needs superpeople they can count on, Hank. We're doing this right, or not at all."

Hank nodded. "How's Reed doing?"

"I have no intention of getting between him and Sue. He did insist on immunity for her and Johnny, as a condition for his continued assistance. That took some talking with the president, let me tell you." He took Hank by the arm. "Enough of this. Come on—there's somebody you should talk to."

He led Hank over to the recruits. Stature, formerly of the Young Avengers, stood with a green-skinned girl sporting a spiked Mohawk and a brawny, cocky-looking blond guy. Tony checked their IDs on his tablet: Komodo and Hardball.

"Hank, I think you've met Cassie Lang."

Hank stared at Stature. "Of course. But the last time I saw you, you were..." He held his hand three feet off the ground.

Stature smiled. She shot up, using her powers to rise up to eight feet in height. "Not anymore."

"Dr. Pym invented the size-changing serum you use, Cassie." Tony watched as she shrank back down to normal size. "I think you could learn a lot from him."

"That's why I'm here. To learn."

"See, Hank? Cassie's late father was the second Ant-Man, and now she's the heir to your serum. In a way, they're like your children."

"You forgot one of my 'children,' Tony." Hank turned away. "Bill Foster."

Stature shrank down to normal size, grimacing. Komodo and Hardball just watched.

"Tony," Hank continued, "can you just *offer* me this position? What about S.H.I.E.L.D.? Has Director Hill signed off on it?"

"Don't worry about Hill, Hank." Tony shook his head. "She didn't exactly distinguish herself with the Thunderbolts beta test."

Komodo stepped forward. "Is it true Spider-Man got away?"

"Temporarily."

Stature looked worried. "What are you gonna do, Mister Stark? When you find Cap, and the others?"

"Finding them isn't the problem, Cassie. The point is to make them see reason. That's what S.H.I.E.L.D. doesn't understand."

A nervous, dark-haired girl approached the recruits. "Guys, guys, they want us to do drills in ten minutes. I don't know if I'm ready."

Stature put a hand on her shoulder. "Be cool, Armory. It'll be fine."

Armory held up her left arm. Alien weaponry covered it, flashing and humming with energy. "I don't know if I can control my power."

"No, no. Stop!" A coach with a clipboard approached, pointing behind Tony. "I said sto—"

Then something slammed into the group, scattering them. Tony stumbled and fell to the ground. He spat sand, brushed off his jacket, and climbed to his feet.

A blur of motion sped away from them, too fast to see clearly. *Hermes again,* Tony realized. Then he heard a scream, and a crackling of energy.

Armory had been flung ten feet away. She knelt down in the sand, cradling a bruised leg. Then she pointed her weapon-arm upward, and fiery alien energy flared out of it. A bolt flashed forth, arced over the yard past a construction site—

—straight into the main admin building, punching a hole through the wall.

The yard erupted in panic. Recruits scattered, running for cover. S.H.I.E.L.D. agents scrambled for their armor, dodging Armory's wild, uncontrolled assault.

"*Armory!*" the coach yelled.

Tony crawled over to Hank Pym, who lay sprawled in the sand. Stature was just picking herself up, dazed.

"Hank, I don't have my gear with me. You have to solve this."

Hank stared at him. "I'm not a super hero anymore, Tony."

"No." Tony pointed at Stature. "But *she* is."

"Me?"

A bolt of energy slammed into the ground, three feet away.

"Violet—Armory. She's got this...bad panic reflex," Stature said.

"Cassie." Hank ushered her back behind a maintenance truck. Tony followed them, watching carefully.

"I need you to grow very large," Hank continued. "Thirty feet or so."

She stared, shook her head. "My dad said never to grow that big."

"It's—"

"He said my spine would snap! Square-cube, something."

"The serum has a calcium booster—your bones can handle the strain for a few minutes. Not for long. But it's our only hope right now."

She leaned around the edge of the truck. Tony looked, too: Armory was barely visible, lost in a haze of swirling sand and alien energy. Force-bolts continued to radiate out from her. One struck a Jeep, and it erupted in a fiery blast.

Stature nodded. She squeezed her eyes shut and started to grow. Ten feet tall, then 12. When she reached 15, she stopped and looked down at Hank.

He smiled. Nodded, gestured upward.

She drew a deep breath and shot up.

Hank pointed. "The new building!"

Stature turned to look at the Combat Simulator building. It sat newly installed on its foundation, mortar still wet around the base. The construction workers had fled from the site, huddling behind Jeeps and steam shovels.

Keeping one eye on Armory, Stature crossed the yard in two ground-shaking strides. She reached down and grasped hold of the entire Combat Simulator building, struggling to lift it.

"Use your knees!" Hank yelled.

With a crunch, the building came loose of its foundation. Stature lifted it to waist-level and tottered, nearly falling backward under the weight. She grimaced, shifted her burden, and grew one more foot taller.

Then she turned toward Armory.

The recruits had all run away now. S.H.I.E.L.D. agents held positions in copters and the remaining trucks. But S.H.I.E.L.D.'s authority, Tony knew, had been reduced following the Thunderbolts debacle. They were waiting for his signal, waiting to see what happened next.

Armory spotted Stature looming above her, and screamed again. Her eyes glowed, her alien arm flashed wildly.

"Violet," Stature said. "It's okay. It's me, Cassie."

Armory's eyes focused. The energy receded, just slightly, retreating to an area eight feet around her body.

Stature saw her chance. Slowly, gently, she deposited the heavy building *around* Armory. The panicked girl looked up and around, but didn't move. When Stature was done, the structure enclosed Armory completely, hiding her from view.

"It's okay," Stature repeated. "You're safe now."

She stepped back, eyeing the building nervously. Tony watched, expecting to see force bolts shatter its walls from inside. But nothing happened. The energy-crackle died down, quieted to a low hum.

Tony led Hank out from behind the truck. All around, in the yard, little fires burned. Recruits crept sheepishly out of their hiding places; S.H.I.E.L.D. agents reached for fire extinguishers.

Closing her eyes, Stature shrank back down to normal size. She walked up to the Simulator building, now awkwardly deposited at an angle in the middle of the yard. Almost comically, she knocked on its door.

The door creaked open, catching briefly on a rock. Armory peeked out, her power-arm dormant now.

"Sorry," she said.

Komodo and Hardball rushed to join Stature. Together, they helped Armory over to the main administration building.

Hank frowned at Tony. "You still think this is a good idea?"

Tony turned to him, stunned. "Are you kidding? This incident *proves* it. We just had a potentially deadly super-power outbreak, which was defused quickly with zero casualties. Imagine if that girl were untrained, and her panic attack had occurred within a city."

The coach approached, out of breath. "Sorry, Mister Stark. I just— you can't exactly control a Greek god—"

Hank stepped forward, a stern look on his face. "Where is Hermes now?"

"Prob'ly halfway to Flagstaff."

"Hadn't you better find him before he gets *all* the way there?"

The coach turned to Tony, baffled.

Tony smiled. "Take a S.H.I.E.L.D. regiment if you need one."

The man nodded, hurried away.

Tony turned to Hank, placed his hands on both his friend's shoulders. "Now do you see why I need you here? Normal humans can run drills, keep records, evaluate performance charts. But I need someone with *real powers experience* running this place."

Hank nodded, slowly.

"Thank you," he said softly.

Tony shook his head. "I should be thanking you."

They stood together, watching the S.H.I.E.L.D. teams douse the last remaining fires. Coaches lined up the recruits, counted heads, and barked out orders. An administrator stood arguing with the reluctant crane operator, pointing at the displaced Simulator building. Tony overheard the word "overtime" mentioned, more than once.

"It's all coming together, Hank." Tony's voice was low, thoughtful. "We should have done this years ago. Soon the world will be a better, safer place."

A better place, he thought. And yet, he couldn't silence a small voice inside. A tiny regret in the scheme of things, but a failure that nagged at him nonetheless.

If only Peter Parker were here, too.

PART FIVE
CLARITY

TWENTY-SIX

"PASSING level twenty-three." The Punisher's voice was low and gravelly, shot through with static. "Captain, I once broke into Rykers Island to take out a mob boss. But I've never seen security protocols like this."

Cap frowned, conscious of Cage, Falcon, and Tigra standing just behind him. They'd crowded into his new comm room, which had been outfitted with equipment from a decommissioned nuclear sub. Cap had called in a favor with a navy contact, who'd delivered the drab gray fixtures, old-style push-button consoles, and a bright red landline phone with a long spiral cord. The younger Resistance members had remodeled the framework, ripping out sonar displays and replacing them with brand-new flatscreens showing mission status, intelligence on the Initiative camps, and hacked Stark hero dossiers. An array of hard drives and a pair of Mac Pros linked the whole system together.

Cap felt oddly at home here.

"Punisher." Cap leaned forward in his chair. "Describe what you see."

"I'm climbing up the maintenance shaft, through a constant stream of blue, semitransparent balloon-like objects. They're just floating in the air, like bubbles in a stream."

"Those are artificial antigens." Falcon leaned forward. "Sue Richards said Reed based the Baxter Building's security on the human immune system, this month."

"Don't even brush against any of those things," Cap said. "You do, and the whole system will attack you as an invading organism."

Punisher laughed harshly. "Relax, Captain. Nothing can read me while I'm wearing the dampers. I'm invisible to all cameras, trip-beams, and overgrown T-cells."

Cage frowned. "Where the hell you lay your hands on that kind of hardware, Castle?"

"Let's just say Tony Stark's warehouse manager should invest in better locks. And don't worry, I swept everything for tracking devices."

Tigra shrugged at Cap, mock-impressed. Her furry arm rested lightly on his shoulder. Suddenly he was very aware of Tigra's presence: her warmth, her curves, her wide cat eyes.

"Passing level twenty-eight now," Punisher said.

"Keep me posted, soldier."

"Aye-aye, Captain."

Cage frowned. "Punisher's a walking arsenal, Cap. Is Sue worried about him bein' in that building with her kids?"

"Reed sent the children away for a while. Thankfully." Cap swivelled in his chair, turned to the others. "So where do we stand?"

Falcon pointed to a screen showing a news report. "Johnny Storm's team just foiled an invasion of Philadelphia by the Mole Man. Went off textbook perfect: They roped off the area, protecting the citizens. Then they met up unexpectedly with Doctor Strange, made a contact. I'm gonna follow that up right after this."

Cap zoomed in the screen, focusing on a red-caped man with a dark blue tunic, Fu Manchu mustache, and a high, majestic collar. "Strange is a powerful mystic. I think even Tony's afraid of him."

"He's also pretty reserved…no commitments yet. But with his help, our team got the job done fast. Knocked Moley back down to the lower level of Dirtville, and got the hell out of there before S.H.I.E.L.D. arrived."

Tigra frowned. "Doesn't seem to have helped our poll numbers."

"This isn't about polls, Greer." Cap turned toward her, looked into her lovely green eyes. "And it's not about one incident. We have to show the people we're doing the right thing, every day."

She smiled. Cap turned away, suddenly uncomfortable.

"How's, uh, Spider-Man doing?" he asked.

"Still groggy, but recovering fast," Cage said. "Dude's got an amazing constitution."

Cap nodded. "Don't push him, but I need to talk to him as soon as he's up and around. He's the only person who's been to that secret prison and came back on his own two feet. Speaking of which, what's the status of those Negative Zone gateways?"

Falcon typed in a sequence, and a United States map appeared on one of the screens. Red lights blinked over Chicago, Sacramento, Albuquerque, and just off the shore of New York City.

"These portals are scheduled to go live over the next eight days." He pointed to the offshore icon. "The Rykers Island one will be activated first, day after tomorrow."

"At that point, they'll start moving all East Coast prisoners through there," Cap said. "They'll stop using the Baxter Building for transport. Our window of attack is closing fast."

"We could use some backup," Tigra said. "Is that where you sent Sue Rrrrrichards?"

"Yes."

Tigra looked at him, questions in her lovely eyes. But he said nothing else.

"The Initiative camps are springing up fast too," Falcon said. "Stark's latest press release says forty-nine young heroes have signed up for training."

"Camps or jail." Cap felt it again, the dark hard thing growing inside him. "Japanese-Americans were offered that choice, once. The Jews of Germany got both, wrapped up in one sadistic package."

Falcon and Cage exchanged troubled looks.

"Uh, Cap...nobody likes bein' locked up less than this ex-con right here." Cage pointed a thumb at his own broad chest. "But you gotta admit there's a difference between trainin' camps and internment camps."

"Or *concentration* camps," Falcon said.

"There's also a difference between living free, and being told what to do by an oppressive government. A government that maintains its power by scaring the hell out of its own people."

Tigra raised an eyebrow.

"Stark Enterprises," Cap continued, "has spent the past decade building a security state for the people of this country to live in. Did you really think they weren't going to *use* it?"

The speaker crackled. "Ahoy, Captain," Punisher's voice said. "I'm in their data center."

"Good." Cap leaned forward again. "Now I need everything you can find on this big 'Number 42' complex, with special emphasis on the Negative Zone portal leading to it. Size, how much space there is to move around, how far the prison itself is from the portal entrance. What kind of guards it has, how the security works." He paused. "Think you can handle that without shooting somebody in the head?"

"Maybe. If nobody interrupts me. Be in touch soon."

Cage turned to leave. "I'll check on Spidey."

"And I better look into this Doctor Strange thing." Falcon moved to follow Cage, then turned back. He laid a hand on Cap's shoulder.

"Cap, you an' me been through a lot. The Red Skull, the Kree invasion, the Secret Empire..."

"Spit it out, Sam."

"I hope you know what you're doing."

He walked away. Cap watched him go, then turned to stare at the U.S map for a long moment. He felt suddenly very tired.

Then Tigra's strong, soft hands were massaging his shoulders. "Alone at last," she said.

"Greer..."

"You're incredibly tense, you know that?" She leaned over, made a purring noise in his ear. "Leads to bad decisions."

He turned to face her. Her lovely, sharp face was covered with soft, beautifully patterned fur; wet lips glistened below a tiny, catlike nose. Greer Nelson had once been an ordinary human woman, until a mystic ritual transformed her into the ultimate warrior of the Cat People. Her strength and agility were now much greater than a human's. And so, Cap knew, were her passions.

Cap had known men and women who hooked up casually, almost mindlessly, in wartime situations. Correspondents, civilian contractors, sometimes even soldiers. He'd never allowed himself the indulgence. But...

"I heard from Hawkeye yesterday," Tigra said.

Cap blinked. "What?"

"He's doing well. They're giving him a whole Initiative team to run. He wanted me to tell you."

Cap frowned, turned away.

"Cap." He turned; her tone of voice was different now, softer. "What's the endgame here?"

He pointed at a screen. "The prison—"

"No no, I don't mean that. I mean...ultimately, what are we trying to accomplish? Registration is the *law*. No matter what happens, they're just going to hunt us forever, right?"

"Laws can be overturned." He straightened up, faced her directly. "If we can achieve a critical mass of superhumans working with us, solving problems and helping people all over the world, we can win out over the forces of fear. I believe that. I *have* to believe that."

A strange look crossed her face. "I guess you do," she whispered.

He leaned in to her, drawn by her scent. She hesitated, then moved to meet his lips.

"Jackpot, Mon Capitan."

Cap sighed. Tigra laughed.

"What have you got, Punisher?"

"Specs, schematics, all kinds of plans. I'm transmitting 'em now."

"Good." Cap grimaced. "Thank you."

"I don't think you're gonna like it. That place has more protection than any incarceration facility I've ever seen. It's gonna take a lot more than your team of grunts to get in there."

A data signal flashed in front of Cap. He tapped it, and the label PROJECT 42 appeared on one of the large screens. Blueprints began to flash up in rapid sequence, all watermarked with the Fantastic Four's distinctive "4" logo.

Cap glanced over at Tigra. She smiled back at him, a wistful, playful smile.

The moment was gone. The spell was broken.

"I'll tell the others," she said.

"Receiving, Castle." Cap stood up, stared hard at the incoming data stream. "Just keep it coming."

TWENTY-SEVEN

THREE miles out, Sue started to hear something. She checked the instrument panel, wondering how a radio transmission could have reached her here, five miles beneath the ocean's surface. The board was clear; no transmission showed on its log. Yet still she heard it. A dirge, a mournful chant. A dark, throbbing, inhuman melody.

Sue peered forward, gazing through the cockpit of the mini-sub, struggling to see through the gloom. But this far down, all was darkness. Eerie mutated fish flickered in and out of view, bony carapaces briefly illuminated by the sub's forward lights.

Then she remembered: *The Atlanteans are telepathic.* She wasn't actually hearing anything—her mind could sense their thoughts, coming from somewhere in the darkness ahead. That, in itself, was alarming. The Atlanteans remained a mysterious people, but nothing the Fantastic Four had ever seen indicated they could mentally transmit messages at such a distance. Sue had been to Atlantis twice before, and both times the approach had been silent, uneventful.

Maybe something was wrong in Atlantis. *If so,* Sue thought, *that'll make it doubly hard to ask him for help.*

The dirge continued, like a parasite lodged in a dark corner of her brain.

At least I'm close.

A glow appeared directly ahead, like a giant stone jellyfish squatting on the ocean floor. Slowly Atlantis loomed into view, a sunken city surrounded by void, its ancient towers chipped and battered but proud nonetheless. The city glowed from within, illuminated by unknown sorcery combined with science beyond that of the surface world.

A stone wall circled the base of the city, pocked with battle-scars from long ago. As Sue approached, a pair of Atlantean warriors appeared out of the gloom, kicking fiercely as they sped toward her vehicle. They wore sparse military uniforms that left their powerful chests bare, and helmets with large fins on them. The lead warrior brandished a long spear; the second one held a compact, glowing energy weapon.

Sue reached into her pack, held up a stone amulet to the inside of the cockpit window. On it was carved the personal seal of Prince Namor, sovereign ruler of Atlantis. The lead warrior peered at the amulet, nodded, and gestured sharply to his fellow. They lowered their weapons and waved Sue on.

She arced the sub up and forward, swooping over the seawall. The telepathic song was stronger now, like a thousand voices bowed in angry prayer. Yet she couldn't see many Atlanteans. Last time she'd been here, a phalanx of six warriors had received her. Today the wall seemed to be guarded by a skeleton force, and even fewer citizens milled around inside.

Just inside the seawall, she parked the sub and secured its controls. She donned a bubble-helmet and air supply, checked that her suit was watertight, and picked up a small carry-pack. Then she swam free and started toward the center of the city. Somehow she knew: That was where the mind-song would be strongest.

She passed a variety of architectural styles: Doric columns, Dravidian pyramids, Byzantine domes. All slightly different from their surface counterparts, adapted to the needs of an underwater culture. Doorways appeared at all levels, even out of penthouse apartments; balconies opened straight onto the sea, without railings. A civilization of swimmers wasn't confined to the ground, and they had no fear of falling either.

If the ancient Greeks could fly, Sue thought.

Still she saw very few citizens. A pair of Herders passed by, shepherding a huge mole-like aquatic beast. Two elderly men—Judicators, she guessed—hurried past her, clearly late for some event in the heart of the city. But except for the two guards outside, she saw no Warriors, the caste that accounted for sixty percent of the city's population.

When she reached the Avenue of Poseidon, she saw why.

Thousands of people, the majority of the city, crowded into the central square, floating and hovering at all levels. Herders, Builders, Merchants, Farmers, Judicators, and many, many Warriors, their finned helmets polished to a fine sheen. Skin shades ranged from deep blue to sea green to a pale, faded yellow. There were racial divides here, Sue knew, ancient tensions she couldn't even begin to understand.

Carefully, mumbling apologies, she pushed her way through and around the people. Several of them stopped to stare. A pink-skinned woman in an air helmet was unheard of in Atlantis, and not terribly welcome either.

When she reached the front of the crowd, she saw him. And all her old doubts rose to the surface again, along with a nagging sense of regret.

Prince Namor floated in the center of the square, addressing the crowd. His muscular frame was cast, as always, in a pose of kingly arrogance. His pointed ears, sharp cheekbones, even the small wings on his feet—absolutely nothing about him had changed since Sue's last visit. He had donned his dress uniform, she saw, a dark blue tunic worn open to display his magnificent chest.

Namor's skin color was Caucasian, the legacy of his human father. But despite his mixed blood, the Atlanteans acknowledged him as their absolute ruler. He seemed ageless, regal, the proud heir to a long-lived people's heritage. Just behind him, a transparent glass coffin floated, glowing lightly with logomantic energy. The coffin was empty.

Namor had taught Sue the basics of Atlantean, and the telepathic component of their language allowed her to understand him clearly. When he spoke, his eyes burned with sorrow and hatred.

"Imperius Rex," he said. Normally it was a battle cry, but here it seemed more of an introduction: *Here I am, your king.*

"Twenty-nine days," Namor continued. "A full turn of the tides it has been, since the violent death of my cousin at the hands of the hated surface people. And so we gather today, the proud inheritors of ancient Atlantis, to enact the age-old ritual."

Oh god, Sue thought, *Namorita.* She'd forgotten: One of the New Warriors had been directly related to Namor. A member of the royal family.

"The time has come for the *regresus.* The return of Namorita—" Namor's voice caught, just slightly. "Of my cousin to the sea. As we all sprang from the leaves and crawling things of the ocean floor, so now shall she be returned to the source of all life.

"Or rather: She *would* be."

Namor gestured to the coffin, floating hollow behind him.

"Behold my cousin's remains. *There are none.* The surface men have not merely robbed us of the royal princess, a laughing light in my life and the lives of all Atlanteans. They have deprived us of every last bit of what she was."

The telepathic wave surged, grief blending with anger like a red tide. Sue winced, made a small involuntary noise.

A blue woman glared at her. The woman nudged a warrior, who stared at Sue. She felt suddenly very pale and exposed.

"They fill our waters with poison," Namor continued. "They boil the ice caps and hunt proud species to extinction. And when one of us, the sweetest and noblest of all our race, ventures forth to live among them, *this* is their response. Total, utter annihilation."

The Atlanteans' thoughts grew darker, angrier still. Two warriors pointed at Sue now, talking in low tones.

"We seek nothing from them, nothing but coexistence. And yet their hatreds—their petty feuds—infest our refuge, thousands of miles away. The superhumans of the North American continent boast of their power, their honor, their prowess at combat and destruction. Yet even as I speak, they battle among themselves over an incomprehensible matter of names and papers.

"Hear me, my subjects: It is my fondest hope that they will *exterminate themselves and leave this world to us.*"

The people erupted in cheers, jostling and waving their spears. Before Sue could react, a warrior's rough hands grabbed her by the arm, thrust her forward. She tumbled in the water, pulled off-balance by her pack.

"My liege," cried the warrior. "Start with this one!"

Two more warriors moved in toward Sue. She flashed on her force field, knocking the warrior back. But the recoil sent her tumbling through the water. She wasn't used to fighting at this depth; her force field seemed unusually thick, hard to control.

She flailed straight into Namor, her force field still up. He snarled and reached for her—and then his eyes went wide.

"Susan Storm," he said.

Sue turned to him, gesturing for help. A dozen emotions flashed across Namor's dark, cruel eyes. Then he reached out a hand to her.

She lowered her force field and allowed him to grasp her arm. He pulled her roughly toward the center of the square. The coffin floated just above, held in place—she saw now—by tiny water-jets attached to its base.

Namor took her by the shoulders, turned her roughly to face the crowd. "This woman," he said, "is one of the world-famous Fantastic Four. She represents the surface-world superhuman community, in all its decadent squalor."

The crowd roared for blood, but kept its distance.

"Tell my people, Susan." Namor glared at her now. "Defend to them the actions of your comrades, of the so-called heroes of your realm." He gestured at the coffin. "Explain how this *atrocity* came to be."

The people raised blue fists, brandished spears and guns. But Sue ignored them, keeping her eyes on Namor.

"Namorita was killed by a super villain," she said. "Not a hero."

"A villain." Namor's gaze didn't waver. "Like myself?"

I was wrong, she thought. *He* has *changed. He's become more bitter, more resentful; there's no joy in him anymore. And yet...*

...he won't allow me to be harmed.

Sue suddenly felt very calm. She reached into her pack, pulled out a small, watertight cylinder made of sculpted marble.

"This urn contains your cousin's ashes," she said. "At least, all we could find. I'm afraid it wasn't very much."

The crowd murmured in surprise. A thousand eyes watched as Namor accepted the urn, ran his hands over its surface.

Sue cleared her throat. "Namor, I—I'm very sorry about—"

"Vashti." Namor gestured sharply, and an old man swam forward. Namor grasped his neck in an intimate gesture, whispered urgently into his ear.

Then Namor took Sue's arm, steered her roughly toward a large, minareted building. "Come with me," he said.

"Watch the damn hands."

But she allowed herself to be led. Behind them, she heard the old man addressing the crowd: "Err, the ceremony will resume tomorrow. Warriors, return to your assigned posts…"

Namor led her straight through a marbled hall, past a sitting room filled with floating chairs, to his royal bedchamber. A huge round bed filled most of the room, topped with rippling, waterproof sheets. As she watched, grimacing, he shrugged off his vest and began removing his formal pants.

"Umm…"

He paused, and a hint of the old playfulness showed in his eyes. "Why are you here, Susan?"

She gestured at the urn, discarded on the bed. "I—"

He whipped off his pants, revealing his normal casual wear: green scaled trunks. When he spoke, there was menace in his voice. "Don't mislead me again."

She nodded, her mouth tight.

"Things are bad, Namor. They've issued what amounts to a superhuman draft, and they're imprisoning people who don't comply. They've already killed one of us."

He waved her on, impatiently.

"Our—Captain America's raid is planned for tomorrow night. You've got one of the fiercest warrior armies in the world out there, Namor. Having you on our side could mean the difference between winning and losing."

Namor stared at her blankly for a long moment. Then he reared back his head and laughed.

"You heard my people," he said. "You felt their grief, their rage. I am their king; their pain, their outrage, is mine as well. Why in the seven seas would I want to help you?"

"Captain America is one of your oldest friends." She could feel her voice faltering. "You fought with him in World War II...you've known him longer than anyone."

"And where is my friend now?" Namor swam through the chamber, gesturing theatrically all around. "Off plotting his little power struggles, no doubt. While he sends *you* here, to take advantage of our unique relationship."

Sue felt very small now, vulnerable in Namor's private quarters. "We don't have a relationship," she said quietly.

Namor eyed her closely, and a sly smile crept onto his lips. He swooped through the water, landing next to her on the edge of the bed.

"Very well," he said. "I will help you, Susan Storm."

Something in his tone made her bones freeze. "It's Richards now," she said.

He pulled back the top sheet, gestured at the bed. "I prefer the Storm."

All the rage, all the frustration of the past weeks erupted inside her. She reached out and *slapped* Namor, as hard as she could given the water resistance. He barely flinched, but his eyes turned cold.

"You're an arrogant, entitled child, who thinks anyone and anything is there for the taking," she hissed. "Always have been."

"You once liked that."

"I'm not finished. You don't respect women, you don't respect yourself. And yet—despite all that—I always thought you had your own brand of honor, somewhere deep inside. Something that made your people want to follow you anywhere.

"But I was wrong. *This* is your price? You'll help us, save your friends and allies from imprisonment, subjugation, and death, if and only if I agree to *sleep with you?*"

He turned away angrily. Shrugged his taut, muscular shoulders. "I grow bored now."

"Tough. That's just tough. Because you want to know something? This is important to me. I have left my husband and my children, which is the hardest thing I've ever done. I miss them so much, miss them every second of every day, I see them everywhere but it's not them, it's just me, it's just in my mind. And I didn't do all that, I didn't tear my life apart, so I could come down here and submit to the whims of some puffed-up, greasy fish-man. *I did it because it was RIGHT!*"

She whirled toward him, but he had drifted away. He floated on the far side of the chamber, his face angry, downcast.

I've done it, she thought. *I've gone too far. Even if he wanted to help, there's no way his pride would allow it now.*

Sue's adrenaline ebbed. She felt ashamed; she felt like a failure. She wanted to cry.

But despite everything, she wanted the slate clean between them. Something inside her couldn't let the whole visit be tainted by dishonesty.

"The ashes." She gestured at the urn. "I, we don't know for sure they're Namorita's. The site was atomized pretty bad. The authorities did their best, but…"

Namor gritted his teeth.

"…but really, Namor. Her ashes, Speedball's, Night Thrasher's or Microbe's. Does it really matter?"

Still he said nothing. Just pointed to the door, his arm rigid, his eyes burning in cold anger.

So she left. She swam away, back through the sitting room and the big foyer, into the open waters of Atlantis. Past the swarms and groups of amphibean men and women, going about their daily business now, pausing as she passed to stare with hostile eyes.

Just like surface people. So small, so provincial. So filled with tiny hatreds, so quick to vilify and demonize others.

No, she thought, *there's one difference. When Namor's people cry, the tears just wash off into the sea.*

TWENTY-EIGHT

"SO Namor's a no-show?"

Johnny Storm snapped shut the cell phone, shook his head.

Cap grimaced, trying not to favor his bad leg as he led the group down the hallway. He felt briefly angry. In the Pacific Theatre, he'd once seen Namor storm an entire Japanese base with only one man—Cap himself—for backup. Back then, Namor would never have let him down.

"Moving on," Cap said. "Who else have we got?"

"Wolverine won't break ranks with the X-Men, so that's out." Falcon consulted his tablet. "And S.H.I.E.L.D. just picked up Hercules outside Chicago. That's a throwdown I would have liked to see."

"Too bad. Tony's already got a Greek god on his side—we could have used one too."

"Black Panther's with us, though," Johnny said. "He's raging mad about the Bill Foster business—he and Storm say they've got our backs."

"Isn't Storm a mutant?"

"She's also Queen of Wakanda, now. Guess that trumps the X-Men's neutrality."

"What about Doctor Strange?"

Falcon frowned. "Said he had to meditate on the situation. Last I talked to him, he was entering the 'Eight-Day Trance of the Faltine.' I wouldn't count on him for tonight."

Cap slammed a fist into his palm. He felt pumped up and anxious, his usual emotional state before a battle. Especially one with as many "ifs" as this.

"It's the first phase of the assault that worries me," he said.

Falcon nodded. "We need as many troops as we can get. I've called in all the reserves, Cap."

Cap stepped through the door to the conference room. An array of bright costumes sat around the table: Cage, Dagger, Patriot, Speed, Photon, Stingray, and at least a half dozen newcomers. Cap recognized ex-villainesses Asp and Diamondback, among others.

Punisher sat alone at one corner of the table, meticulously cleaning a pair of semiautomatic rifles with a can of oil, sitting open in front of him.

Cap seated himself at the head of the table; Johnny and Falcon took seats on either side of him. "Okay, let's get down to business." He pressed a stud built into the tabletop.

Newly installed holographic projectors hummed to life, and a rotating schematic image rose up from the table. It showed a jagged complex of buildings jutting out of a rock, floating in a surreal version of outer space. "The Punisher got us all the specs on the Negative Zone prison. This is a huge, collective holding facility designed and built by Stark Enterprises specifically to hold superhumans. The layout can be found in this three-dimensional schematic."

Cap reached out to the hologram with both hands and pinched it apart. The image zoomed in, cutting inside the buildings to reveal corridors, cells, exercise areas, and medical facilities, all carefully labeled.

All around the table, heroes leaned forward, studying the display.

Photon frowned. "It's full of super villains, right?"

"*Ostensibly* it's for high-risk super villains. But a lot of rebel super heroes are being held there too. A lot of our friends."

"Stark, Reed Richards, and Henry Pym are planning to install puppet heroes in every state," Falcon said. "Eventually there'll be fifty portals leading directly into the prison. Right now..."

He stabbed a button, and the hologram winked out. A new image rose: the soaring spire of the Baxter Building.

"...there's only one."

"But we need to move fast." Cap leaned across the table, his blood racing. "Our intel suggests they're planning a huge assault on the rebel superhuman community, using both S.H.I.E.L.D. and the Thunderbolts. So tonight is our absolute last opportunity."

He looked around the room. Some people looked uneasy, particularly the younger heroes—Patriot, Dagger, Speed.

"Look," Cap continued. "I understand this is difficult. You're all used to battle, to overwhelming odds, even to hiding from the authorities. What you're *not* used to is having to go up against *other heroes*—people whose priorities, in other times and places, would be exactly the same as your own." He looked down, briefly. "Friends, and former friends.

"But you have to be ready. You have to harden yourselves, to be prepared for what's coming tonight. Because if Iron Man or Ms. Marvel comes charging through the air toward you, you need to act swiftly and decisively to *put them down*. Otherwise, you'll be the next guest in their little alien lockup. And worse than that: You'll be letting down everyone else in this room."

Tigra entered the room. "Sounds like we could use some help." She gestured theatrically...

...and in came Spider-Man. He wore his original costume, red and blue with an intricate webbing pattern. He raised a hand, waved shyly.

"Hi, guys."

Johnny Storm grinned broadly and shot to his feet. He crossed to Spider-Man and clasped him in a big, broad man-hug. "Don't scare me like that again, you wall-crawling freak."

"You took a few lumps yourself, Matchstick." Spider-Man winced. "Ease off the ribs, okay? I'm still a little creaky."

"Awww! Mister Sensitive, always playing to the ladies."

"All right, all right." Cap frowned, and the two men separated. "Spider-Man, are you sure you're up to this?"

"Absolutely, Cap." Spidey swept a glance around the room. "Sounds like you're gonna need every extra pair of hands."

Spider-Man took a seat near the door, in a vacant chair next to the Punisher. Punisher peered at a disassembled rifle, squeezed some lubricant into its firing chamber.

"You, uh, you carry those everywhere?" Spider-Man asked.

"You're welcome." Punisher didn't look up. "For your life, I mean."

Cap pointed at the Baxter Building, zooming the display in to the upper floors. "The key spots are *here* and *here*. Reed's main lab, and this server room."

"It's labeled 'The Quincunx.'" Johnny Storm leaned forward, frowning. "I've never seen that room before."

"We should be able to get inside. But it's possible there will be defenses we don't anticipate."

Cage clapped one arm around Falcon and the other around Dagger, who winced. "We got some power here."

"Still. Even with Spider-Man, I'm a little worried about the numbers."

Diamondback, a reformed ex-villainess in sleek black and purple, rose to her feet. "I might be able to help there." She gestured to the far doorway, opposite Cap's chair. "Goldbug? Plunderer?"

The door opened, and two men walked in. Goldbug wore a full-body costume in red and gold, with a metallic headpiece that resembled an insect's mandible. Plunderer's garb was old-school: blue and white spandex with a high collar and half-face mask.

They were both super villains. Not reformed ones, like Diamondback and Asp. Wanted criminals.

Cap hissed in a breath.

Goldbug turned to address Cap directly. "You guys ain't the only ones scared we're heading for a police state, Captain. The super-criminal community's more concerned about Stark's plans than anybody."

"Yeah." Plunderer swept a nervous look across the table full of heroes. "We just came by to let you know we're here if you need us. Only fair if *Iron Man's* got super villains on his side, am I ri—"

A deafening round of gunfire rang out. Cap shot to his feet just in time to hear Plunderer and Goldbug scream in agony. They toppled backward, jerking and spasming, their bodies riddled by a hail of bullets.

Everyone leapt up. The Human Torch flamed on; Spider-Man leapt onto a wall, looking around frantically. Dagger's hands glowed with light-power.

The Punisher stood calmly, his chair kicked out and discarded behind him. Both semiautomatic rifles smoked in his hand.

Spider-Man whirled toward him.

The Punisher arched an eyebrow. "What?"

The dark thing inside Cap boiled over. He vaulted over the table and pasted a sharp fist across the Punisher's face. The vigilante grunted, dropped his weapons, and fell back against the wall.

Cap glared down at him. The Punisher wiped blood from his face, and slowly looked up. Cap tensed, ready to block the next blow.

But the Punisher just sat still, crouched against the wall. He seemed puzzled, like a dog who couldn't understand why he'd been punished.

"You murderous piece of trash," Cap hissed.

"They were—bad guys, Cap." Punisher struggled to his feet. "Thieves. Killers—"

"SHUT UP!"

Cap kicked out, his boot smashing into the Punisher's jaw. Blood spattered against the wall. Before the Punisher could react, Cap reached out and pulled him close. Cap slammed his shield down onto the Punisher's throat, barely pulling back in time to keep from breaking his neck.

Suddenly everyone was in motion. Some of the heroes ran to the dead villains' bodies; others moved to circle Cap and the Punisher. Still others ran from the room, seeking medical help. The hologram hung over the table, forgotten in the chaos.

"Cap," Falcon said.

But Captain America barely heard him. The world had narrowed down, become a tiny tunnel of battle. No more Registration Act, no more secret prison, no more Resistance and Thunderbolts and Fifty State Initiatives. Just Cap—the super-soldier—and his enemy. A mass murderer in a skull T-shirt, who leaned, bruised and bleeding, against the wall before him.

Just me, Cap thought, *and my biggest mistake.*

Still the Punisher made no move against him.

Cap pulled his fist back, prepared to strike again. "Fight, you coward."

The Punisher shook his head, wincing. "Not—" He spat blood. "Not against you."

Cap stared at him for a long moment. Then he lowered his fist.

"Get him out of here," Cap said. "And throw his guns in the incinerator."

Tigra gestured. Patriot moved to join her, and they each took

Punisher by an arm. Still the Punisher made no move against them.

"Let's, uh..." Cage gestured. "Let's get the medics in here. Have 'em remove those stiffs."

Patriot leaned over to Spider-Man. "Why wouldn't he hit Cap?"

"They're both soldiers. Cap's probably the reason Punisher joined the service. Same guy, different war."

Cap whirled on them, glaring at Spider-Man with eyes full of rage. "*Wrong*," he said. "The Punisher is insane."

Spider-Man nodded, a little too fast. "I know, Cap. I know he is."

Cap turned away again, fists clenched. He squeezed his eyes tight, filling his vision with red haze. Around him, he could hear gurneys being wheeled in, machinery being activated.

"This changes nothing. Pre-attack countdown begins now." Cap whirled back to face the group. "Team Liberty, meet me in ten minutes for a strategy session. The rest of you: Get ready."

He gazed across the assembled faces. They all looked alarmed now, more doubtful than before. Dagger's eyes were wider than ever; Photon looked like she regretted joining up at all. Cage had lowered his shades, staring at Cap with his mouth set tight.

Falcon wasn't looking at him at all.

They're not an army, Cap realized. *They're individuals, accustomed to working alone or in small groups. And tonight they'll go up against the full might of Stark Enterprises, S.H.I.E.L.D., and the United States government.*

But they would have to do. *Too much is riding on this. Our own freedom, and that of our friends. The future of our very way of life.*

Tonight, one way or another, that future would be decided.

TWENTY-NINE

SPIDER-MAN'S muscles creaked; his neck ached. A dull fog still filled his head, left over from Jester's grenades. His spider-sense flared almost constantly now, warning him of danger around every corner.

But somewhere on the trip over to the Baxter Building, he'd realized he felt good. Better than he had in a long time. Maybe it was the costume, the lightweight feel of the old blue and reds. The uniform he'd sewed himself, mere days after that radioactive spider had first taken a bite out of teenaged Peter Parker.

Or maybe, he thought, *it's because I'm finally on the right side.*

"While we're young, Parker? Some of us, anyway."

He followed Johnny Storm through the concealed access panel, set low along the wall of the corridor. "Take it easy, Matchstick. This half of 'Team Liberty' is on the—"

He stopped dead, the quip dying on his lips.

The hidden room—the Quincunx—was almost perfectly spherical, 12 or 14 feet in diameter, and big enough to hold four or five people. Its walls, floor, and ceiling were composed entirely of white triangular plates, interlocked in perfect sequence. Like two geodesic domes fitted together, one on top of the other, to form a giant ball.

"An icosahedron," Spidey said. "It's an icosahedron."

"Suuuuuure, Webs."

Blue-white light filled the room, glowing softly from the triangular panels. A single wooden stool rose up from the central floor-plate.

"Like I said," Johnny said. "Never even heard of this room."

"Or you weren't listening when Reed told you about it."

Johnny grinned. "That's possible, yeah."

Spider-Man leapt up, reaching out to a couple of jointed plates along the "wall" of the room. His gloved hands made contact, sticking instantly to the plates with his natural spider-adhesive. He found the chamber disorienting; it was hard to know where, or how, to stand.

A winking caught his eye. The plate under his hand had lit up with a menu:

AWAITING COMMANDS
INPUT PASSWORD/HANDPRINT/RETINA

The same menu beckoned from three other plates, the ones his boots and his other hand adhered to. He pointed down at Johnny's feet; the same thing had happened where he stood.

Johnny pulled off a glove and reached out his hand. When he touched a wall-plate, its display lit up briefly, then changed to:

ID CONFIRMED: JONATHAN STORM
ACCESS GRANTED

The plate swung open, revealing a row of switches and wires. Johnny shrugged, motioned for Spider-Man to look.

"According to the plans stolen by Mister Shooty Pants, this room controls all access to the labs and the Negative Zone portal." Spider-Man reached out a hand to the switches. "Let's see what this one does."

Johnny put his fingers in his ears, comically. Spidey rolled his eyes and flipped the switch. A display lit up on the adjoining panel.

YOU HAVE JUST DEACTIVATED ROBOT BABYSITTER
H.E.R.B.I.E.
DO YOU WISH TO CONTINUE? Y/N

Spider-Man and Johnny exchanged shrugs. Johnny touched YES.

Across the room from them, way up at ceiling level, another plate popped open. Spider-Man frowned, leapt across to land on the curved wall. Once again, another plate had lit up next to the open one.

ADDITIONAL BABYSITTER CONTROLS AVAILABLE.
DO YOU WISH TO CONTINUE? Y/N

Spider-Man looked down at Johnny. "I don't get this. How is a normal person supposed to operate these controls? I'm gonna wind up bouncing all over the room."

Johnny frowned for a moment, then snapped his finger. A small flame rose from it, as if from a cigarette lighter.

"It's not made for a normal person. It's made for *Reed*." Johnny gestured at the small stool. "All his limbs are stretchable, remember? He can sit there, crane his long neck around to read the screens, and work one set of controls with his elongated left hand and another, clear across the room, with his right one. Maybe another set with his long stretchy toes. Or..."

"Let's leave it at toes. But yeah, that makes sense." Spider-Man closed the open plate, jumped back down. "Speaking of Reed..."

"He's in D.C. for sure, giving an update to that Congressional committee."

Johnny reached out, touched another plate.

LIVING QUARTERS LOCK CONTROLS
DO YOU WISH TO CONTINUE? Y/N

Johnny sighed. "This is gonna take a while to figure out."

"Then we better get moving." Spider-Man reached into the open plate, started moving wires around. "Every minute we waste, the whole Resistance gets closer to a big long stretch in Prison 42."

CAP was on edge. Every step of this operation hung by a thread. Sue Richards had managed to hide the group from view, long enough to sneak them past the S.H.I.E.L.D. guards outside the Baxter Building. And the Punisher's stolen intel had gotten them inside and upstairs without being detected.

But there had been some dicey moments. Sue's powers could keep a phalanx of heroes invisible—but she couldn't keep them *quiet*. A sneeze from Dagger had almost given them away.

Now they stood massed in the corridor, nearly two dozen renegade super heroes trying to be unobtrusive. It was almost funny. Sue held her hands to her head, sweating with the strain of maintaining such a wide invisibility field.

Cap leaned in to her. "Just a little longer, Sue."

She nodded.

A pair of S.H.I.E.L.D. agents stood guard at the door to Reed's lab.

Cap gestured to Cage and Dagger, and the two of them moved forward. Dagger fired off light-daggers at one of the agents, shattering his weapon and stunning him. Cage lumbered forward, launched a powerhouse fist at the second agent's stomach. The agent doubled over in pain, fumbling for his weapon. Cage followed up with a decisive chop to the head.

Cap ran up, caught the agent as he fell. Stripped off the unconscious man's glove and lifted his hand up to the doorplate. The door slid open.

Cage grinned. "We're in, baby."

Cap nodded, motioned the group forward.

Reed's lab was as cavernous as ever—and even messier. Whiteboards, gadgets, and paper plans were strewn everywhere. Liquids bubbled from beakers, remnants of experiments set up and then forgotten in haste.

Sue staggered. "Cap...?"

"You can let the field down now, Sue."

She slumped back against a table, exhausted. The Resistance faded into view.

Cap frowned. Something felt wrong here; this was all too easy. *Two S.H.I.E.L.D. agents to guard the only Negative Zone portal on Earth?*

Falcon crossed past Cap with T'Challa, the dark-clad Black Panther. As ruler of the African nation of Wakanda, the Panther had worked with the Fantastic Four several times and knew their systems. "Thanks for coming, T'Challa. I know it's in Wakanda's interests to stay neutral."

"Forget it, my friend." T'Challa lowered his face-mask, revealing noble features. "Had I answered your first summons, our friend Bill Foster might still be alive. As my wife has reminded me."

He smiled sadly across the room. Storm, weather-goddess of the X-Men and T'Challa's recent bride, spread her arms, acknowledging her husband with a small burst of lightning.

Falcon motioned the Panther toward the Negative Zone portal, which stood dark and quiet. Cap moved to join them.

"What you make of it, T'Challa?"

The Panther frowned, tapped a keyboard beneath a dark screen. "It's off," he reported. "No systems active, no energy coursing through it at all."

Falcon turned to Cap. "Something's wrong. Punisher's intel said they kept it running all the time."

"We do. Unless we're expecting saboteurs."

Cap whipped around toward the voice. An entire wall hummed and began to slide apart, revealing a large chamber beyond. Light streamed in from a picture window, illuminating the normally dark lab.

In that chamber stood the She-Hulk. Ms. Marvel. Hawkeye. Stature, 8 feet tall and filled with determination. Mister Fantastic.

The Thunderbolts stood with them: four super villains, each one a living weapon. Bullseye, the master marksman. Lady Deathstrike, deadly cyborg assassin. Venom, a petty thug possessed by an alien parasite, his long snaking tongue dripping acid. The withered, skull-like Taskmaster, trainer of other super villains.

New allies, too. Wonder Man. Captain Marvel, the newly revived alien warrior. Spider-Woman. Doc Samson. The Sentry, hovering and glowing with unearthly power. Hermes, the swiftly vibrating Greek god. Even Henry Pym had suited up as Yellowjacket, his latest hero guise.

And still more: fresh recruits, straight from the Initiative camps. Blue and red and yellow costumes; a sea of fresh young faces, fliers and cyborgs, mutants and aliens and ordinary hand-to-hand fighters. Young and old, black and white and brown and other colors too, races never before seen on Earth.

Led, as always, by a gleaming figure in red and gold. He stepped forward.

"Tony," Cap said.

Cap swept his shield around the room, motioning the Resistance back. They took up position behind him, facing the newcomers.

Iron Man's voice was calm. "You've walked into another trap, Captain. This time we've got a few extra allies backing us up."

Cap glared at the Thunderbolts. "You must be very proud."

Bullseye widened his eyes, smiled a cruel smile. Venom flicked his long, hungry tongue across his grotesque mouth.

"We've had a mole on your side all along," Tony continued. "Now would be a good time to surrender."

"If you're talking about Tigra, I know all about her."

Tigra whipped her head toward Cap. "What?"

Cap turned to look at her, with mixed feelings. "You overplayed your hand a little, back at headquarters. Though you did make me think."

Tigra stared at Cap, a hint of regret in her eyes. Then she jumped, light as a feather, across the room, to stand with Iron Man.

"I'm an Avenger," she said.

"It doesn't matter," Tony said. "Even if some of the intel Cap's fed us is false, we still hold all the cards. This little 'Occupy' movement is over. *Now.*"

Captain America glanced back at his troops. Cage and the Falcon looked furious, ready for battle. Photon, Stingray, Patriot, Dagger, Speed, Asp, Diamondback, and the others: They seemed truly united now. All hesitation had gone. They would fight for him, he knew, until the end.

They won't be enough. But maybe they won't have to be.

Cap stepped forward, glared into Iron Man's glowing eye-lenses. He felt strong, fierce, unstoppable. Like David facing off against Goliath; like Washington sailing down the river. He could hear the cavalry thundering just over the rise, the Marines about to storm the beach.

The chimes of freedom.

"Be reasonable," Tony said. "You're outnumbered two to one. How can you hope to defeat us?"

Cap stood his ground. Didn't move, didn't even blink.

"Step by step." Slowly, a dark smile crept onto his face. "Brick by brick."

THIRTY

THE Invisible Woman ducked into the Quincunx room. Johnny and Spider-Man whirled toward the door, searching frantically. Spider-Man leapt up, looked up, down, and around.

"Sis?" Johnny called.

Sue willed herself to become visible. "Yeah. Listen, we've got trouble."

"No kidding." Johnny gestured to a bank of open panels, near eye level on the opposite wall. "Reed's file system is as tangled as his limbs."

Spider-Man pointed to a screen showing a maze of circuit-board diagrams. "Plus, this old Atari emulator keeps freezing up on me. I'm never gonna realize my childhood dream of becoming world Centipede champion."

Sue studied the cluster of panels. Six adjacent panels had lit up to form a continuous display screen, showing a schematic of the Negative Zone prison. Small information icons hovered over the individual prison cells; she touched one, and the label DAREDEVIL came up. Several surrounding plates had been flipped open, revealing a rainbow of multicolored wires, switches, and microcircuitry.

Johnny pointed at the schematic. "We've tapped into the prison's mainframe remotely. We even separated the cells holding heroes from the ones with villains in them."

"Yeah." Spider-Man placed a hand on Johnny's shoulder, patronizingly. "*We* did a nice job with that."

Johnny ignored him. "But it's not accepting any of our commands. We can *see* the cells and who's in which ones, but we can't do anything."

Sue reached for an open panel, flipped a switch. "This should get us into Reed's virtual keychain."

Johnny cocked his head at her. "You've been in this room before?"

"Oh, sure. Reed and I like to come in here for..." She stopped, smirked, and turned away. "Never mind."

"No way. No. *Way.*"

Spider-Man crept up the side of the room, craning his neck to see the display. "Don't mind me. Just a fly on the wall over here."

Sue sighed. This was like having *two* little brothers.

She reached over to a second open panel and flipped another switch. One of the screens flickered, changing to a long list of words:

```
ATTILAN PLAYGROUND

GAMMA GAMMA KREE

INITIATIVE RUSCH

FIVE FIREFLY FILLION

DOUBLE DUTCH ALEC

BALLMER WOZNIAK BETA
```

On and on, scrolling down off the screen. Sue swore.

"Sis? What does it mean?"

"It's a list of Reed's passwords. One of these is the one we need." She frowned. "But I don't know which one."

Johnny slapped his forehead. "Leave it to Big Brain to be his own, final layer of security. There's hundreds of passwords here, and only *he* knows which one goes with which system."

```
ECHO MACK BENDIS

ALPHA ALONSO ALPHA BETA

LARRY MAC NIVEN

TERA BYTE GEO

HESTER PRIN PHILLIP
```

Spider-Man shook his head, staring at the screen. "I feel like I just contracted dyslexia."

"This is serious, boys. Tony Stark has ambushed us again, down in the lab. He and Cap are doing that thing right now, where they circle around each other like gunfighters."

Spider-Man hissed in a breath. "That ended real well last time."

"I barely managed to slip away before Reed saw me. He's not really out of town—another thing he didn't tell me, I guess."

```
OCTO DECA MEGA

MILLER SIN MILLAR

HAWKING NEGATIVE Z

SIERRA CHARLIE PEGGY LIPTON

RUNCITER TAVERNER ELDRITCH
```

Spider-Man jumped up in the air, startling both Sue and Johnny. "That one!" he cried.

Sue frowned. "What? Which one?"

He jabbed a gloved finger at the screen. "That one! *That's it!*"

Johnny stared at him. "'Peggy Lipton'?"

"Sixties TV actors. Trust me!"

Sue turned back to the main display, the prison schematic. She called up a virtual keyboard and began to type.

She realized she was holding her breath. Cap and the others were at Tony's mercy, right now. If this didn't work...

The display blinked once, and for a terrible moment Sue thought she'd locked herself out of the system. Then the schematic reappeared, with the transparent words overlaid:

ACCESS GRANTED

"All right!" Johnny clapped his hands. "I knew we could do it."

"Again with the *we?*"

Sue ignored them. She reached out to the touchscreen, began tapping individual cells. One by one, they turned green. She pinched and zoomed the schematic, moving around the prison, checking each cell's label carefully.

"Now the portal," she said. "And then we're—"

A loud klaxon went off, startling her. Throughout the room, the lighting dimmed. Sue whipped her head around and saw: Every screen, except the ones she was working on, now glowed with the dark red word ALERT.

"I think Team Liberty just went public," Spider-Man said.

"It doesn't matter." Sue turned to them. "I've got to stay here, finish activating the portal sequence. You two get down to the lab, help Cap."

"Sis—"

"Believe me, Johnny. You're gonna be in more danger than me."

She turned back to the screen, resuming her task. A command menu labeled NEGATIVE ZONE PORTAL came up before her.

Johnny kissed her once on the head. "Come on, Webs. Let's go be heroes."

"Yeah." Sue grimaced, wincing as the loud alarm continued. "And when you see Reed, give him a good slap for me."

TONY Stark had won. His forces fanned out slowly, surrounding the so-called Resistance. Cap's forces stood their ground, not moving. But there was no doubt now: They were trapped here in Reed's laboratory.

Every step of this operation had been planned, drilled, checked, and rechecked. The experienced Avengers formed the front line; the Thunderbolts provided backup, their murderous tendencies kept in check by the nanomachines running through their veins. A small army of Initiative recruits formed a circle at the fringes. And if, by some fluke, a rebel or two managed to escape, S.H.I.E.L.D. copters hovered just outside, waiting to scoop them up.

There was nowhere to run, no gambit left for the rebels to play. And yet, here stood Captain America, glaring straight at him. Eyes like black ice. Smile of a dead man.

Tony wanted very, very badly to hit him.

Tony raised his faceplate, forcing the anger down. "If you knew about Tigra," he said slowly, "why did you let her keep working with you?"

"If I'd exposed her, you might have moved against us sooner."

"But she led us here. She told us your entire plan."

Cap turned dark eyes on Tigra. "Not all of it."

"In God's name, what do you *want?*" The anger boiled over; Tony felt himself losing control. "I've done *everything* to help you. I offered you amnesty, more than once. I talked the United States government out of shutting us all down! Do you know what *could* have happened here?"

All eyes were on Tony now. Reed Richards snaked his way to the front of the group.

"What do you want?" Tony repeated. "Do you expect everyone to just let you do whatever you want, and damn the consequences? Exactly *what war do you think you're fighting?*"

Cap glared at him, and the smile faded from his face. "There's only one war."

"Excuse me." Reed's elongated neck swooped up to face Cap and Tony. "Where is Susan? I saw her before."

"Not now, Ree—"

A grinding noise filled the room. Tony whipped his head around, searching for the source. Lights flashed, alerts rang out. A large display screen lit up with the words: PROJECT 42 GATEWAY / ACTIVE.

"The portal," Tony said.

A small clump of Initiative kids stood near it; they backed away, watching as the swirling chaos of Negative Zone space faded into view. Reed Richards swooped his rubber body through the air toward the portal.

"Reed!" Tony called. "Turn that off."

Reed stared for a moment at the portal. Then his head wobbled, as if at the end of a spring, and reversed course. He stretched his torso toward a control console across the room.

She-Hulk, Hawkeye, Wonder Man: One by one, the Avengers turned to Tony, questioning looks in their eyes.

The rebels started to stir, to flex their muscles. A hard smile crept over Luke Cage's face.

"Initiative forces," Tony continued. "Maintain your positions."

Tony turned back to Cap. The super-soldier's face was stone cold now, ready for battle.

"What's your plan?" Tony gestured dismissively. "Escape into the Negative Zone?"

"Not exactly."

Stature stretched herself up to 10 feet in height and pointed at the portal. "Mister Stark! Look!"

Within the portal, silhouetted against a roiling antimatter nebula, a cluster of colorful dots appeared. Human shapes, and humanoid, all growing closer and larger with each passing second. Some flew under their own power, and some shot along on tiny rocket-jets. All in formation, and all moving rapidly toward the portal's opening.

Wiccan. Hulkling. Daredevil. Cloak. Valkyrie, Nighthawk, Hercules. And dozens more behind them.

"The cells," Tony whispered.

"This should even the odds a little," Cap said.

Daredevil's grim red form drew closer. Nighthawk's wings beat wildly, propelling him through the dark matter of Negative Zone space. Cloak's dark, angry form swooped ahead of the others, almost filling the portal.

Luke Cage smacked a fist into his hand.

Then Cloak broke through the portal, his cape swirling wide. Daredevil followed, and then the others. Hercules, the Greek god of legend, laughed as his enormous legs touched down on the lab floor.

The rebels seized their chance. The lab broke out into chaos.

Falcon took to the air. Hawkeye ran to follow, drawing his bow and aiming shakily upward. "C'mon, Falc," Hawkeye called. "Cap's crusade—it's over, man."

"Doesn't look over to me," Falcon said.

Down below, Wiccan and Hulkling hugged Speed and Patriot quickly. Then they turned to Stature, their estranged teammate. Her eyes went wide with panic, and she looked around. Then Komodo, Hardball, and Armory—Stature's fellow Initiative trainees—rushed to her side. Armory let out a fierce energy blast, and the battle was joined.

"Don't hurt them," Stature said.

The Black Widow ran to intercept Daredevil. He swung his billy club at her and jumped away, vaulting over a disassembled space-flier cockpit. She followed, stingers flashing, murder in her eyes.

Dagger leapt, ballet-style, over the fray, touching down right next to her returned partner. Without even a shared glance, they took up defensive positions back to back. Dagger fired light-bolts at Initiative trainees, dazzling and stunning them. Cloak hurled them into the chill depths of his cape.

"Avengers!" Tony said. "Don't panic. Follow protocols—"

He turned, just a second too late. Cap's fist slammed into his exposed face, spinning him around. Tony crashed back against a computer display, shattering it in a shower of sparks.

Tony shook his head, blood flying from his jaw. Raised his hand, fired off a repulsor beam. Cap leapt back, dodging in midair—

—and then the door blew open from outside. Smoke blew in from the corridor outside, silhouetting a phalanx of body-armored S.H.I.E.L.D. agents. Maria Hill swept past them, leading them into the battle-damaged room.

Still groggy, Tony reached out a hand to her. "Maria—don't. Let my people—"

But Hill wasn't listening. She made urgent hand-signs, maneuvering her agents carefully around the battles breaking out all over the room. Asp and Diamondback stood grappling two-on-one with the powerful, black-clad Wonder Man. Photon ran to join Cage and the Panther, firing energy-bolts into a clutch of half-trained Initiative kids. They screamed and scattered.

Tony cast a quick glance at Cap—just as a massive tangle of limbs and flesh crashed onto the floor between them. Tony jumped back, startled. He barely recognized the two gods, Hercules and Hermes, grappling and wrestling as they tumbled across the floor. Their battle was savage, deadly, punctuated by cries of triumph and howls of agony. They were also laughing.

The gods passed by, crashed together into a wall. When Tony looked up, Cap was gone.

Rebels continued to pour out through the Negative Zone portal. A sea of costumes, red and blue and gold and silver. Humans, aliens, cyborgs, mutants. And all of them very, very angry.

Maria Hill ignored them all. She pointed sharply at Reed Richards, who stood locked in battle with the beautiful rebel called Asp. Reed's body was coiled around Asp, squeezing the breath from her. She gasped, firing venom-blasts at his dodging, stretching arms and head.

Grimacing with pain, Tony flipped his helmet down into place and flew up into the air, heading toward them.

At Hill's command, a half dozen S.H.I.E.L.D. agents surrounded Asp. Reed Richards's eyes went wide; he uncoiled rapidly, slinging his body away like a rubber band—just as Hill's agents opened fire on Asp with tranq guns. Asp staggered, fired off a final blast, and went down.

"Maria," Tony called.

Hill didn't respond. Her agents grabbed the startled Reed Richards, pulled his malleable shoulders down to her level.

"Doctor Richards," Hill said. "Show me how to regain control of this building's defenses."

Reed looked around, dazed. His eyes flickered from the raging Negative Zone portal, to the dozen little battles wreaking havoc on his lab. "What have I done?" he whispered.

"Doctor Richards. We need to shut down that portal." She pulled out a magnum, pressed the barrel to Reed's head. *"Now."*

Reed turned to look at her, then at the gun. As if they were insects invading his sealed, sterile experiment.

Tony reached out his hand and blasted Hill's gun to pieces. She recoiled, grabbed her hand in pain.

"There's no need for that," Tony said, hovering just above her. "Reed is our ally."

Hill cradled her hand, glared up at him.

"Reed." Tony wafted in for a landing. "She's right."

Reed stared blankly at Tony for a moment, then nodded. He reached out a long arm and gestured at a console, halfway across the room.

Tony shot up into the air, surveyed the battle. In between Reed and the console, She-Hulk was grappling with the savage Valkyrie. Val's sword flashed, grazing She-Hulk's shoulder. She-Hulk howled with rage and brought down both fists on the warrior-woman's head.

Tony swerved in midair and fired on Valkyrie with both repulsors. Val went down. She-Hulk grimaced in pain, but reached up her good arm to give Tony a high-five.

The S.H.I.E.L.D. agents stepped over the downed Valkyrie, pausing to shoot off a tranq dart into her, just in case. Reed led them toward a small computer screen with a keyboard attached. Miraculously, it was still intact.

Tony arced over the group, landing next to them.

"This is it," Reed said. "I can shut down the gateway from here."

"Well, get it done," Hill growled.

Tony turned back to the battle. Stature and Yellowjacket fought back to back, holding off the attack of the other four, rebel Young Avengers. A nasty aerial fight had broken out in the center of the lab, where the ceiling was highest: Stingray and Nighthawk of the rebels, aided by the flashing weather-goddess Storm, dodged and weaved to avoid Ms. Marvel's powerful force bolts.

"Lock down this room, too," Tony said. "I don't care how many criminals they manage to spring from the Zone. If we can trap them in the lab, we'll wear them down eventually."

Reed nodded. His fingers stretched and tapped across the keyboard.

Tony gritted his teeth. *This is still salvageable,* he thought. *It won't fall apart. It can't—not after all we've sacrificed. All I've sacrificed.*

"Reed?"

Reed was frowning at the display screen. "Someone else is controlling this. From the Quincunx..." He stopped, staring at the screen.

Hill threw up her hands. "What?!"

"The pattern of keystrokes...I recognize it."

Hands shaking, Reed opened a chat box and typed a single word:

SUE?

A force bolt blasted past them, burning a hole in the wall. Hill gestured, almost casually, and a pair of S.H.I.E.L.D. agents formed a blockade behind them, firing tranqs into the rebels.

When Tony looked back, Reed was staring at the screen again. The chat window showed a short, return message:

GO TO HELL
DARLING

"Reed!" Tony took him by the shoulders. "You can do this. You have to do this."

Reed stared at him for a long moment. Tony thought he saw Reed start to nod—

—and then something slammed into Tony's back with a dull, wet noise. Before he could react, a powerful force lifted him up off the floor. He spun around in midair, boot-jets firing at full—and found himself tangled in sticky webbing.

"I'm back, Shell-Head. And I brought my *can opener.*"

Spider-Man's fist slammed into Tony's helmet. Tony howled in pain. A dozen armor alarms went off, but his helmet seal held.

Tony reached out a hand, fired a repulsor at Spider-Man. The wall-crawler scuttled along the lab wall, dodged—*blasted spider-sense!*—but caught a bit of the blast on the edge of his upper torso. His blue-red uniform tore open, exposing burned flesh beneath.

Tony twisted in midair, still caught in a net of webbing. He fired pinlight-beam repulsors, burning off it bit by bit, slowly but surely.

"Should have kept the new suit, Peter."

"I couldn't, *boss.* Too much blood on it."

"BAXTER BUILDING MAIN LABORATORY." The piercing computer voice filled the air. "SECURITY SYSTEMS ACTIVATED. SIXTY SECONDS TO LOCKDOWN."

"Reed!" Tony yelled. "Silence that thing. We don't need to *warn* them—"

Spider-Man leapt toward Tony, both his fists clasped together. He struck Tony's torso with a loud clang, then leapt away quickly. Tony stumbled back, firing off repulsors, but Spidey was moving too fast to get a target lock. Tony crashed down, scattering a group of Initiative trainees.

Tony climbed to his feet—and noticed that the battle pattern had changed. The Resistance forces stood together now, their backs to the large window in the side chamber. They'd managed to form a barricade against all of Tony's forces: the Avengers, Thunderbolts, and Initiative trainees. S.H.I.E.L.D., too.

And the rebels weren't just brawling. They stood arm to arm, in a straight line. Even their aerial forces had joined them; Falcon hovered with Stingray, Nighthawk, and Storm above the rebel line, blasting and thrusting to keep the Initiative fliers back. All with a single goal: protecting something, or someone, over by the window.

Then Spider-Man was on Tony again, punching and firing off webs.

Tony activated his chest-beam, set it to widest spread. Spidey flew backward, yelling in pain.

"THIRTY SECONDS TO LOCKDOWN."

The thought hit Tony like a blast of ice: *Peter was a decoy. To keep me from realizing what's going on...*

He flew up into the air. Blasted Stingray hard, with both repulsors and chest-beam, smashing a hole in the rebels' aerial blockade.

...over there.

Tony swooped over the line, dodging Storm's lightning bolts and Falcon's grasping arms. Then he stopped short as he saw:

Captain America stood at the huge glass wall-window, bashing at it with his shield. Next to him, Dagger fired off a wide spread of light-knives, weakening the glass in a dozen spots. Cage punched at a single spot, very hard, several times in succession. Hercules hurled himself at the glass, his massive body slamming into it and bouncing back, again and again and again.

Johnny Storm had joined them, too. He fired off flame-balls, softening the glass, yellow and white flames glinting off its surface.

Beyond the window, evening had fallen. A thousand tiny lights illuminated the spires of Manhattan, lit up against the chill autumn night.

Oh no, Tony thought. *No no no no no—*

"FIFTEEN SECONDS TO LOCKDOWN."

"It's now or never." Cap raised his shield, called to the others. *"Freedom!"*

"Cap!" Tony yelled. "Please—"

Too late. Light-daggers flashed, street-toughened fists lashed out. Fireballs flamed bright; god-muscles flexed and released. Captain America lashed out with his shield to strike the final, shattering blow.

The glass splintered, burst outward in a thousand shards. Captain America and the others tumbled after it, into the open air.

Cold air blasted in. With a rebel cry, the rest of the Resistance turned to follow their leader. They ran, jumped, and flew out into the dark sky.

Spider-Man swung out last, his webline anchored to the ceiling. As he let go of the line, swooping out into the sky, he turned and shot Tony another Nazi arm-salute.

Tony hovered, shocked and horrified. *Evening in Times Square,* he thought. *There are thousands of people down on the streets. Thousands of innocent bystanders, people I've vowed to keep safe. And now we've brought our battle straight into their lives.*

He clenched his fists. *This is bad, very bad. This isn't contained any longer; it's now a public brawl. The one thing I tried, above all else, to avoid.*

"ALERT: OUTER PERIMETER BREACH."

Hill ran up beneath Tony, staring out the shattered window, barking orders into her shoulder-comm. Reed stretched up next to her, his eyes wide with shock. The rest of the Initiative forces scrambled up to join them, looking to their leader.

Ms. Marvel, strong and loyal as always, flew up to stand right before Tony. "Orders?"

He swept his gaze across her beautiful form, then down and around past his assembled forces. She-Hulk and Black Widow, determined and sure; Hawkeye and Reed, torn by old loyalties. Stature and Hermes and the children from the Initiative, just beginning their super hero careers. The deadly Thunderbolts, sneering and snarling, human weapons kept in check only by S.H.I.E.L.D.'s technology.

Tony turned, then, and gazed out into the night sky. S.H.I.E.L.D. copters dipped low, buzzing and whirling, awaiting orders.

He swept his arm forward, and soared out through the window. Then he turned back, setting his armor's speakers to maximum.

"SHUT 'EM DOWN," he said.

THIRTY-ONE

"ALL the fliers, grab a friend," Cap yelled. *"Now!"*

Floor after floor of the Baxter Building whizzed by, frighteningly fast. The lights of Times Square glared bright, painting the falling heroes in a surreal palette of bright hues.

The Human Torch flamed on, arcing upward to grab hold of Sue and Dagger. Nighthawk's wings beat furiously as he scooped up Daredevil, Valkyrie, and Cage. Storm grabbed her husband, and Spider-Man shot webs out toward the side of the Baxter Building, slowing his own fall.

Falcon swooped down and grabbed Cap up by the arms.

"Like old times, right, Cap?"

"Not exactly." Cap shot him a grateful glance. "Get me some altitude?"

Falcon titled his head up and soared upward, carrying his partner along. Cap felt the night air on his face, invigorating him. He looked down.

The chaos of Times Square spread out in a thin wedge, cars crawling by around a central triangle of food stands, military recruiting areas, and pedestrian seating areas. The Square was crowded with people: commuters and tourists, street performers and ticket scalpers, all lit by streetlamps and arc-bright billboards. They ran like ants now, away from the barrage of glass and bodies plummeting down from the Baxter Building.

Riot-suited S.H.I.E.L.D. agents rushed into the square, waving batons and herding the crowd south, through clumps of metal tables surrounding dumpling trucks and hot dog carts. Local cops poured out into the streets, clearing the major routes of cars. Official vehicles screeched up to block intersections.

If they just let us go, Cap thought, *this'll be over fast. But if Tony lets his troops loose on the ground...*

"HO, MORTALS!" Hercules screamed down past Cap and the Falcon, his fall unchecked. "MAKE WAY FOR THE SON OF ZEUS!"

Laughing, Herc struck the sidewalk with a thundering crash. Pavement split, people scattered; water burst up from a shattered hydrant.

Dammit, Cap thought.

Two and three at a time, the Resistance touched down in the square. The Torch first, with Sue and Dagger in tow. Storm and the Panther. Spider-Man swung down to join them, shooting out webbing to dam the gushing hydrant.

Cap gestured, and Falcon turned back toward the Baxter Building. The hole was still visible in the side of Reed's lab. A few brightly colored figures peered out, but Cap couldn't make them out from this distance. Four S.H.I.E.L.D. copters hovered just outside.

And down below...

A cruel figure in deep blue and white stalked out the main entrance of the Baxter Building, his features lit in flashes by a Broadway theatre ad. Bullseye. The ghoul-faced Taskmaster followed, then Lady Deathstrike. And Venom, in his dark mockery of Spider-Man's costume, his inhuman tongue flicking around hungrily.

The Thunderbolts. Tony Stark's mercenary army, his own troop of supposedly tame super villains. Loose among the panicked citizens of New York.

Behind the Thunderbolts, heroes swarmed out of the Baxter Building. She-Hulk, Black Widow, Doc Samson. With a sinking feeling, Cap knew: *This battle isn't over yet.*

The Thunderbolts whispered quickly among themselves. Lady Deathstrike pointed a long, unnaturally sharp finger, and the others turned to look. Cap squinted and saw their target: Stingray was just wobbling in for a rough landing on the blue-paved pedestrian area. He carried Asp, who struggled in his grip. She slipped, banged a leg badly in the landing.

"Gliding ain't flying," Cap said.

Falcon looked down at him. "What?"

Below, the Thunderbolts took off at a run. They dodged across screeching traffic, heading straight for the dazed Stingray and Asp.

Cap tensed. "There." He pointed at the villains. "Get me down there."

Falcon grabbed Cap tighter and dove. The gigantic ads of Times Square lit their descent: Broadway shows, fast food, electronics equipment. A documentary called *Inside Stamford: Anatomy of a Tragedy.*

"What's our play?" Falcon asked.

"I can handle it. You help the others."

"You're gonna take on *all four of 'em?* Those are heavy hitters!"

"I need you to make sure our guys are all safe. If I need help, I'll yell."

Falcon let out a sigh, audible even over the rush of wind. He swooped down to a height of twelve feet. Cap looked down just in time to see Venom wrap his malleable alien body around Stingray, knocking him off his feet. Lady Deathstrike and Taskmaster grabbed on to the dazed Asp, holding her up before Bullseye—who just stood smiling, licking his lips.

Cap slapped Falcon's arm. Falcon nodded and dropped him.

Cap plummeted down, over the panicked, swerving cars. Later, he would remember: In that brief moment, falling through the air toward his enemies, he felt as alive as he ever had in his life.

Then he struck down hard, crashing down on Lady Deathstrike's neck. Asp seized the chance, shooting off a bioelectric charge at Taskmaster. He cried out and staggered back.

But Bullseye was already in motion. The assassin, who specialized in using any object as a weapon, grabbed a briefcase from a startled businessman. The man started to protest, then caught a glimpse of Bullseye's eyes and fled in terror.

Bullseye snapped open the briefcase, incredibly fast. He grabbed out four ordinary pens and fired them like missiles, straight at Cap and Asp. Cap barely managed to raise his shield in time to block them.

A gurgling noise alerted him to Stingray's plight: Venom's long tongue was wrapped around Stingray's neck now, slowly choking him. Cap pointed, and Asp nodded. She reached out her arms, sending a fierce charged bolt straight at Venom. The alien shuddered, spasmed, and released his prey.

Stingray ran to Cap. "Thanks," he said.

"Couldn't desert Resistance members in need," Captain America replied.

Asp smiled. "I thought you'd be off with Falcon and…and the Torch…"

"You're *all* my troops. Now go—help the others."

Asp shot him a last, grateful glance as they ran off. Then a flash of light caught Cap's eye. Purely on instinct, he swiveled his shield around just in time to block Taskmaster's ray-blast. He kicked backward, catching Lady Deathstrike in the stomach an instant before her cyborg claws could grab his throat.

Cap was completely in the moment, now. All around him, little fights were breaking out: Resistance versus Initiative, heroes versus heroes. A few S.H.I.E.L.D. agents swarmed onto the blue pedestrian area, brandishing their weapons. Civilians pointed in panic, ran for cover. Cars screeched, swerved, crashed into lampposts.

Lady Deathstrike reached out long claws, slashed Cap across the chest. Blood spurted. "Some rebel leader!" she said.

Cap staggered back, and realized: *I've lost the advantage.*

Before he could recover, Venom punched him in the stomach. "Yesssss." Cap could feel his hot breath, foul and alien.

"This is the living legend of World War Two?" Bullseye kicked high, his boot catching Cap in the face. "Who was he fighting, Bing Crosby?"

Cap's head snapped back. The world swam before his eyes. All around him, brightly colored costumes fought a desperate ballet. Above, the lights of the square wavered and flashed before his eyes...

...and he smiled.

Lady Deathstrike held his head firmly now, gripping it from behind in her unnaturally long fingers.

"What's so funny, Captain?"

Cap smiled through blood-splattered teeth. "I'm just thinking about my pal up there..."

A regal figure swooped down out of the night sky. Behind him, a high-tech airship popped open...and dozens of tattooed, blue-skinned warriors poured out.

"...who's about to kick your butts into next week."

Prince Namor arrowed downward, fists clenched. He reached back, motioning his warriors to follow. "IMPERIUS REX!"

Again, Cap smiled.

Now the Resistance had a fighting chance.

SUE Richards gazed up at Namor, watched the graceful arc of his descent. His imposing figure crashed into Bullseye, fists first, knocking the assassin to the ground. The warriors of Atlantis followed, four or five each swarming over Venom, Taskmaster, and Lady Deathstrike.

Unbidden, the thought came to Sue: *At least there's one man in my life I can count on.*

She stood, invisible, pressed against an alcove next to the Baxter Building main entrance. Ben had loitered out here many times after an FF meeting, puffing that stogie. Before he gave up smoking, of course.

"Iron Man to all points." Sue looked up sharply, saw Tony's gleaming figure hovering above the fray. *"Continue evacuation of the area and contain the battle to midtown. I want no civilian casualties. Repeat: NO CIVILIAN CASUALTIES!"*

The battle had resumed quickly, down here on the ground. Just across Broadway, Luke Cage and Diamondback grappled with Wonder Man, while Ms. Marvel shot force-bolts at Cage from the air. Falcon leapt and swooped above Hawkeye, who stood with bow drawn, shouting up at his enemy. Hercules shrugged off the Black Widow's stinger-blasts, smiling as She-Hulk moved in to join the fray.

Sue searched around for Reed. She caught a glimpse of his attenuated, 15-foot-long body a block north, coiled around Patriot and besieged by Atlantean troops. Johnny soared overhead, dodging and firing off flame-balls at Captain Marvel, the two of them framed by a 30-foot lingerie ad.

A hail of glass rained down on Sue—more debris from the upper floor. A group of civilians stood huddled against the building; Sue flashed on her force field, shielding them, and herself, from the new barrage. Then she heard a familiar grunt from across the square.

She dropped her invisibility field. "Ben!"

The Thing smiled, that crooked smile she'd grown to love. He stopped to backhand She-Hulk, knocking her away from Hercules. Herc turned, regarding Ben with a look of disappointment.

Ben clomped across the street, his arms spread wide. "Ya didn't really think I was gonna sit this one out eatin' croissants?" He reached out, hugged Sue tight. "We got people to protect!"

Then his eyes went wide with alarm. Sue whipped her head around and saw—

—a glint of light—

—the Taskmaster's ghoulish, desiccated face—

—his energy gun, light flashing red —

"SUSAN!"

And then the air was filled with blue. Reed Richards threw himself in front of the Taskmaster's blast, taking it full-on in the back. He cried out in pain and went limp, spasming like a rubber sheet in midair.

"Reed!" Sue pulled free of Ben, whipped herself around.

Reed collapsed to the sidewalk, his long limbs sprawling out into the street. The traffic had almost all fled now; Ben held up a hand to a bus, which screeched to a halt. Then he leaned down over Reed's smoking body.

"Aw, man," Ben said.

Sue ran over and bent down to touch her husband. Reed's heart was tough to locate in his elongated form, but she'd had practice. She felt around his chest, avoiding the smoking hole in his uniform. Felt the beat beneath her palm: *Bu-bump. Bu-bump.*

She exhaled in relief. Then she turned to face the Taskmaster, who stood against the Baxter Building wall, recharging his weapon. The last pedestrians had fled at his first shot; he was alone.

"I got 'im, Suzie."

"No, Ben." Sue concentrated. "He's mine."

She reached out with her force field, shaping it into an invisible, hammer-shaped bludgeon. Taskmaster looked up, snarled at her—then realized what was happening. His eyes went wide with fear.

She slammed the field downward, flattening Taskmaster against the sidewalk. Smashed it down once, twice, slamming him down again and again with tremendous force.

When she was done, the Taskmaster lay limp in a two-foot circular depression, surrounded by cracked concrete. Above, on an ad for a children's musical, a cartoon lion looked down blankly.

Ben stared at her. "Whoa."

Sue knelt down, cradled Reed's elongated body. A faint, pained sound issued from his lips.

She looked up, grimacing at the chaos all around. Flying heroes fought up above; fierce battles continued on the ground, fought with fists and guns and force blasts. All around, Namor's Atlantean legions fanned out, assisting the rebels.

The tide was turning.

Hercules hefted Doc Samson into the air, hurled him at a bus. Tourists poured out the door in panic, just before the huge, green-haired scientist slammed into the bus windows. The vehicle crashed down on its side, narrowly missing an old woman.

Ben reached down for Reed, but Sue held out a hand. "Go help people," she said. "I've got him."

Ben glanced at her, unsure. Then he turned sharply as Doc Samson lifted the bus, tossed it through the air toward the laughing Hercules.

Ben touched her once on the shoulder, then hurried off.

Sue reached under Reed's limp body and lifted him up. His stretched-out limbs flopped out at unnatural angles. He mumbled incoherently as she carried him off through the chaos. A drop of blood fell from his lip.

"Stupid," she whispered, trying not to cry. "Stupid, stupid man."

THIRTY-TWO

DOWN below, Times Square was really taking a beating. Storm fired lightning bolts down at the dodging Ms. Marvel, cutting up chunks of pavement with every strike. She-Hulk threw Hulkling into a public bench, shattering it to splinters. Hercules was a one-man wrecking crew.

Tony Stark hovered, studying the chaos. It was all spiraling out of control. *Cap!* he thought. *Why are you doing this?*

"Stark."

The voice was like a mini-migraine in his ear.

"Yes, Maria."

"I've got eight more battalions ready to drop."

He glanced upward. More copters had assembled, buzzing angrily in the air. Below them, the S.H.I.E.L.D. Mobile Command Center swooped down low. That would be Maria.

"Negative. I can contain this."

"I think we're a few stages past that, Stark. And I'll remind you: There are now foreign terrorists aiding the fugitives on U.S. soil. Which gives S.H.I.E.L.D. clear authority."

"What foreign—" He stopped, swiveled to look down again. The

Atlantean warriors had spread out all through the square, armed with both spears and energy-weapons. A few of them had inserted themselves into a battle involving Cloak, Dagger, Hawkeye, and She-Hulk; another group skirmished with S.H.I.E.L.D. agents on the eastern side of the square. Eight or nine more warriors stood triumphantly over the Thunderbolts' bodies.

"Stand by, Maria."

"Stark—"

"Damn you! Just give me a minute."

Tony triggered boot-jets to full and shot upward. He gave the Mobile Command Center a curt wave as he passed it, then zigzagged around the S.H.I.E.L.D. copters. When he'd cleared the skyline, he swooped around the copters and whirled around to look down. He needed to get a full view of the situation.

As always, the sight of Manhattan at night took his breath away. Headlights creeping down avenues, thousands of people—millions—stalking the streets. All those lives, all those souls. So glorious, yet so helpless...

Tony shook his head. *When was the last time I slept?*

Then a bright flash of light caught his attention, along with a faint crashing sound. Ms. Marvel's force bolts; he couldn't tell who had made the impact—Hercules, maybe, or She-Hulk. Even from this height, without triggering lens magnification, he could see the damage being done. Not just in Times Square itself, but to the surrounding area. Explosions, stinger-bolts, bodies flying into buildings. Black S.H.I.E.L.D. helmets formed a perimeter guard around the three-block area, but a lot of civilians were trapped inside the combat zone.

A flying figure gestured—*Sentry?*—and a huge, smoky explosion rose up from the middle of the square.

Panic gripped Tony, bone-deep and sudden. *No,* he thought. *Not another Stamford. Never again.*

He aimed sensors down and activated a mobile CapeSearch protocol. Images flickered before his lenses: Spider-Man and Daredevil facing off against Black Widow and Captain Marvel. Cage and She-Hulk, circling like boxers. Falcon in midair combat with Ms. Marvel. Hawkeye in front of a food truck, grappling with—

—Captain America.

"Target," Tony said softly. And he dove.

Cut off the head, he thought, *and the Resistance will fall.*

Times Square loomed into view, incredibly fast. More images of little battles: Photon vs. Tigra. Dagger backed up against a wall by Stature and Yellowjacket. Hermes in furious motion, whizzing around and around the Human Torch.

Captain America flipped Hawkeye over his shoulder. Arrows flew wildly; Hawk crashed into a metal table with a cracking noise. Cap stared at Hawk's unconscious body, started to speak—

—and then Tony struck.

But Cap had raised his shield, faster than even Tony's armor could detect. Tony's fist struck the shield, which absorbed most of the impact. Cap jabbed the shield forward and Tony leapt back, rising up into the air slightly. He touched down right in front of the U.S. Armed Forces recruiting center wall: a 12-foot high, brightly lit American flag shining into the pedestrian seating area.

Tony dropped into a crouch, facing his enemy head-on. Giant flag at his back.

"You and me again, Cap."

Cap glared. "Things are a little different this time, Tony."

"You're right. This time I'm not gonna fall for some antique

S.H.I.E.L.D. gadget."

He leapt for Cap, repulsor rays firing. Cap raised the shield again, deflecting the rays. But Tony was on him, knocking him backward. Tony raised a metal-sheathed fist and cracked it against Cap's jaw.

Cap grunted, pushed Tony off him. "And this time I've got more allies."

"You mean those Atlantean mercenaries?"

Tony raised his hands, triggered repulsors again—

—and then something landed on his back, light as a feather. "Hi, dad. Miss me?"

Spider-Man. *Again.*

Tony whirled, glared at the wall-crawler with bright glowing eyes. Tony rose up into the air, tilted side to side, trying to shake him off.

Below, a news van screeched up. A coiffed newswoman tumbled out, yelling frantic instructions to a photographer and technicians.

Spider-Man gripped Tony's shoulders, one in each hand. "Don't want to go too high, Tone."

"If you're trying to gum up my armor again, forget it. I can neutralize your webbing now."

"I figured you'd fix that." Spider-Man pressed his thumbs into the shoulder-joints of Tony's armor. "But some things are harder to fix."

Too late, Tony realized what the wall-crawler was doing. He turned sharply in midair, but Spider-Man held on tight.

"Microcontrollers in your armor," Spider-Man said. "Delicate little buggers. You told me you were having trouble with them, remember? Way back, when we were bestest buds?"

Spider-Man *squeezed.* The microcontrollers, nestled in Tony's shoulder-joints, made a low snapping noise—first one side, then the other.

"Never got around to dealing with that, did you?"

Tony's arms snapped up, rigid, and he tumbled out of the sky. Spider-Man leapt free just before impact. Tony crashed down awkwardly, straight onto his chestplate.

He gasped, struggled to catch his breath.

Dimly he registered that civilians were clustered around now, recording video on their phones. At least eight or nine, silhouetted against that gigantic flag display.

"You know who could have helped with those microcontrollers? *Bill Foster.*" Spider-Man leaned down, his blank eye-lenses filling Tony's field of view. "Too bad."

Tony struggled to his knees. The controllers were rebooting, but for the moment he was vulnerable. "P-parsifal," he said.

"What's that, boss?"

"*Parsifal!*"

A massive bolt of lightning cracked down, splitting open the pavement between Tony and Spider-Man. Spidey leapt up, momentarily disoriented. Then a meaty hand grabbed him around the waist and lifted him up into the air.

The Mighty Thor stood like a vengeful god of old, dangling his prey between two enormous fingers. His hammer flashed in his other hand. He leaned in close to Spider-Man and hissed:

"HAVE AT THEE."

Then he flung Spider-Man up and out, clear over the recruiting center. Spidey twisted, flailed in midair, and dropped out of view behind the low building.

Thor clomped off after him, shaking the pavement with each step. He reached out a hand to swing himself around the recruiting center, and a section of the big flag—a cluster of red and white LEDs—sparked and shattered under his grip.

Two S.H.I.E.L.D. agents glanced at Thor, touched their shoulders to radio for assistance. A small clutch of civilians followed, camera-phones held up to catch every move. Then they all disappeared behind the sparking wall of the recruiting center.

Across the Square, Hercules's body smashed into an office building. Glass rained down; a small explosion erupted from the impact spot.

Tony's armor clicked once as the left-shoulder microcontroller finally engaged. He straightened up, took a look around. *This is bad,* he thought. *Millions of dollars' worth of damage already. And the Resistance will fight until their last member drops.*

And then, for the first time, he felt a different kind of despair. A deeper, more personal sadness. *It's gone too far,* he realized. *All of it. There's no going back between us, no dusting off wounds and shaking hands in grudging admiration. No teaming up against Galactus or Doctor Doom. Not now, and not ever again.*

It's over.

He looked up and saw Captain America advancing on him. Face bloody, fire in his eyes. Moving in for one last battle, one final contest of shield and steel. Two gladiators made old before their time, squaring off for one final bout in the ring. Two men who had once been friends.

Tony tried to crouch for battle, but his right arm still hung loose. So he lifted his left hand, fired repulsors, and prepared to embrace his destiny.

SPIDER-MAN landed in a crouch in the middle of Broadway. He whirled around, searching for cars; but the local authorities had finally managed to clear the street. He raised his web-shooters—

—but before he could fire, Thor was on him again, bodyslamming him like a wrestler. Spidey fell to the street, the breath knocked out of him, Thor's massive bulk crushing him against the pavement.

Not Thor, he reminded himself. *Clone Thor. Clor.*

Spider-Man wrenched his arms back, pressing his palms against the pavement. He tensed his muscles and *pushed.* Thor flipped off of him, and he rolled out of the way.

Thor raised his hammer, calling down lightning. "BASE VILLAIN," he said.

Spidey leapt to his feet, dodging lightning bolts. He stumbled backward, almost falling into a curious woman in a business suit. "Stay back!" he called. "That isn't a real thunder god, but it's twice as nasty."

"THE THUNDER. IT IS…MINE."

Spider-Man stopped, studied Thor for a moment. The clone seemed slower now, confused. Spider-Man moved toward him cautiously, ready to dodge at any second.

"You know, Clor—can I call you Clor? This is all kind of funny." Spidey took another step. "Tony tried to make me into a junior version of himself, and it didn't take. So he trotted *you* out. His own private super hero, grown exactly to his specifications."

Thor's hammer flashed. But he made no movement.

"Trouble is, you didn't work quite right either, the first time out." Spider-Man studied him. "Y'know what I think, Clor? I think they upgraded you after the chemical factory. Gave you the power of speech, for one thing. Step in the right direction, though your patter could use some work."

A network news crew approached. A cameraman poked his way in, dangerously close to the battle.

"But I think maybe they put in some safeguards, too. I think they put you on a leash. I bet even Tony Stark wouldn't set you loose again, unless he was sure you wouldn't start massacring people."

Thor turned toward Spider-Man, his hammer raised. He reared back to throw it—and then his gaze dropped to the civilians below. His arm went slack.

"You know," Spider-Man continued, "I was worried about replacing you. Not you—*Thor*, I mean. The real one. When Tony asked me to join the Avengers, I wasn't sure if I had what it took to compete with a god.

"'Cause I knew Thor, buddy. I fought with him. And you know something, imposter?"

Spider-Man tensed, leapt through the air.

"Thou art no Thor!"

The clone whipped around, but Spider-Man was already on top of him. Webs shot out, clinging to Thor's face. The thunder god howled, clawed at his eyes.

Spidey grabbed Thor's huge hammer-arm in both hands, wrenched it back. Thor toppled to the ground with a massive crash. Spidey leapt up into the air and brought both fists down together on Thor's neck.

An electric shock surged through Spider-Man's body. He yelped, pulled back both hands, and stared. Thor's throat had torn open, revealing a bizarre mixture of cell tissue and sparking, electronic wires and circuits. The clone's arms flailed, jerking all around.

Spider-Man reached out and grabbed the hammer out of Thor's twitching hand. "And this," Spidey said, "art no Mjolnir, neither."

Spidey slammed the hammer down onto "Thor's" throat. The clone spasmed, arched his back, and let out a metallic howling noise. His chest cracked open, revealing a glowing, sparking central power unit.

"Or is that 'ain't'? Middle English gives me a headache."

Spider-Man struck again, a hammer-blow straight to the power unit. Pulled his hand back just in time, as a massive electrical short-circuit ripped all through Thor's mutilated, spasming body.

Thor blinked once, twice. Then he was still.

A crowd had gathered now, staring in awe and horror. Spidey turned toward them and they backed away, almost like a single organism. He looked down, saw the stain of blood and machine oil on his gloves and chest.

All around him, the battles continued. Cage and the Thing squared off against She-Hulk and Wonder Man. Daredevil and the Black Widow stalked each other up and down lampposts and benches, their moves deadly and precise. Above, a half-dozen costumes tumbled through the air, force bolts lighting up the night.

Spidey slumped back against a wall, momentarily exhausted. With Thor gone, he felt oddly quiet, alone in a private, important moment. *I've proved myself,* he realized. *I'm as good as any of them. No matter what Tony Stark, Captain America, or anyone else thinks.*

Whichever way this battle went, there would be hell to pay. If Cap prevailed, Peter would be a wanted fugitive. If Tony won, he'd have to face charges. Either way, the future looked grim.

But right now, Spider-Man was victorious. He'd won.

Today, he thought, *I am an Avenger.*

CAP brought his shield down hard, smashing it across Tony's helmet. The playboy's head snapped to the side. He let out a strangled cry.

One more blow, and Tony's helmet cracked. His faceplate clicked open, revealing split skin and bloody bruises. Once, Cap might have felt sorry for him. But not today.

"Arrogant little rich boy," Cap hissed. "You had it all. Born with a silver-plated rattle in your crib."

"Ugggh!"

"Not me. I'm just a fighter, a soldier. A man trained to seize any chance, find the crack in any enemy's armor."

Tony said nothing.

Cap paused, gestured around him. "See those Atlantean warriors? They're my cavalry, Tony. They're gonna pound your forces into fish food."

"S.H.I.E.L.D. has...tranqs. Made specially...for mermen."

To the north, the S.H.I.E.L.D. copters were just dropping to the ground. Agents swarmed out the doors, leaping the last few feet, not even waiting till touchdown.

"Then we'll fight even harder."

Tony reached up with trembling hands and pulled off his faceplate. His face bled from a dozen cuts; his lip was split. One eye was almost swollen shut. But as Cap watched, a kind of peace seemed to settle over his face.

"What are you waiting for?" Tony grunted. "Finish it."

Cap paused for just a second. Then he pulled his fist back—

—and a hand clamped down on his shoulder, from behind. "Lay off him, man!"

Cap whirled, swinging his shield at the attacker.

"Uhhh!"

The attacker fell back against a pedestrian seating table, striking his head on the round metal leg. Cap jumped to his feet, then stopped at the sight that confronted him.

The man wore a tracksuit and glasses. Short graying hair, a face that had seen a few scraps. But not a hero, not a villain; neither an Avenger nor a Resistance member. Just an ordinary man.

The man rubbed his head. "What are you *doin'?*"

Behind him, a clutch of other bystanders stood just in front of the sparking flag display. A tall businessman with a loosened tie. A big girl with teased-out hair hair. Black guy in shades. Sharp-faced Japanese woman, and a blond fireman in full uniform. Trim businesswoman in a tailored suit and heels.

Cap frowned at them. "I—"

The fireman pointed. *"Get him!"*

Then they were all on Cap, grabbing for him, pulling him down. His eyes went wide with shock; he couldn't even fight back. They swarmed over him, tugging at him, dragging him down to the pavement.

Tony Stark struggled to rise. Cap could feel Tony's good eye on him, watching the scene.

"What do you think you're doing here?" the Asian woman demanded.

"Let me go!" Cap struggled, still stunned. "Please. I don't want to hurt you—"

"*Hurt* us?" The businesswoman's face showed shock. "Are you trying to be funny?"

The fireman hauled Cap roughly to his feet, and gestured around.

Cap took in the scene. Heroes fought heroes; S.H.I.E.L.D. agents and Atlantean warriors traded shots, while civilians ran panicked for cover. Fires burned in a dozen spots, from gas mains and trash cans and office windows. To the north, half a building had collapsed, rubble blocking the entire street and half a pedestrian area.

"People are worried about their jobs, their futures, their families." The black man lowered his sunglasses, glared at Cap. "You think they need to worry about *this*?"

Cap opened his mouth to reply. And stopped, struck dumb.

Tony's words, from the press conference, came back to him: *moment of clarity.*

"Oh my God," Cap whispered.

Falcon swooped low overhead. "Cap!" he called. "Stand back, I'll—"

"No!"

"What?"

Falcon spread his wings, touched down in front of the half-smashed American flag display. The civilians stepped back, releasing Cap.

Tony Stark staggered to his feet. Spat a tooth, but held his fire.

"They're right, Falc." Cap lowered his shield, bowed his head. "We were...we were supposed to be fighting for the people. But that's not what we're doing anymore." He gestured around. "We're just *fighting*."

The Human Torch swooped in. "What are you doing, Cap? You want them to throw everybody in jail?"

"We're beatin' 'em!" Falcon gestured at a troop of S.H.I.E.L.D. agents, on their knees before the fierce Atlantean warriors. "We can win this!"

Cap turned, ran his eyes across the civilians who'd attacked him. Their faces showed fear, but also determination. They knew their cause was right.

"We can win," Cap repeated. "Everything but the argument."

He raised his shield slowly, tossed it to the Falcon. Falcon caught it in surprise, and stared at it for a long moment. Then he turned to glare at Cap, a horrible look of betrayal and accusation. He threw the shield to the ground and shot off into the sky.

The shield rolled down the street, past Cage. He didn't move, just shook his head as it passed by. Hawkeye ran for the shield, grabbed for it, and missed.

Tigra snatched it up, stared across its shiny surface at Captain America. There was something in her eyes that might have been understanding.

Maria Hill ran forward, accompanied by her S.H.I.E.L.D. guard. At her signal, the agents took aim at Captain America. But Tony Stark raised a hand.

All around him, the heroes gathered together. Paused in their battles, looked to their leaders for guidance. Another S.H.I.E.L.D. troop ran up, followed closely by a pair of local cop cars.

Namor soared on to the scene, stopped in midair, and locked eyes momentarily with Cap. Then Namor shook his head, held up his hand, and let out a low whistling sound. All around the square, Atlantean warriors began to retreat from their battles.

Slowly Cap reached up and pulled off his mask. Revealed bruises, cuts, and decades' worth of scars.

"Steven Rogers," he said. "United States Armed Forces, Honorably Discharged. Serial Number RA25-262-771."

Maria Hill stepped forward, her leather-garbed form dark against the bright stars and stripes of the recruiting center.

Cap held out his hands. "I surrender."

Hill lowered her shades…the first time Cap had ever seen her unsure of herself. "I, uh, he should be processed by local authorities first."

Tony nodded. His face was swollen, unreadable.

Two New York cops moved in, wide-eyed. The tall one pulled out cuffs, snapped them on to Cap's wrists.

Spider-Man webbed his way on to the scene. He was saying something, calling out to Cap. But Cap couldn't hear him.

The other Resistance members looked around, eyeing the Avengers and S.H.I.E.L.D. agents nervously. Cage looked exhausted; Johnny Storm was stunned. Ms. Marvel hovered above, alongside the brightly glowing Sentry. One by one the battles slowed, the powers faded.

Fires blazed all around; the noise of sirens and rescue vehicles suffused the air. Everyone seemed dazed, shell-shocked. No one wanted to make the next move, fire the next shot.

The cop gestured toward his squad car. Cap moved toward the open door, ducking his head.

"Stand down, troops." Cap paused, just long enough to register the stunned, betrayed looks on his followers. "That's an order."

The door slammed shut behind him, and the War was over.

EPILOGUE ONE
INVISIBLE

My Dear, Sweet Susan:

Forgive my erratic handwriting. You know how difficult I find it to slow my thoughts to the point where a keyboard can translate my sentiments into linear sentences. A handwritten letter like this one takes an even longer, more excruciating period of time to compose.

But you wrote me your thoughts in this form when you left. So it seemed fitting, symmetrical even, for me to respond in kind.

Sue Richards stood in her rented room on the Brooklyn waterfront. Mattress on the floor, rusted teakettle heating on the stove. The letter felt cold in her hand.

It has been nearly two weeks since that terrible battle. I hope you were pleased by the general hero amnesty offered in the wake of Captain America's surrender. Certainly I was pleased that you accepted it.

I saw you across the square, during the cleanup. But I felt it was inappropriate to discuss our future while our adrenal glands might still impair our judgment.

You looked so beautiful, so vibrant and clear-eyed. Like the girl I first met, wise beyond her years, with a raging fire for justice in her heart. It seemed as if all the years melted away and I was a nervous suitor again, fumbling for the right words to say to such an exquisite creature. That day, as so many times before, I failed.

When I returned home that night, I cried for a full ninety-three minutes.

The kettle whistled. She crossed to the stove, poured a cup into a cracked mug. Watched for a long moment, while the teabag steeped and the water turned a warm, dark color.

She took a tentative sip. Hissed in a breath, and resumed reading.

By now you will have seen the launch of the Initiative. When it is completed, it will comprise at least one super hero team in every state. I'm sure you can appreciate the pressure I, and all the others involved, have been under: creating new heroes, revamping old ones. Building a super-powered force for the twenty-first century.

The public seems very pleased, overall, with the new arrangement. How frightening the world must have seemed to them before: vigilantes roaming the streets, amateurs with the power of nuclear weapons, villains whose atrocities never seemed to reap genuine consequences.

It's a wonder we were tolerated for as long as we were.

Of course, not everyone is happy with the new order. Some have moved to Canada, where Registration laws do not apply. Here in the U.S., a small band of Captain America's followers are rumored to be still at large, forming a new, more radicalized underground movement.

And then, of course, there is Cap himself.

But on the whole, our experiment has been an enormous success. What once seemed like our darkest hour has been transformed into a great opportunity.

Perhaps the most heartening thing, for me, has been the new life the Initiative has given to old friends. Hank Pym has thrown himself into the job of training new heroes. Tigra felt some guilt over her betrayal of Captain America, I think, but she too has become a valued member of our team. First, last, and always, she's an Avenger.

Our remit has now progressed beyond simple enforcement of law and order. We're now working directly with the U.S. government, tackling everything from environmental crises to global poverty.

Tony in particular. Can you believe the new job the President has handed him?

But utopian ideals and favorable opinion polls mean nothing to me, my darling, without you by my side. No matter what we achieve in this New America, it can never be Heaven to me unless I have you.

So I promise you: no more traps, no more clones. None of the painful things we had to do on that path toward respectability.

I could never, would never try to pressure you. You know where I am, and I've reprogrammed the rebuilt Baxter Building locks to admit you once again. The choice is yours, and yours alone.

But I hope, beyond all hope, that you will return to the family who needs you more than

A rustling noise at the door. Sue whirled, feeling pent-up and angry: *That better not be the creepy guy with the dogs again.* She flung open the door.

Reed stood there, wearing a sadly dated suit and tie. His limbs were normal-length; he wasn't using his powers. He held a small bouquet of daisies, already starting to wither.

"I couldn't wait," he said.

She smiled, felt tears rising. "That's the sorriest batch of flowers I've ever..."

And then they were in each other's arms, sobbing and mumbling apologies. His breath was warm in her ear, his tears hot on her shoulder. She reached out, pulled him closer.

His body began to stretch involuntarily, forming a thin blanket, reaching out to cover her in a full-body embrace. But it didn't feel confining or stifling. It felt right.

"...too much futurism," he said, his thoughts spilling out too fast. "Learned I need to moderate my logic. Tony's learning that too, I think. And also, also you should know: The Negative Zone prison is being closed. Tony didn't want to do it, but I insisted. It was the price of my continued involvement in his plans. Probably the last chip I'll ever be able to play with Tony, but..."

"Reed." She pulled back, framed his face in her hands. Stared into his wet, suffering eyes. "Reed, can I tell you something? Something that might shock you?"

He stared, nodded.

"Tony Stark is not a partner in this marriage."

A moment passed, a long quiet beat in that shabby room on the docks. And then Reed Richards laughed. It was a lovely human sound, a sound Sue hadn't heard for a long, long time. She laughed back, then leaned forward and kissed him.

Tears mingled with laughter, and Sue let Reed into her heart in a way she hadn't for a long time. She felt warm, loving, loved.

And very, very visible.

EPILOGUE TWO
SPIDER

"IT'S very dry here, dear. Good for my sinuses, I suppose. But I do miss the squirrels—"

"Stop, Aunt May. Please. I don't want to know where you are."

"Oh. Of course, Peter. I'm sorry."

"No, Aunt May, *I'm* sorry. Sorry you have to—oh, dammit. Hold on a minute."

The phone crackled in Spider-Man's ear. He held it out and wiggled its old-style, spiral cord. He planted his feet on the brick wall, three stories up, and adjusted the wire connecting the phone to the junction box.

"Peter? Are you still there?"

"Yes, Aunt May. Sorry. I didn't want to use my cell, so this setup is a little bit jury-rigged."

A little trick Daredevil had taught him: *Landlines are still harder to trace.*

"I'm worried about you, Peter. Are you getting enough to eat? Do you have a place to stay?"

"Yes and yes."

That's a world record, Parker. Lying to your aunt twice in three words.

"I miss you, Aunt May. I promise, things will calm down soon and you can come home."

"I'm not worried for myself, Peter. But Mary Jane seems a bit on edge."

"Can I speak to her again?"

"Of course."

"Wait." Spider-Man flattened himself against the building wall, sheltering against the chill autumn breeze. "Aunt May, are you still proud of me?"

"Of course I am. Especially when you *don't* talk like a silly little boy."

He laughed.

"Here she is, dear."

There was a pause on the line, long enough that Spider-Man worried they'd been disconnected. He looked around at the five- and six-story buildings, old and weathered, dotted with lights in the windows. The renovated doorman buildings with fancy names, the old rent-controlled brownstones, the bodegas that never closed. The Upper West Side had been the site of his very first apartment, with Harry Osborn.

"Petey?"

Her voice was like a shot of warm coffee, soothing and exciting at the same time. A memory rose to his mind: Mary Jane coming up to visit that first apartment, dancing her way inside, stopping to flirt with both him and Harry. Bright red hair, even brighter lipstick, and a smile that seemed to burn right through him.

For a moment he couldn't speak.

"Tiger, what's going on? Are you there?"

"Yeah, MJ. I'm here."

"What's the situation? Are we safe yet?"

"I'm not sure." He swallowed. "You know they offered us all amnesty..."

"Yeah. You're taking it, right?"

"I...I don't think I can."

Another pause.

"It's just..." He paused, lost for words. "I've been through so much with Tony. To jump back into that fire again...they'd probably make me do training in Montana or something. But that's not really it. I guess...I'm just a loner, you know?"

"I know." Her voice was hard, unhappy.

"And I know it affects you—"

"Cable news is buzzing with rumors, Tiger. Something they're calling the 'Secret Avengers.' They say it's connected with Doctor Strange."

"I'm not in touch with them."

That was a half-truth. The Falcon had sent him a brief text, a street address in the Village that sounded like Strange's house. But Peter hadn't replied.

"I'm sorry, MJ. About uprooting you, saddling you with Aunt May—"

"We're fine, Peter. May's much more adaptable than you give her credit for, and I spend half the year on the road anyway. I've already picked up a few modeling gigs here." She laughed. "You know, it's funny."

"What?"

"On our wedding day...when you didn't show. Afterward, all you talked about was what a terrible thing you'd done to me, to your aunt, to our friends. You apologized so many times, tried so hard to make it up to me. But you never realized what was really bothering me. It never occurred to you that what I was worried about, the thing that woke me up screaming at night, was what had happened to *you*."

He blinked.

"How are you, Petey?"

"I..."

"And don't give me some glib spider-quip. You're not talking to Professor Octopus Man here."

He took a deep breath.

"I've lost my job, MJ. I've got no apartment, no friends I can talk to without endangering them, no clothes except the ones on my back. The cops are after me again, and Jameson has launched a blistering new anti-Spider-Man crusade that makes all the crap he's done before look like a kid's birthday party.

"Every shred of my normal life has been blown apart. Except for you, I've got no contact left with the normal, human world. I'm really, truly alone.

"But you know what? I can sleep at night."

"I guess...I guess that's what matters."

"Some things are just *wrong*, MJ. And somebody's gotta stand up for what's right."

"Then that's all there is to say."

"Yeah. Except...MJ, I really want you to know, I always—"

"Save it, Parker. You'll tell me in person, soon enough." She drew in a deep breath. "Just water my damn tomatoes, okay?"

"Every day."

The line went dead in his hand.

"I promise," he said.

Spider-Man reached out and yanked the cord out of the junction box. He hurled the phone through the air, three stories down. It whizzed past a young woman, startling her, and landed square in the middle of a public trash can.

"Slam dunk," he whispered.

A scream rang out, faint in the cold air. Five, maybe six blocks away.

Webbing shot out toward a lamppost; powerful legs tensed, then sprang up into the sky. Passers-by pointed upward, whispered excitedly. And once again, as so many times before, the amazing Spider-Man swung off into the night.

EPILOGUE THREE
AMERICA

"YO, Steve."

Skritch skritch.

"Steve! You there?"

"Yeah, Raheem. I'm here."

"What you doin' over there? I hear some crazy *skritch-skritch* on the other side'a this wall."

"Sorry if I disturbed you, Raheem. Just doing a little drawing."

"Drawing! On the wall?"

"That's right."

"You a artist?"

"I was a commercial artist, for a while. I've done a lot of things."

"Huh."

"I'll try and be quieter."

"Don't trip, brother. Anything's better'n bein' bored all the time."

"Actually, Raheem, I like having time to think."

"You a strange one, Steve. See if you can get yourself transferred to death row, you'll have plenty of time."

Skritch skritch skritch.

"Sound like chalk. How they let you get chalk, anyway?"

"A guard did me a solid."

"You trade for it?"

"He owed me a favor. From before."

"Pretty small favor. Sound like you got scammed."

Skritch skritch. "I only needed three colors, anyway."

"You losin' it, Steve. How long you been in this joint?"

"Thirteen days."

"You sure? Seem like more."

Steve Rogers stepped back, holding up the red chalk in his hand. The cell was Spartan: bed, bench, bare metal toilet. But the wall facing him was covered with a meticulous chalk rendering of an American flag. He reached out and added the final strokes to the red stripe at the bottom.

The thirteenth stripe.

"I'm sure," he said.

Steve frowned, then turned back to the hand-drawn flag. The upper left quarter was a solid block of blue. He placed the red chalk down on his bunk and picked up the white, juggled it lightly in his hand.

Tomorrow, he would start in on the stars.

EPILOGUE FOUR
IRON

THE Iron Man armor hung in the air like a scarecrow, spread out on tiny gravity nullifiers. Tony Stark peered at the chestplate, then frowned at the right-hand shoulder joint. "Controller test," he said.

Both arms snapped upward instantly, in perfect formation.

Tony smiled. In the helmet, he caught a glimpse of his own reflection. The new Armani suit fit perfectly. The scars from his battle with Cap had nearly healed, with the help of some minor but expensive plastic surgery. He ran a finger along his upper lip; still slightly swollen, but the goatee had grown in to cover it.

"So. Director of S.H.I.E.L.D.?"

He turned, looking down one of the crisscrossing walkways dotting the interior of the Helicarrier. Miriam Sharpe, the woman who'd lost her son at Stamford, walked cautiously toward him, casting her eyes around at the buzz of technicians and repairmen working at consoles below. Maria Hill followed, her head lowered.

Tony smiled, held out a hand to Mrs. Sharpe.

"Why not? It makes perfect sense. I have close links to both the government and the superhuman community, and with Nick Fury gone..." Tony looked up brightly, turned to Hill. "Could we have a couple of coffees over here please, Deputy Director? Cream and plenty of sugar?"

Hill shot him a look that could ground planes. She turned and stalked away.

"I have something for you." Tony rummaged in his jacket pocket, pulled out a small Iron Man figure. "Your son's toy."

Sharpe frowned. "I gave it to you."

"And it helped me more than you can know. But I don't need it anymore."

Smiling shyly, she took the toy. Clutched it tight, like an old memory.

"'Scuse me, Director?"

Three S.H.I.E.L.D. agents moved toward them, carrying a huge metal plate and a canister of sealant. "Just repairing the last of the blast damage from...you know. Captain America's little tantrum." The agent nodded past Tony's hovering armor, at the wall. A discolored, dented patch hung like a bruise.

Tony snapped his fingers, and the armor collapsed into his hands. He folded it quickly into his briefcase. "Let's let the men work."

He took Sharpe by the arm and led her down a small flight of steps.

"You won the war," she said.

"Yes, and now we have to win the peace. I want everyone to understand, to get enthused about this new way of working."

An elevator door opened. He ushered her inside and pressed a button. The elevator dropped, fast enough that his stomach lurched.

"Did you hear the state of Colorado just requested the Thunderbolts as their official team?"

She smiled. "I heard you have to fire a couple of the nutcases."

"Nevertheless, it's still a tremendous step. Giving offenders a second chance...it's something I've always tried to do."

The elevator door opened. A thin walkway led to a bank of windows, blazing bright in the midday sunlight.

"Do you know why we called our prison 'Number 42'?" he asked.

"Nope."

"Because it was number 42 of a hundred ideas Reed and I wrote down, the night your son was killed. A hundred ideas for a safer world, and we aren't even at number fifty yet. Isn't that exciting?"

At the end of the walkway, the chamber opened up into a multifaceted observation blister with a curved, transparent floor. They were on the bottom of the Helicarrier now; sunlight streamed in, reflected in all directions by the glass.

"Cleaning up S.H.I.E.L.D.," Tony continued, "is idea number forty-three. Believe you me, ma'am, the super hero community just found the greatest friend it'll ever have. Do you really think I'd let anyone else guard my friends' secrets?"

Sharpe turned away. She looked down at the Iron Man toy in her hand.

"You're a good man, Tony Stark." A tear welled up in her eye. "You risked everything to give people heroes they could believe in, again."

He smiled, felt a swell of pride. "I could never have done anything different."

"I believe you. This is the beginning of something wonderful."

Tony leaned on the railing, stared down through the glass at the city of New York. Laid out like a magical kingdom, ripe and full of promise. Sunlight glinted, clear and bright, off its proud spires.

No clouds today.

"The best is yet to come, sweetheart." When he looked back up, there was steel in his eyes. "That's a promise."

THE END

ACKNOWLEDGMENTS

A novel is not a graphic novel, and this particular, brilliant graphic novel required a lot of restructuring to work in prose form. My thanks to Marvel's Ruwan Jayatilleke, Jeff Youngquist, and David Gabriel for trusting me to do justice to their most popular, most powerful story line of recent years. They gave me all the tools and then let me work, providing just the right amount of guidance whenever I needed it.

I had two editors on this project: Axel Alonso, editor in chief of Marvel, and Marie Javins, the book's primary editor. Axel schooled me on the moral compass of the Punisher and suggested some excellent plot twists; Marie asked all the right questions, cleaned up my prose, and worked long hours polishing the manuscript. Together, they pushed me in all the right directions.

Tom Brevoort, editor of the original CIVIL WAR series, provided valuable input at the early stages. Tie-in stories by J. Michael Straczynski, Ron Garney, Dan Slott, and Stefano Caselli served as important source material for the novel. Steve McNiven's artwork, on the main series, was both a constant inspiration and a source of frustration—it really does take a thousand words to capture a battle that he could show in one strong, powerful panel.

Mark Millar, an old friend and one of the smartest, most genuine guys in comics, encouraged me to take his story and make it my own. Hopefully I've done that without screwing up the structure, which was as airtight and breathtaking as any comics event in recent memory; or the powerful emotional core of the story.

My wife, Liz Sonneborn, was unfailingly supportive as I took notes late into the night, pulled out my hair over minor plot points, and paced around the house muttering obscure questions like, "Is it too confusing to have two characters called Hawkeye in one book?" (Answer: Yes.)

Finally, I owe a huge debt to all the writers and artists who've contributed to the Marvel Universe over the years. CIVIL WAR couldn't have existed, in any form, without their contributions. Hopefully, together, we've done them justice.